AI Income Streams Monetizing from Home

Your Ultimate Guide to Turning SMART
AI tools into Home-Based Income

BY NELSON PARRISH

TABLE OF CONTENTS

TABLE OF CONTENTS

INTRODUCTION

"If you don't find a way to make money while you sleep, you will work until you die."

— Warren Buffett

The first time I heard this quote, it hit me like a wake-up call—harsh, but undeniably true. If money never stops moving, why should we be the only ones stuck in place? That question sent me on a mission. How can we get our hard-earned money to work for us instead of the other way around? And that's when I discovered the game-changer: Artificial Intelligence (AI).

For years, the idea of earning passive income seemed like something only the super-intelligent and the rich could achieve. You'd hear stories about landlords with a dozen properties or investors with insider knowledge of Wall Street, but where's your success story? But now, with AI stepping into the scene, this dream is more achievable than ever for anyone wanting to upgrade their income game. It's like AI has swung open the gates of opportunity, giving anyone with an internet connection the tools to build multiple streams of income from home. Yes, even if you have zero tech skills and only a few free hours each day, you can still earn an income. How big? It will depend on you.

I wasn't always an AI believer. When I first started exploring it, I was intrigued but sceptical. AI sounded complex, almost too good to be true. Could these so-called 'smart tools' really automate work and generate income? I didn't have to wonder for long. The answer was a resounding yes!

From self-publishing books to running my e-commerce clothing brand, AI quickly became my silent business partner. It handled the tasks that used to drain my time—writing, designing, marketing, and customer service—allowing me to focus on growing my business instead of just keeping up with it.

Let's be real—most traditional ways of making money from home demand a lot of time, effort, and upfront investment. I remember my first attempt at freelancing back in the early 2000s. It was hyped up as an 'easy' way to earn extra cash while working from home. But reality hit fast. Instead of quick wins, it quickly turned into hours of unpaid proposals, revisions, and never-ending client demands. Don't get me wrong. Freelancing was great, but it was not the passive income dream everyone talked about. And it sure didn't leave me with much freedom or time. There were no shortcuts back then.

The same goes for other traditional side hustles. Starting a small business requires a huge learning curve, not to mention financial investment. Investing in stocks felt risky, like gambling with money I couldn't afford to lose. Everything seemed to require much time or money upfront—two things I didn't have much of.

AI changed the game completely. With AI, you don't need to be an expert. You don't need a massive initial investment. All you need is a willingness to learn and experiment. Whether you're into writing, graphic design, online sales, or even digital marketing, there's an AI tool that can help you do the work faster, better, and with much less effort.

The best part? You don't even need to work 9-to-5 anymore. These AI tools work around the clock, giving you the freedom to live your life. You can earn money while cooking dinner, taking the kids to school, or dare I say while you are sleeping. The flexibility AI offers is a game-changer, especially if you're juggling multiple responsibilities.

I'll never forget the first time I woke up and checked my email, only to see that a chatbot had handled several customer inquiries overnight, and I had made sales while I was asleep. It was like magic. I wasn't at my desk, but my business had kept running, thanks to AI.

The ability to automate doesn't just stop at e-commerce, either. You can automate content creation, social media marketing, email campaigns, and more. Once these systems are set up, they run with minimal oversight, which means you're not tied to your desk every hour of the day. Your AI tools become your personal assistant, doing the work while you're off living your life.

We're at a point where AI is no longer this futuristic concept. It's already here and incredibly accessible. Tools that used to cost thousands of dollars or require expert knowledge are now available to anyone with an internet connection. And the earlier you start, the more time you'll have to learn, adapt, and maximize your earning potential before AI becomes a standard tool everyone will be using. So why not get ahead?

In the following chapters, we'll discuss ways you can use AI to generate income, from writing and design to automating entire business models. I'll walk you through the platforms, tools, and strategies you need to know about, even if you're a beginner. Whether you're looking to supplement your current income or make a full-time career out of it, AI is your ticket to doing it all from home.

The future of work is changing, and AI is leading the way. So why not hop on board and let smart tools do the heavy lifting for you? Trust me, once you see how AI can help you generate income effortlessly, you will wonder how you ever lived without it.

CHAPTER 1

Introduction To AI

Imagine having a virtual assistant who sorts out your emails, writes a blog post, or manages your online store, all before you brush your teeth in the morning without hiring a human. It sounds like a dream, right? Well, it's not; AI can do all that and more within a short time. AI is quietly changing how the world works; making money is now easier than ever,

Artificial Intelligence (AI) is often seen as a complex technology reserved for experts, but that perception couldn't be further from the truth. I used to think the same way—until a friend casually mentioned that AI had written her entire website's content. Skeptical, I expected something robotic and uninspiring. Instead, the writing was polished, engaging, and indistinguishable from human work. AI isn't just for tech professionals but a tool anyone can use to streamline work and drive results.

AI can help run your business, create content, or manage your tasks. For some years, it has been transforming industries left and right. Unlike humans, AI never sleeps, never complains, and doesn't need coffee breaks. In fact, it makes jobs so easy, you might wonder what you were doing all this time without it!

For our first chapter, you'll understand what AI is and how it is transforming the world around us and see how it can fit into your life even if you're just starting out. Trust me, if I, who was once tech-challenged, can do it, so can you.

What is AI?

Artificial Intelligence, or AI, has quickly become one of the most talked-about technologies of the modern age, but what exactly is it? In simple terms, AI refers to machines or software systems that can perform tasks that typically require human intelligence. These tasks include things like understanding language, recognizing patterns, making decisions, solving problems, and even generating creative content.

Think of AI as the brain behind a machine. Though it doesn't quite think like humans, it's capable of learning from data, making sense of complex information, and executing tasks more efficiently than ever before. Whether it's your voice assistant responding to your questions or a recommendation engine suggesting the perfect movie for you, AI is quietly working behind the scenes, making life easier and processes faster.

At its core, AI mimics certain functions of the human brain, like learning and problem-solving, but it doesn't have emotions or consciousness. What makes AI so powerful is its ability to process huge amounts of data in ways we can't—spotting patterns, predicting outcomes, and automating processes that would take humans far longer to do. From predicting the stock market to writing articles, AI has shown that it's more than just a buzzword. It's a tool that can change how we work and live.

AI Isn't Too Technical; Anyone Can Use It to Earn

Most of the AI tools out there are designed to make your life easier, not harder. But I get it; using AI can sound intimidating. The good news is that it really is not. If you can operate a smartphone or navigate Netflix, you can use AI to start making money. It really is that simple.

Let me tell you about my friend Jason. He runs an online fitness coaching business, helping clients stay in shape with personalized workout plans. He's an expert at training and nutrition, but when it came to the digital side of his business—marketing, content creation, and client communication—he was drowning.

Jason spent hours manually responding to inquiries, posting on social media, and trying to keep up with his growing client list. It got to a point where he was working more on admin tasks than actually coaching his clients. That's when he decided to try AI.

Within weeks, Jason automated client onboarding with AI chatbots, used AI-powered design tools to create professional social media posts in minutes, and even had an AI assistant draft personalized meal plans based on client preferences. The result? More time to focus on what he loves—helping people reach their fitness goals—while his business runs smoothly in the background.

Jason didn't need to be a tech expert to make it work. He just needed the right AI tools. And if he can do it, so can you.

The truth is AI is user-friendly. Tools like ChatGPT or Jasper (for writing), Canva (for design), or MidJourney (for generating images) have interfaces that are so simple and easier to figure out than most social media platforms. Many AI programs are just plug-and-play. You put in a few details, and the AI handles the rest.

Are you still worried it's too technical? Well so was Dominic at first. He is a musician. He's the type who spends hours jamming on his guitar but can't figure out how to send a calendar invite. One day, he discovered AI tools that could help him mix and edit his music. Instead of paying someone else to do it, with my help, he figured out how to use AI software to create professional-sounding tracks right from his laptop. He has no fancy studio, no tech knowledge, just a simple program that does the heavy lifting while he does what he loves: making music. So he saved money and time and had full control of editing his music all thanks to AI.

To the best part; many AI tools are super affordable, or even free! You probably think anything this powerful must cost a fortune, but nope. You can access AI-powered tools for just a few dollars a month or even nothing at all. Sure, there are some premium options if you want all the bells and whistles, but if you're starting, the free versions are more than enough to complete the job.

Take chatbots, for example. You don't need to build some fancy, complicated system. Platforms like ManyChat or Drift make setting up an AI chatbot as simple as dragging and dropping. Remember Jason and his fitness coaching business? He uses a chatbot to answer basic customer questions like "How much does the coaching plan cost?" and "Do you offer customized workout plan?" The customer gets instant replies without you needing to be glued to her phone, but we will discuss this in more detail later in the book.

But it's not just entrepreneurs and freelancers who can benefit. AI can be your secret weapon if you're looking for a side hustle. The possibilities are endless, from generating passive income through automated sales funnels to creating AI-driven e-commerce stores.

So, let's put this myth to rest: AI isn't too technical for the average person to use. All it takes is a little curiosity and a willingness to embrace how it can help you work smarter, not harder.

How AI Is Transforming Industries

The world is changing fast, and AI is at the center of it. Whether browsing for new shoes online or watching a movie recommendation on Netflix, AI is quietly working behind the scenes, making everything smarter and more efficient. But it's not just about fancy tech or big companies; it's about how you can take advantage of AI and its growing influence across different industries.

AI is here, opening doors for individuals to tap into new income streams, whether you're a freelancer, an entrepreneur, or someone just looking to make money. So, which industry is AI impacting?

Retail and E-Commerce

Think about the last time you bought something online. You probably noticed how eerily accurate the product recommendations were, right? That's AI at work. AI is a game-changer for the retail world, from predicting what products customers are likely to buy to automating inventory management.

Small online stores can run like well-oiled machines with tools like Shopify and AI-driven chatbots. You can set up an ecommerce store with AI handling everything from customer service to inventory forecasting, allowing you to sit back and watch the sales roll in. Whether selling handmade crafts or dropshipping products, AI helps you manage your store like a pro.

Content Creation

Creating high-quality content used to take hours, if not days. Well, not anymore. AI has made time-wasting a thing of the past. Whether writing blog posts, generating video scripts, or editing videos, AI can do it faster and better.

Take copywriting, for example. Tools like Jasper and ChatGPT can help you write compelling content for websites, ads, or social media posts in a fraction of the time. Are you more into design? AI tools like Canva make it incredibly easy to create professional-grade graphics, even if you have zero design experience. If you're into video, AI-powered editing software cuts down hours of tedious editing into mere minutes. Content creators use these tools to pump out high-quality work and make money on platforms like YouTube, Etsy, and TikTok.

Real Estate

Real estate isn't exactly the first thing that comes to mind when you think about AI, but it's one of the sectors benefiting the most from AI's influence. From AI-powered algorithms predicting property prices to chatbots handling tenant inquiries, real estate professionals use AI to streamline their operations.

You don't have to be a real estate mogul to get in on this. AI tools can help you identify the best properties to invest in, forecast rental income, and automate managing multiple properties if you're a landlord.

Finance and Investing

You've probably heard about AI in finance, especially regarding automated trading or robo-advisors. These tools analyze markets 24/7, finding the best investment opportunities without the emotional decision-making we humans tend to struggle with. But it's not just for Wall Street pros. People use AI-powered investing apps daily to grow their wealth, whether through stocks, cryptocurrency, or even real estate crowdfunding. Platforms like Betterment and Wealthfront make it easy for anyone to start investing with just a few clicks, all thanks to AI.

Freelancing and Remote Work: AI as Your Business Partner

The freelancing world has exploded, and AI is one of the main reasons it's easier than ever to run a successful freelance business. Whether you're offering graphic design, writing, or digital marketing services, AI tools are there to back you up. They can help you write faster, design more efficiently, or automate project management tasks.

For example, freelance writers use AI to draft articles, create social media content, or generate marketing copy quickly. Graphic designers can whip up logos, branding materials, and social media graphics with the help of AI-powered platforms like MidJourney or Canva. If you're into marketing, AI tools help you analyze data, target the right audiences, and automate client reports.

Education and Tutoring

AI isn't just making industries more efficient; it's also revolutionizing education. If you've got expertise in any subject, AI can help you reach more students and streamline your tutoring or teaching services. For instance, you can use AI tools to create interactive learning materials, automate lesson plans, or even provide feedback to students without spending all your time grading.

Online tutoring platforms use AI to pair students with the best tutors, optimize lesson structures, and track progress. Whether teaching language skills, coding, or even guitar lessons, AI allows you to scale your tutoring business while maintaining a personalized touch.

Health and Wellness

Believe it or not, AI is also making waves in the health and wellness sector. From fitness apps that track your progress and suggest personalized workout plans to AI-powered nutritionists that help you eat better, there are income opportunities here if you're passionate about wellness.

For instance, if you're a personal trainer or health coach, you can use AI to design custom workout routines for clients. Apps like MyFitnessPal or Noom use AI to help people reach their fitness goals, and they create a business opportunity for anyone who wants to coach or sell wellness products online.

AI is everywhere, and so are opportunities. No matter what industry you're interested in, AI creates new ways for individuals like you to earn a living. AI isn't just the future of work; it's the present. It's already transforming industries, and by embracing these tools, you can position yourself at the forefront of this revolution, ready to create, automate, and thrive in ways you never thought possible.

Case Studies of Successful AI Marketing

AI-driven marketing has emerged as a transformative force in today's rapidly changing market. Leading businesses worldwide are harnessing AI to revolutionize their marketing strategies, resulting in significant growth and competitive advantages. But how are they doing it?

The following case studies uncover the strategies and successes that define AI marketing's vanguard.

First, consider the case of Netflix. This entertainment giant has successfully leveraged AI to personalize content recommendations for its millions of subscribers. By analyzing viewing habits, search patterns, and preference data, Netflix's AI algorithms suggest content that aligns with each user's interests. This tailored experience enhances customer satisfaction and boosts engagement, driving watch time and reducing churn. The captivating aspect here is not merely the technology itself but how it augments the user experience in a symbiotic relationship; the more users engage, the better the system becomes.

Another notable example is the cosmetics retail company Sephora. Through integrating AI-powered tools, Sephora has transformed the online and in-store shopping experience. Their Virtual Artist feature, which uses augmented reality and machine learning, allows users to try on products virtually before purchasing. This innovation has amplified online sales and enriched the in-store experience by reducing returns and increasing customer satisfaction. AI here acts as a bridge, seamlessly connecting the digital and physical shopping worlds.

Meanwhile, let's take a closer look at Coca-Cola. The beverage giant utilizes AI for massive-scale data analysis, allowing it to understand consumer behavior and preferences more deeply than ever before. By leveraging AI to process social media data, customer reviews, and consumption patterns, Coca-Cola can ideate new products and marketing campaigns aligned with precise consumer desires. Essentially, they are not just responding to market demands but are also predicting and shaping them. AI enables Coca-Cola to stay one step ahead while nurturing brand loyalty.

AI's influence isn't limited to content streaming, cosmetics, or beverages. The apparel industry, too, has embraced AI with open arms. Take, for example, H&M. The clothing retailer uses AI technology to analyze returns and exchange data, thus gaining insight into the fit and preferences of their customers. This data drives the recommendation engines on their platforms and informs inventory management, ensuring popular items are stocked efficiently. The beauty of AI here lies in its ability to provide precise, actionable insights from complex datasets, translating directly into enhanced consumer experiences and optimized operational efficiency.

Now, let's focus on Spotify, the music streaming service. Spotify has perfected the use of AI to craft personalized playlists and recommendations. Whether it's the "Discover Weekly" feature or daily mixes, AI's role in processing billions of data points from listening histories and patterns ensures a unique musical journey for each user. This personalization keeps users engaged, fostering a sense of intimacy and curation that feels artisanal yet is underpinned by sophisticated machine algorithms. It epitomizes the delicate balance AI strikes between technical prowess and human touch.

But success with AI marketing isn't confined to established giants. Startups, too, leverage AI for market entry and brand building. Consider Stitch Fix, a company that combines AI with human expertise to deliver personalized style recommendations to its customers. Their AI algorithms analyze customer feedback, style preferences, and data across hundreds of data points to curate clothing recommendations. Human stylists then refine these recommendations, resulting in a hybrid approach that feels bespoke and personalized, resonating well with customers who value efficiency and a personal touch.

AI marketing also shines in customer service automation, where chatbots and virtual assistants are revolutionizing the interaction paradigms. Brands like H&M and Sephora aren't only using AI for product offerings but employing it to enhance customer support. These tools can handle inquiries beyond basic FAQs, using natural language processing to understand and respond to nuanced customer queries in real time. The result is a streamlined, 24/7 service capability that enhances consumer satisfaction while optimizing resource allocation.

AI marketing approaches have also been deployed significantly in governmental and non-profit sectors. For instance, UNICEF uses AI-driven analysis to optimize its fundraising campaigns. By predicting the likelihood of previous donors contributing again, AI helps strategize outreach and engagement effectively, resulting in increased donations. Here, AI goes beyond mere profitability, aiding in generating social impact in meaningful ways.

The many applications showcased in the above case studies highlight AI's surprising versatility and effectiveness in marketing. It's not just about having access to advanced technology; it's about creatively applying these tools to solve distinct business challenges. Successful companies understand the nuanced balance between harnessing AI's data-driven precision and maintaining a human touch in their engagements. This duality ensures that marketing strategies are efficient, scalable, and deeply resonant with consumers. As you navigate your journey as an entrepreneur, tech enthusiast, or investor, consider these case studies as a beacon of what's possible when you integrate AI into your strategy. AI's potential is vast, and these examples are but the forefront of what an innovative marketing world can achieve.

Why Start Now?

You've probably heard the saying, "Timing is everything," and when it comes to AI, now is the perfect time to jump on board. But why now? Why is this moment so ripe for diving into the AI world?

1. The Technology is Ready, And So Are You
A few years ago, AI felt like something from a sci-fi movie. It looked cool but a little out of reach for the average person. You had to be some Silicon Valley genius to understand how it worked. But that's no longer the case.

Today, AI tools are user-friendly, accessible, and fun to use. Platforms like ChatGPT, Jasper, and MidJourney are built for you, the entrepreneur, the freelancer, the creative, or the side hustler who wants to make money with ease. Click a few buttons, and let AI do the heavy lifting.

2. AI is Everywhere, and It's Democratizing Opportunity
It's not just tech giants like Google or Amazon that benefit from AI anymore. AI is everywhere, from small businesses to solo entrepreneurs, leveling the playing field. Whether you want to start an ecommerce store, become a freelance content creator, or dive into AI-driven investing, a tool (or ten) can help you do it.

The best part? AI is making once-complex tasks simpler for everyone. Automating your social media, writing blog posts, and designing logos would have required serious skills or a whole team in the past. Now, thanks to AI, you can do it all from your laptop in your pajamas.

3. The Market is Hungry for AI Solutions
There's no denying it, AI is a hot topic across industries right now. Businesses, from startups to Fortune 500 companies, are scrambling to integrate AI into their operations, and they need people who can help them make the transition. This creates a massive demand for AI-powered services and products.

If you can offer something as simple as AI-optimized marketing, AI-generated content, or an automated customer service solution, there's a market waiting for you. The early adopters of this technology are already seeing huge gains, and the wave of demand is only growing.

4. Passive Income with AI is Now Easier Than Ever
Who wouldn't want to make money while they sleep? The dream of passive income is now more attainable with AI, and there are

many ways to set up automated revenue streams. Think about e-commerce platforms that use AI to run 24/7 or content creation tools that churn out high-quality work without constant supervision. Subscription models, automated sales funnels, AI-driven product recommendations—all of these can work in the background to generate income while you focus on scaling your efforts. You set it up once, let AI take over, and watch the profits roll in. That kind of passive income stream was almost impossible for individuals to manage a decade ago.

5. AI Can Scale Your Efforts Like Never Before
The ability to scale has always been one of the biggest challenges for entrepreneurs and small businesses. You have a great idea, a small team (maybe just you), and tons of ambition—but only 24 hours a day. Enter AI.

AI tools allow you to scale your business in ways that used to be unimaginable. You can automate tasks, personalize marketing to thousands of customers at once, and even handle multiple projects without breaking a sweat. It's like having a virtual team of experts working for you, except you don't have to pay salaries or worry about HR headaches. This scalability makes AI the ultimate wealth-building tool for anyone, whether you're just starting or already have a business ready to grow.

6. The Competition is Still Low, But Not for Long
Here's the secret: even though AI is everywhere, not everyone is taking advantage of it yet. We're still in the early stages of the AI revolution, which gives you a golden opportunity. Those who jump on the AI bandwagon are now setting themselves up to stay ahead of the competition when the masses finally catch on.

It's like getting in on the ground floor of a skyscraper that's about to be built. The earlier you start, the higher you can climb. But the window of opportunity won't stay open forever. The more people realize how easy and profitable AI can be, the more crowded the market will get. By acting now, you're positioning yourself as an expert, a leader, and a wealth-builder in the AI economy.

7. AI is Here to Stay; It's Not a just a trend
If you're wondering whether AI is just a trend, let me reassure you, it's here to stay. AI will become even more integral to how we work, live, and build wealth in the coming years. AI is infiltrating every corner of our lives, from healthcare to finance, education, and entertainment.

The good news? You don't have to catch up later when everyone else is scrambling. By starting now, you'll be ahead of the curve, armed with the knowledge and tools you need to succeed in an AI-driven world. By the time others figure out how to use AI, you'll already be using it to build multiple income streams.

Start small, explore the tools, and see what works for you. Before you know it, AI will work for you, not vice versa.

CHAPTER 2

Unlocking Your Earning With AI-Powered Freelancing

What comes to mind when you hear AI-powered freelancing?

Imagine breaking free from the grind of endless tasks—pitching clients, managing deadlines, chasing payments—and stepping into a world where innovation does the heavy lifting for you.

AI tools like ChatGPT, Jasper, and MidJourney are your secret weapons, empowering you to work smarter, not harder while unlocking income potential you never thought possible. These tools are designed to be intuitive and beginner-friendly. Whether you're starting fresh or already a seasoned pro, AI has got you covered. AI-powered freelancing lets you take on more projects, deliver exceptional work, and wow your potential clients with innovative solutions—all while freeing up more time for the things you love.

In this chapter, you'll unlock the secrets to using AI to supercharge your freelancing journey—no technical background or expensive tools required. You'll learn how to choose the right AI platforms that fit your skills, whether you're a writer, designer, marketer, or something entirely unique. With just a little guidance, these tools can transform your ideas into polished, professional results in a fraction of the time it would usually take.

Imagine crafting high-converting sales copy in minutes, building entire branding packages overnight, or generating stunning visuals that clients can't wait to pay for—all without burning out. The best part? You can do it all from your laptop, in your own space, and on your own terms. AI takes the heavy lifting off your plate so you can focus on being creative, productive, and profitable.

Throughout this chapter, I'll walk you step by step through how to build a scalable income stream by offering freelance services powered by artificial intelligence. Whether you're just starting out or looking to grow your client base, you'll find practical tips, and easy-to-follow strategies that will help you work smarter and earn faster. This is your moment to break free from the traditional grind and embrace a more flexible, empowered way to earn from home. Let's dive in and make it happen.

Smart Writing, Smart Money: Copywriting

If you're reading this book, chances are you're looking for ways to generate income from home using modern tools that simplify the process—and copywriting with AI is one of the most accessible paths you can take. You don't need a degree in marketing or years of experience to get started. With the right AI tools at your fingertips, even beginners can create compelling copy that grabs attention and drives action.

Think of these tools not as replacements for your creativity, but as collaborators. They're like having a writing partner who never sleeps—always ready to help you brainstorm, polish your wording, and crank out content faster than ever. Let's say you're crafting a sales page for your online product or writing an email campaign for a client. Tools like Jasper or Copy.ai can whip up several versions of a headline or body copy in seconds, giving you options to play with and refine. This kind of flexibility means you're never stuck staring at a blank screen again.

Now, if you're feeling a little overwhelmed by all the AI tools we've just mentioned—don't worry. That's totally normal. You don't need to master everything at once. We'll walk through each tool step-by-step in the coming pages, showing you exactly how they work, how to use them effectively, and—most importantly—how to monetize your new skills from the comfort of your home.

By the end of this section, you won't just know what these tools do—you'll know how to use them to start making real money, whether it's through freelance gigs, launching your own content-based business, or building a passive income stream. You're not just learning about AI—you're learning how to turn AI into opportunity.

The beauty of AI-assisted copywriting is that it's scalable. Once you get the hang of it, you can start offering freelance services, create your own content for affiliate marketing, or even launch a niche blog that generates income through ads and sponsored posts. The low barrier to entry makes it ideal for anyone looking to pivot into the digital economy—especially from the comfort of home.

Of course, while these tools do a lot of the heavy lifting, it's your unique voice and understanding of your audience that truly make the copy shine. AI helps speed up the process, but human insight gives it heart. That's why your role is still essential. The more you practice and experiment with different types of content—emails, social posts, product pages—the better you'll become at guiding the AI and refining the final result.

Ultimately, learning how to use AI for copywriting is like gaining a superpower that multiplies your productivity and opens new doors. Whether you're building your personal brand, helping small businesses, or launching your own digital venture, mastering these tools gives you the flexibility to work on your terms, from anywhere, and get paid for your words.

So don't be intimidated. Dive in, play around with the tools, and start experimenting. This is one of the most beginner-friendly ways to generate an income using AI—no fancy setup, no need to go viral, just solid, smart writing with a little help from your digital assistant.

Top AI Tools for Copywriting: Boost Your Writing Efficiency

To embark on your copywriting journey, the first step is getting comfortable with the AI tools that can boost both your writing process and your final results. Think of these tools as your digital writing assistants—they help you write smarter, faster, and with more confidence, even if you're just getting started.

Let's begin with **ChatGPT** and **OpenAI's GPT-4**. These are two of the most advanced language models available right now. You simply type in a prompt (like "Write a friendly product description for a handmade candle"), and the AI will instantly generate polished, professional-sounding content. Whether you're writing ad copy, social media captions, blog intros, or email newsletters, these tools help spark ideas and overcome that dreaded blank-page syndrome. They're great for brainstorming, getting quick drafts, and even rewriting your content in different tones or styles.

Next up is **Jasper**, a favorite among marketers. Jasper comes loaded with pre-made templates specifically designed for writing high-converting content—think landing pages, sales emails, product reviews, and more. For example, if you're trying to write a Facebook ad, Jasper will guide you through a few simple inputs (like product name, tone of voice, and a few key benefits), then it will spit out a full ad copy you can tweak or use as-is. This makes it ideal if you want to get into freelance copywriting or create compelling marketing content for your own business.

Then there's **Copy.ai**, which shines when it comes to short-form content. It's perfect for quick and catchy writing—like Instagram captions, product descriptions, or taglines. The interface is super beginner-friendly, so if you're not a tech wizard, don't worry. You'll find it easy to navigate and fun to experiment with. Copy.ai also includes an idea generator, which is helpful when you're stuck and just need some creative juice to get started.

If you're looking to dive into longer-form content like blog posts, ebooks, or informative guides (kind of like the one you're reading right now), **Writesonic** is your go-to tool. It's designed to create in-depth content with structure and flow. You can feed it a topic or headline, and it will generate sections, intros, conclusions, and even SEO-friendly paragraphs. It's a time-saver for bloggers, affiliate marketers, and content creators who want to publish consistent, quality work without spending hours writing from scratch.

The beauty of all these tools is that *they don't replace you*—they *enhance* what you're already doing. They help you write faster, think more clearly, and even learn new ways to structure your content. Instead of spending hours rewriting the same paragraph, you can get a solid draft in minutes and spend your time refining your message or testing out what resonates with your audience.

And if you're totally new to writing or feel unsure about how to get started, don't stress. In the next few chapters, we'll break down each tool step-by-step. You'll learn how to use them effectively, how to practice and sharpen your skills, and how to turn your writing into income—whether that's through freelancing, selling templates, creating ad copy for small businesses, or building your own content brand online.

How to Master AI Tools for Effortless Copywriting

Mastering AI tools for copywriting can drastically improve both the speed and quality of your content creation. Whether you're writing website copy, social media posts, email marketing campaigns, or product descriptions, AI-powered copywriting tools can help streamline the process while ensuring your copy is engaging, persuasive, and targeted to your audience.

Step 1: Selecting the Right Tool for the Job

The first step in using AI for copywriting is choosing the appropriate tool. Platforms like **Jasper, Copy.ai,** and **Writesonic** specialize in generating high-quality copy across a variety of content types. Each platform offers templates tailored to specific needs, such as writing blog posts, Facebook ads, or landing page copy. For example, if you're working on a Facebook ad, a short, engaging copy template would be ideal. For a more detailed blog post, you might use a long-form content template that structures the post into sections like an introduction, body, and conclusion. The right template ensures you have the correct structure to start with, saving time on formatting and allowing you to focus more on refining the message.

Step 2: Crafting Detailed Prompts

Once you've chosen the right template, the next step is crafting a clear and detailed prompt for the AI tool. The quality of the content generated depends largely on the clarity of your instructions. The more context you provide, the better the AI can deliver tailored results. For example, if you're writing a product description for a new fitness tracker, a vague prompt like *"Write a product description for a fitness tracker"* won't yield great results. Instead, provide specifics:

"Write a product description for a sleek and affordable fitness tracker designed for young professionals who want to track their daily steps, monitor their sleep quality, and set fitness goals. Highlight features like waterproof design, long battery life, and customizable watch faces."

The more specific you are, the more likely the AI will generate copy that aligns with your target audience and effectively communicates your product's unique selling points.

Step 3: Refining the AI-Generated Copy

AI tools can produce great drafts, but the copy often needs a human touch to make it sound authentic and aligned with your brand's voice. After receiving the AI-generated copy, read through it carefully, and adjust the tone and style to suit your audience. For example, if the AI produces content that's too formal for your brand, you might want to rewrite sections to sound more conversational or friendly. Conversely, if your brand requires a more authoritative or professional tone, refine the copy accordingly.

Additionally, you should ensure that the copy follows a logical flow, includes persuasive language, and uses a strong call to action. For example, if you're writing a landing page for a product, the call to action (CTA) should be clear and compelling, like *"Get started today with a 30-day free trial!"* or *"Shop now and enjoy 20% off your first order!"*

Step 4: A/B Testing and Optimization

Once the AI-generated copy is refined, it's a good practice to A/B test different versions of your copy to see which performs better with your audience. Tools like **AdCreative.ai** can help optimize ad copy by generating multiple variations, allowing you to test different headlines, body text, or calls to action to determine which one drives the most engagement or conversions.

For example, if you're running a Facebook ad campaign, you could create two versions of the ad copy: one that highlights the benefits of your product and another that emphasizes the product's affordability. After running the ads for a period, you can analyze which version performs best and use that as the basis for future campaigns.

Step 5: Rewriting and Repurposing Content

AI tools can also help you quickly rewrite or repurpose content for different formats. If you have a blog post that's performing well, you can use an AI tool like **QuillBot** to rewrite it in a different style or condense it into a summary for social media. This can save time and effort while maintaining a consistent voice across multiple platforms.

For example, you might have a blog post about "10 Ways to Improve Your Digital Marketing Strategy." Using AI, you could quickly generate Twitter posts, Facebook captions, or even email newsletter excerpts that distill the key takeaways from the post. Repurposing content like this can help you keep your messaging consistent while maximizing the reach of your content.

Example Scenario: Writing a Sales Page for an Online Course
Imagine you're launching an online course on digital marketing. Using **Jasper** or **Copy.ai,** you start by selecting a sales page template. You input a prompt like:

"Write a compelling sales page for an online course called 'Mastering Digital Marketing,' which covers SEO, social media advertising, and email marketing. The course is aimed at small business owners who are new to digital marketing and want to increase their online sales. The

course is priced at $199 and offers a 14-day money-back guarantee."

The AI tool will generate a sales page with an engaging headline, a description of the course modules, testimonials (if provided), and a clear call to action to encourage sign-ups. You'll refine the language to ensure it speaks directly to the pain points of your target audience, perhaps emphasizing how the course will help them "gain a competitive edge" or "grow their business online."

Once you've refined the copy, you can run A/B tests on your sales page to see which headline or CTA drives the highest conversions. You might find that a version with "Boost Your Business Today" performs better than one with "Start Your Marketing Journey" as the CTA, and you can optimize your future marketing campaigns accordingly.

Step 6: Finalizing and Formatting

Now that you've got your AI-generated copy cleaned up and sounding great, it's time to give it that final polish so it's ready to shine on whatever platform you're using. Think of this step as the last mile before launch—it's where presentation meets performance.

If you're writing for a website, you'll want to make sure your copy is optimized for SEO (Search Engine Optimization). This means including keywords that people are actually searching for, writing a clear and catchy meta description, and adding alt text to any images you include. Don't worry—this might sound technical now, but we'll break it all down later. What matters is that your copy isn't just well-written—it's discoverable.

For social media, your content needs to be punchy and engaging. Shorter is often better here. Use a bold hook to grab attention in the first line, then guide the reader with a quick value-packed message. Add relevant hashtags to boost visibility, tag collaborators or brands if needed, and include eye-catching visuals like a graphic, reel, or carousel. A good post can drive traffic, build your brand, or even land you clients—all from the comfort of your home.

If you're writing email campaigns, structure is everything. People skim emails, so break things up with subheadings, short paragraphs, and bullet points when needed (we'll dive into email copywriting soon). A powerful CTA (Call To Action) should stand out—whether that's "Shop Now," "Download Your Guide," or "Book a Free Call." Keep your tone friendly and conversational, like you're talking to a friend. That personal connection goes a long way in getting people to click.

This might feel like a lot right now—but breathe. You're not expected to master it all instantly. The cool thing about this book is that everything that seems unfamiliar or confusing at this point will be explained in bite-sized, beginner-friendly steps as we go. You'll learn the strategy behind the writing, the formatting tricks that work, and how to actually get paid for this skill.

Whether you want to work with clients, launch your own brand, or build a passive income stream with digital products—you're already on the right path. You're not just learning how to write with AI. You're learning how to monetize it. So, take your time, ask questions, and refer back to this guide whenever you need. You've got this.

How to Monetize AI-Powered Copywriting

Let's now dive into how you can transform copywriting into a profitable income stream.

One of the most straightforward ways to monetize your copywriting skills is by offering your services on freelance platforms like Upwork, Fiverr, and Freelancer. These platforms connect you with clients looking for copywriters to create engaging content. Start by creating a professional profile showcasing your copywriting expertise, even if you're new to the field. Include samples generated by AI tools like ChatGPT or Jasper to demonstrate your capabilities. Initially, focus on smaller projects to build your portfolio and gather positive reviews.

As you gain experience, expand your offerings by creating larger service packages that encompass comprehensive deliverables, such as full website content or email marketing campaigns. Highlight your use of AI tools to emphasize quick turnarounds without sacrificing quality, which is a strong selling point for many clients. Over time, work to establish long-term relationships with clients by offering ongoing services like weekly blog posts or monthly newsletters. Adjust your rates as you build your reputation and expand your client base.

Here's the exciting part: AI-enhanced copywriters can realistically earn between $25 to $150 per piece of content, depending on the niche, word count, and complexity. For example, a beginner might start by offering short email sequences or product blurbs at $30–$50 per piece. As your skills grow—and with AI accelerating your workflow—you can easily scale up to higher-ticket gigs like website copy or long-form blog posts at $100 to $300+ each.

Let's break it down: even if you write just 2–3 pieces a day at $50 each, you're looking at $3,000 to $4,500 per month working part-time. Many experienced AI-powered copywriters offering premium services or monthly retainers hit $7,000 to $12,000+ per month once they build up a steady client base.

Want even more leverage? Package your services into niche offers—like "AI-powered email funnels for online coaches" or "SEO blog content for eco-friendly brands." Use AI to generate fast results, and brand yourself as a specialist. The key is using AI not just to write faster, but smarter—and positioning yourself as the creative strategist who gets results.

This is not just about writing—it's about building a business. With low overhead, high scalability, and nearly unlimited demand, AI-assisted copywriting is one of the most exciting and accessible home-based income streams available today.

Creating Preset Packages for Passive Income (Even if You're Just Starting Out)

If you're new to the idea of making money from home and don't know where to begin, creating preset service packages is a great way to start building your income—no experience needed! A preset package is simply a bundle of services or digital content that you offer at a fixed price. Think of it like a menu of done-for-you services, such as writing blog posts, crafting product descriptions, or putting together social media captions.

Here's how you can get started—step by step:

Step 1: Decide What You Want to Offer
First, think about your skills or interests. Can you write? Create social media posts? Help small businesses with marketing? Even if you're not sure, AI tools like **ChatGPT** can help you write product descriptions, emails, blog posts, and more—so you don't need to be an expert.

Step 2: Build a Simple Website
Use easy website builders like **Wix, Squarespace,** or **WordPress. com.** You don't need to know how to code—just choose a template, customize it with your name, a few images, and a section that describes your services.

Step 3: Create Your Packages
Start with 2 or 3 options:

- **Basic Package:** 5 product descriptions

- **Standard Package:** 10 product descriptions + 5 social media captions

- **Premium Package:** 20 product descriptions + 10 social media captions + 3 email marketing sequences

You can always adjust these later, but having clear options makes it easy for someone to buy from you.

Step 4: Automate Your Payments
Connect your site to **PayPal** or **Stripe**, so customers can pay you directly online. Most website builders have built-in tools to help you do this with just a few clicks.

Step 5: Use AI to Deliver High-Quality Work
Once someone buys a package, use tools like **ChatGPT, Jasper,** or **Copy.ai** to help you write the content. You can prompt the AI with something like:

"Write 5 product descriptions for handmade scented candles."

And the AI will give you a great starting point. You can tweak it, polish it up, and send it to your customer. Fast, simple, and professional.

Even if you're starting from scratch, this method can help you build confidence and income at the same time. By setting up your offers once, you create a system that can keep earning for you—day or night. Let your website and AI do the heavy lifting, while you focus on delivering value.

Provide Monthly Content Retainer Services

If you're looking to build consistent income from copywriting—especially from the comfort of your home—offering monthly content retainers is a smart and scalable option. Think of it like a subscription service, but instead of streaming shows, your clients are getting fresh, high-quality content delivered every month.

Here's how it works: many small businesses, coaches, and online brands need regular content to stay visible, engage their audience, and boost sales. But hiring a full-time copywriter is often out of their budget. That's where you come in. By offering a **monthly content retainer**, you're providing them with a steady stream of copy—like blog posts, email newsletters, or social media content—at an affordable, predictable rate.

Start simple. For example, you can offer a **starter package** that includes:

- 2 blog posts per month
- Weekly social media captions
- Basic content planning or a mini content calendar

This low-risk entry point makes it easy for clients to say "yes" without feeling locked into something huge. And with AI tools like Jasper, Writesonic, or ChatGPT, you can generate solid drafts quickly and polish them up with your personal touch. In fact, you could use Jasper to batch-create an entire month's worth of Instagram captions, or let ChatGPT outline and help draft blog posts in just a few hours. That means you could take on multiple clients while still working reasonable hours.

Once your client sees the value you bring (especially when their posts start getting likes, shares, or even sales), they'll often want to scale up. That's your opportunity to offer **expanded packages** with:

- Additional blog posts
- Email marketing sequences
- SEO optimization
- Content repurposing (e.g., turning a blog into social posts or newsletters)

And don't be afraid to charge what you're worth as you grow. As long as you're delivering consistent, quality content, businesses are happy to invest—especially when they realize they can rely on you to take content creation off their plate completely.

To keep things organized and professional, use tools like Google Drive for content delivery, Notion or Trello for planning, and set clear timelines for when content will be submitted each month. You'll look super organized (even if you're writing in your PJs), and your clients will love how smooth everything feels.

Monthly retainers give you income you can count on, month after month—and with AI tools on your team, they're 100% doable. You don't have to hustle for new clients every week. Just build a few great relationships, deliver killer content consistently, and let the momentum build.

The best part? You're creating real value and getting paid for it—on repeat.

Another great way to monetize copywriting is by providing a content retainer service. Small businesses often lack the resources to hire full-time copywriters and are willing to pay for ongoing content creation on a retainer basis. Offer a monthly package that includes blog posts, email newsletters, or social media copy. Begin with a low-cost starter package that includes, say, two blog posts per month and weekly social media captions. This allows clients to test your services with minimal risk. AI tools can help you produce quality content fast, ensuring you meet monthly deadlines with ease. For example, Jasper can generate a month's worth of social media content in a couple of hours, letting you fulfill retainers for multiple clients. As clients benefit from your work, offer to expand their package to include more content or additional services, like SEO optimization or email marketing.

Create a Niche Copywriting Service

Choosing a niche for your copywriting services can help you attract clients more easily and command higher rates due to your specialized expertise. Consider areas such as e-commerce product descriptions, health and wellness blogs, or technology whitepapers. Engage with communities on platforms like LinkedIn or industry-specific forums to identify specific copywriting needs within your chosen niche. Utilize your AI tools to generate high-quality samples relevant to your niche, which will enhance your portfolio. For instance, if you're targeting e-commerce clients, create compelling product descriptions using tools like Jasper or Copy.ai. These tailored samples will demonstrate your understanding of the niche and make it easier to attract and secure clients. Promote your niche services using LinkedIn, social media, and industry-specific job boards to promote your niche services. Your messaging should clearly state how you understand the unique needs of your niche and have the tools (AI) to meet them efficiently.

Run AI Copywriting Workshops for Businesses

Many organizations are eager to learn how AI can support their marketing efforts. By organizing workshops, you can teach employees how to use AI tools for content creation, editing, and brainstorming.

Develop a comprehensive agenda that guides participants through the capabilities of AI tools, demonstrating how they can enhance productivity and maintain high-quality content. To reach a wider audience, consider offering virtual workshops through platforms like Zoom or Google Meet. This format makes it easier for businesses with remote teams to participate. You can charge either a per-participant fee or a flat rate for the entire team, depending on their size and needs. By sharing your expertise, you not only generate income but also position yourself as a thought leader in the copywriting field.

Expand Your Skills and Offer Additional Services

As the copywriting world continues to evolve, it's vital to stay current with trends, technologies, and best practices. Consider investing in additional training or courses on advanced copywriting techniques, SEO, or digital marketing strategies to further enhance your service offerings. By continuously developing your skills, you can provide more comprehensive solutions to your clients and stay competitive in the market.

Final Thoughts: Making AI Copywriting Work for You

AI-powered copywriting isn't a get-rich-quick scheme, but it is a smart way to boost your productivity, improve your writing, and create new income opportunities. Whether you're freelancing, building a niche service, or selling copywriting packages, AI can help streamline your process—BUT success still depends on your effort, strategy, and ability to deliver quality work.

The key is to use AI as a tool, not a replacement for skill or creativity. It can speed up content creation, help you overcome writer's block, and generate ideas, but your personal touch is what makes the copy truly engaging. Clients value originality, strategic thinking, and the human element—things AI can't fully replicate.

So, where do you start? Pick a tool, experiment with different types of content, and take on small projects to build confidence. Over time, you'll develop your own workflow, refine your skills, and find ways to scale your income. With consistency and the right approach, AI-powered copywriting can become a sustainable and profitable way to earn from home.

The AI Blogging Revolution: Automate, Optimize, Monetize

If you've ever dreamed of turning your passion into a business, blogging is one of the most accessible and powerful tools available today. With the help of AI, you can now create content, build an audience, and generate income without needing a whole production team or marketing background. Whether you're a fitness coach sharing training tips, a food lover posting recipes and kitchen hacks, or just someone with a hobby you can't stop talking about—there's room for you to grow and monetize your blog into a successful business venture. With AI tools, you can generate blog topics, write articles, design social media graphics, and even automate email marketing to keep your audience engaged.

And the best part? Your blog becomes an income-generating machine. From affiliate marketing and sponsored posts to selling your own digital products or online services, there are endless ways to monetize your content. Whether you want a side hustle or a full-time income stream, blogging—powered by AI—is one of the smartest and most scalable ways to do it.

Essential AI Tools That Will Transform Your Blogging Game

Creating high-quality content consistently is one of the biggest challenges bloggers face. You can spend hours brainstorming ideas, writing blog posts, and optimizing for SEO, but without high-quality content, your blog won't attract the traffic necessary to generate revenue. This is where **Jasper** comes in.

Jasper is one of the most powerful tools for content creation in the AI space (formerly known as Jarvis). Jasper is an advanced AI writing assistant designed to help creators write high-quality content faster and more efficiently. Whether you're working on blog posts, website copy, product descriptions, or email newsletters, Jasper can do the heavy lifting. It generates well-structured, engaging content based on just a few prompts, saving you hours of writing and editing time.

But Jasper isn't just about speed—it's also smart. It has features that help optimize your blog posts for SEO, so your content ranks higher on Google and attracts more organic traffic. Simply input your target keywords, audience tone, and topic, and Jasper can deliver a full draft complete with headings, subheadings, and even calls to action. It can also tailor the content style to match your brand voice, whether you want it to sound professional, friendly, casual, or inspirational. It even comes with pre-built templates for specific content needs, like "blog post intro," "product review," "how-to article," or "listicle," which makes it easy to stay consistent and productive.

Jasper's ability to generate content quickly means more posts, more traffic, and more monetization opportunities. Whether you're monetizing through affiliate marketing, sponsored posts, or digital products like travel guides or eBooks, AI can make your blogging journey more profitable by creating content faster and with fewer roadblocks.

Once you have great content, the next step is making sure it gets seen by the right people. That's where SEO (Search Engine Optimization) comes in. Optimizing your blog posts for Google's search algorithms is crucial for driving organic traffic. However, optimizing every blog post manually can be exhausting. That's where Surfer SEO comes into play, an AI tool that specializes in attracting views to your blog. Surfer SEO analyzes top-ranking articles, suggested keywords, and recommended improvements to your blog's structure, increasing the chances of exposure.

With tools like Surfer SEO, you don't need to be an SEO expert to optimize your blog for search engines. AI tools take care of the technical side, leaving you more time to focus on creating content and monetizing your blog.

Take my friend Emily, a wellness blogger who struggled with SEO for years. Despite writing valuable content, her blog posts never ranked as high as they should have. After using AI tools, she was able to automate her SEO process by optimizing her content for the keywords that matter most to her readers. As a result, Emily's content began ranking higher in search results, attracting more organic traffic, which directly boosted her ad revenue and affiliate commissions from wellness product promotions.

Repurposing Content Creation with AI

Creating new blog posts consistently can be exhausting, but with Quillbot, you can repurpose existing content to reach a wider audience and increase your traffic. Quillbot's AI-powered paraphrasing tool can take your existing blog posts and turn them into new, fresh content that can be republished across multiple platforms, or even in different formats like social media posts or eBooks.

For example, Ryan, a mental health blogger, had a wealth of valuable content on his site, but he struggled to keep his posts fresh and engaging. Using Quillbot, he repurposed his most popular blog posts into shorter, shareable content for social media, email newsletters, and lead magnets to grow his email list. This helped Ryan generate passive income by promoting affiliate products related to mental health and wellness through his email campaigns.

Repurposing content with AI not only saves you time but also expands your reach, creating more monetization opportunities through affiliate sales, product promotions, and email marketing.

Once your content is live, AI can help you promote it effectively. Tools like MarketMuse help you strategize and ensure your content is competitive. By suggesting relevant topics and high-ranking keywords, MarketMuse ensures your blog posts attract targeted traffic, increasing your monetization potential.

Additionally, tools like Rytr can assist with generating promotional emails and social media content, which are essential for driving traffic back to your blog. By automating the process of content promotion, you free up more time to focus on growing your blog and diversifying your income streams.

Monetizing with Affiliate Marketing and Sponsored Content

Before diving into specific strategies on how to monetize your blog, it's important to understand that monetizing your blog is not a one-size-fits-all approach. The income potential of your blog depends on several factors, including the niche, audience size, and the value you offer. Some bloggers choose to focus on passive income, while others actively promote products and services.

Turning blogging into a reliable income stream involves multiple approaches, each leveraging the reach and value your blog provides.

One of the incredibly popular and beginner-friendly way to monetize a blog is through affiliate marketing. This strategy allows you to earn money by recommending products or services to your readers—whenever someone clicks your unique affiliate link and makes a purchase, you receive a commission. Simple, effective, and scalable.

Take Sarah, for example—a travel blogger who shares destination guides, packing tips, and hotel reviews. Throughout her posts, she includes affiliate links to her favorite travel gear, booking platforms, and even travel insurance. Every time a reader follows her recommendation and makes a purchase, Sarah earns a commission—sometimes a few dollars, other times much more, depending on the product.

The beauty of affiliate marketing is that it works behind the scenes. Once the content is live, those links keep working for you 24/7, turning your blog into a passive income engine. The key to maximizing this income stream is to promote products that genuinely align with your niche and audience—things you either use yourself or truly believe in. And instead of sounding salesy, your recommendations should be seamlessly woven into valuable, informative content that helps your readers.

With the right strategy and growing traffic, affiliate marketing has the potential to generate hundreds to thousands of dollars per month, even while you sleep.

Another popular monetizing strategy to generate passive income from your blog is by monetizing with ads. Platforms like Google AdSense make it incredibly easy to start—you just apply, get approved, and place ad code on your site. From there, every visitor becomes an opportunity to earn, as you get paid based on impressions and clicks.

To maximize your earnings from ads, focus first on growing consistent traffic. The more visitors you attract, the more your revenue potential increases. Strategic ad placement is also key—try embedding ads in your sidebar, header, or directly within your content to find what draws the most engagement. It's all about experimenting and optimizing.

Once your blog reaches a certain threshold—typically around 50,000 sessions per month—you can level up to premium ad networks like Mediavine or AdThrive. These platforms pay significantly more than AdSense, often between $10 to $40 per 1,000 impressions, depending on your niche and audience. That means with strong traffic, your blog could easily bring in $1,000–$5,000+ per month just from ads alone.

While ad revenue takes time to build, it can become a steady, scalable income stream—especially when paired with great content and the power of AI-driven SEO to bring in long-term traffic.

Sponsored Content
As your blog begins to gain traction, sponsored content becomes a powerful and rewarding monetization strategy. This involves partnering with brands who pay you to write about their products or services—

whether it's a detailed review, a tutorial, or a feature within a relevant post.

The key to attracting sponsorships is to build a blog that radiates credibility, consistency, and niche expertise. With the help of AI tools that streamline content creation and scheduling, you can maintain a steady publishing rhythm and establish yourself as a trusted voice in your niche. Brands notice this—and they're always on the lookout for influencers and bloggers who align with their mission and audience.

Imagine a wellness blogger who writes about meditation, healthy eating, and mindfulness. As her readership grows, a wellness brand might approach her to feature their organic supplements or fitness app in a blog post. She can charge anywhere from $100 to $1,000+ per post, depending on her traffic, domain authority, and social engagement.

To successfully land and leverage sponsored content deals:

- Cultivate an engaged audience that values your recommendations - brands love to work with creators who inspire action.

- Proactively reach out to companies in your niche with a well-crafted pitch and media kit showcasing your stats.

- Always disclose sponsored content transparently to maintain reader trust and comply with advertising guidelines.

Over time, sponsored content can evolve from one-off deals into long-term brand partnerships, adding a reliable and potentially lucrative income stream to your blogging business—all from the comfort of home.

Selling Digital Products and E-books

Selling your own digital products is not only one of the most profitable ways to monetize a blog—it's also one of the most empowering. With no inventory to manage or shipping logistics to worry about, you can turn your knowledge and creativity into products that generate income passively and at scale.

Think eBooks, online courses, printable planners, design templates, or niche-specific guides. Once created, these products can be sold over and over again—making them an ideal income stream for anyone looking to monetize from home with minimal ongoing effort.

Take Liam, for example. A blogging expert, he designed a beginner-friendly course teaching others how to start and grow a blog. By promoting the course through his blog and email list, Liam started earning $2,000–$5,000 per month—simply from sharing what he already knew. That's the beauty of digital products—you build once and earn endlessly.

Many bloggers who sell niche products like meal plans, fitness programs, or business templates can make anywhere from $500 to $10,000+ per month, depending on traffic, pricing, and marketing. High-ticket courses or memberships can even bring in $50,000 or more per year once established.

To successfully monetize through digital products:

- Start with your audience: What do they struggle with? What would make their lives easier? Create a solution in digital form.

- Use your blog as a funnel: Offer free content that leads naturally to your paid product, building trust and interest.

- Promote effectively: Leverage social media, newsletters, and AI-generated content to drive traffic to your product pages.

Platforms like Gumroad, Podia, Shopify, and SendOwl make selling digital products seamless. Meanwhile, AI tools like ChatGPT or Jasper can help you craft landing pages, sales copy, and automated email sequences to convert readers into customers—on autopilot.

With the right strategy, selling digital products can become a scalable, evergreen income stream that grows with your brand. Whether you're aiming for a few hundred dollars in side income or building toward a full-time living, it's all possible—right from home.

Subscription-Based Content

For bloggers who consistently deliver high-value, engaging content, subscriptions and memberships offer a powerful way to generate reliable, recurring income—month after month. Instead of relying solely on ad clicks or one-time product sales, this model rewards you for building a loyal community that's willing to pay for exclusive access and deeper value.

Platforms like Patreon, Substack, and Buy Me a Coffee make it easy to offer premium content, behind-the-scenes updates, downloadable resources, or one-on-one interaction through tiered memberships. You can offer different levels of perks—from bonus blog posts and downloadable eBooks to live Q&As, private community chats, and more.

Take Clara, a food blogger, for example. After building a solid audience, she introduced a $5/month membership that gave subscribers access to premium recipes, detailed cooking tutorials, and personalized kitchen tips. Within just a few months, she attracted 500 subscribers—bringing in $2,500 per month in passive income. This recurring revenue allowed her to focus less on chasing one-off sponsorships and more on creating what she loves.

Depending on your niche and audience size, bloggers can earn anywhere from a few hundred dollars to $10,000+ per month in membership income. And since you control the value and pricing, the earning potential only grows as your audience expands.

To successfully monetize with subscriptions:

- Provide irresistible value: Whether it's exclusive content, tools, or personal access, make sure paying members get something they can't find for free.

- Build connection: Let your subscribers feel like part of a special community. Engaging directly and consistently keeps them invested.

- Use AI to scale: AI tools like ChatGPT or Jasper can help you quickly create unique, premium content—from bonus blog posts and digital downloads to automated newsletters for members.

Offering a membership model is more than just a revenue stream—it's a relationship with your most dedicated readers. And when you treat that relationship with care, the rewards—both financially and creatively—can be incredible.

Offering Consulting or Coaching Services
If you've built trust and authority in your niche, one of the most rewarding ways to monetize your blog is by offering coaching or consulting services. This model transforms your knowledge into a high-ticket income stream, allowing you to work directly with clients who are eager to learn from your expertise.

For example, imagine you're running a blog on personal finance. You could offer one-on-one coaching sessions to help readers create customized budgeting plans, improve their credit scores, or develop investment strategies. By leveraging your blog content as proof of knowledge, you can attract serious clients who are willing to pay for tailored advice.

This method can be extremely lucrative—coaches and consultants in niches like business, health, marketing, and finance often charge $100 to $300+ per session, with monthly packages bringing in $1,000 to $5,000 or more, depending on your experience and the value you offer.

To successfully monetize your blog through consulting or coaching:

- Position yourself as an expert: Publish high-quality, informative blog posts, case studies, or results-driven content that demonstrates your authority.

- Use your blog to funnel leads: Offer free value—like webinars, downloadable guides, or email series—to attract and warm up potential clients.

- Promote your services clearly: Create a dedicated page on your blog outlining your services, pricing, and testimonials. Use strong calls-to-action in your blog posts and emails.

- Automate with AI: Use tools like ChatGPT to help create coaching resources, prep documents, client templates, or even scripts for discovery calls—saving you time and adding polish to your services.

Whether you're offering business strategy sessions, fitness coaching, or mindset mentoring, consulting allows you to deliver high-impact value while earning significantly for your time and expertise. And as your client base and reputation grow, so does your income potential.

Final thoughts on turning your blog into an income stream

Monetizing your blog is not a "get-rich-quick" process—it takes time, consistency, and strategy. By using the proven methods outlined in this chapter, you can start to generate income from your blog while providing valuable content to your readers. Whether it's through affiliate marketing, selling digital products, sponsored posts, or offering consulting services, there are multiple ways to monetize your blog.

Remember, the key to successful monetization is building a strong, engaged audience. Once you have that foundation, you can explore the various methods of monetization that suit your niche and expertise.

By leveraging the strategies in this chapter, you'll be well on your way to turning your blog into a reliable income source. The opportunity to earn from your passion is within reach, and now it's time to take action and unlock your blog's full potential.

From Pen to Profit:

Monetizing Writing and Publishing with AI

Venturing into the world of self-publishing can be daunting, yet with the right strategies and tools, it's an exciting journey that could lead to personal satisfaction and financial success. AI can significantly streamline self-publishing, making it easier for authors or anyone with a passion to produce, market, and sell their books from home just using their laptop or a computer.

This section will not only guide you through the key AI tools that can help you unlock new income streams in writing and publishing but will also enable you to create and publish your own books from the comfort of your own home!

We will explore how AI tools can assist you in content creation, SEO optimization, and even marketing, giving you the blueprint to monetize your work more effectively. Whether you're already a professional writer or just a beginner, by the end of this chapter, you will be able to write and publish your own books too!

Unlocking Writing and Publishing Success with AI Tools

In the ever-evolving landscape of digital content creation, the idea of turning a passion for writing into a profitable venture is now more achievable than ever before. Gone are the days when writers had to spend endless hours perfecting their craft while also struggling with the daunting task of marketing, promoting, and monetizing their work. Today, Artificial Intelligence (AI) has revolutionized the way writers and publishers approach their business, offering a smarter, faster, and more efficient path to creating content and generating revenue.

AI tools have transformed the entire writing and publishing process, allowing writers to focus on what they do best—crafting compelling content. Whether you're an established writer, a blogger, or an aspiring self-published author, AI can help you streamline your efforts, optimize your content for SEO, and reach a wider audience—all while

41

improving efficiency, reducing burnout, and freeing up more time for creativity. From brainstorming ideas and generating outlines to editing drafts and designing covers, AI supports you at every stage of your publishing journey, making it easier than ever to turn your ideas into a polished, profitable book.

One of the key ways AI enhances the writing process is through content generation. Tools like **Jasper**, an AI-powered writing assistant, allow writers to create high-quality blog posts, articles, product descriptions, and even eBooks in a fraction of the time it would take manually. With Jasper, you simply provide a few key details in the form of a prompt, and the tool produces a well-structured, coherent piece of writing that's almost ready to publish. The best part? The content is SEO-optimized, which helps improve search engine rankings and makes it easier for your audience to find your work. By leveraging Jasper , you can publish more frequently and drive more traffic to your site, leading to increased opportunities for ad revenue, affiliate marketing, and sponsored content.

Here are some of the most essential AI tools that every writer and self-publisher should know about—each one plays a unique role in streamlining the writing, editing, and publishing process from start to finish.

ChatGPT and **Jasper** are top-tier content generation tools. ChatGPT shines when it comes to brainstorming, outlining, and drafting ideas quickly, making it a reliable creative partner for writers. Jasper, on the other hand, is equipped with pre-built templates for everything from blog posts and sales pages to long-form book chapters. It's designed with SEO in mind, helping you create content that's not only readable but also discoverable.

Sudowrite is a dream tool for creative writers. It uses AI to spark ideas, develop characters, enhance dialogue, and suggest plot twists. Whether you're writing a novel, short story, or script, Sudowrite acts like a writing coach and creative companion, helping you push through writer's block and elevate your prose.

To ensure your content is clean, clear, and professional, **Grammarly** and **ProWritingAid** are indispensable. Grammarly focuses on grammar, tone, and clarity, while ProWritingAid offers deeper style analysis and readability reports. Together, they help polish your writing to a high standard.

When it's time to format your manuscript, **Vellum** makes the process seamless. With its intuitive interface and beautiful templates, you can easily create professional-quality eBooks and print-ready layouts that meet the standards of major self-publishing platforms.

For authors looking to maximize visibility and sales, **Publisher Rocket (formerly KDP Rocket)** is a game-changer. It helps you uncover profitable keywords, analyze competitor books, and find the best niches within your genre—making it easier to attract the right readers and increase book sales.

Finally, for striking and original book covers, **Ideogram** is a powerful AI design tool that brings your visual concepts to life. Whether you need a clean, minimalist eBook cover or a bold, genre-specific paperback design, Ideogram helps you create stunning graphics that grab attention and reflect your story's essence.

Step-by-Step Guide: Mastering the Art of Writing and Publishing with the Power of AI Tools

Now that we've covered the essential AI tools for writing and publishing, let's dive into the step-by-step process of how to actually write and publish your book.

Step 1: Creating An Outline

An outline is like a blueprint for your book—it contains the full breakdown of chapters and the core content that will shape your story or message. To create an effective outline, begin by brainstorming ideas. **ChatGPT** and **Jasper** can help by generating potential book titles, chapter outlines, and even short story ideas based on your prompt. For instance, if you're writing nonfiction, you could input something like: *"Create an outline for a book called 'A Guide to Home Gardening for Beginners',"* and the AI will deliver a structured chapter list, complete with subtopics and research pointers.

For fiction writers, **Sudowrite** is especially powerful. This AI tool is built for creative storytelling and offers features like "Story Engine," "Describe," and "Character Generator." Let's say you're writing a fantasy novel—Sudowrite can help you build a detailed world, generate vivid character profiles, and even suggest plot twists to maintain tension. If you're stuck, you can use the "Expand" feature to take a sentence or paragraph you've written and watch it grow into a full scene, written in your tone and style. For example, you might type: *"My hero discovers a hidden map in the attic,"* and Sudowrite can expand it into a full narrative scene with dialogue, sensory details, and emotion.

With tools like these, outlining becomes a creative, collaborative experience. You're no longer staring at a blank page—you're bouncing ideas off an intelligent assistant that's ready to help with structure, pacing, and creativity. By leveraging AI in your outlining phase, you're setting yourself up for a smoother, faster, and more inspired writing journey.

Step 2: Writing the Manuscript

Now that your outline is ready, it's time to bring your book to life—one chapter at a time. Use your outline as a roadmap, and start drafting each section with intention. This is where AI tools really shine.

ChatGPT is excellent for generating well-structured content for nonfiction books. Simply input a prompt like, *"Write an introductory chapter on sustainable gardening for beginners,"* and it can provide a clear, informative draft to build upon. You can then tweak the tone, add personal insights, or expand with more research as needed. Really make sure you are taking your time on each chapter and perfecting it as you go.

If you're working on fiction, **Sudowrite** becomes your creative sidekick. Say you're writing a sci-fi novel—use Sudowrite to describe the intricate setting of a futuristic city, explore character motivations, or get help continuing a tricky scene. You can even use the "Describe," "Expand," or "Rewrite" functions to enhance emotional beats or deepen your world building with just a few clicks.

Writing a book isn't a race—it's a journey. As you move through each chapter, remember that you're building something meaningful, something that has the potential to inspire, educate, or transport your readers. Whether you're working on a practical guide or an epic fantasy, each word you write brings you closer to your finished masterpiece.

Take your time and be intentional. Let the AI tools support you, not rush you. Use them to spark ideas, to keep you moving forward when motivation dips, and to elevate your writing to its highest potential. Every draft, every revision, every little tweak is a step toward something you'll be proud to share with the world.

Think of your manuscript as a living creation—one that grows richer the more care and attention you pour into it. So breathe, stay curious, and trust the process. With patience, creativity, and the right digital tools by your side, you're not just writing a book—you're crafting a legacy.

Step 3: Formatting your Book to Amazon Standard

Once your manuscript is ready, use Vellum to format your print book and eBook. Vellum ensures a professional look that's consistent across devices and platforms. You can do this by uploading your draft to design and format your eBook and print-ready version with customizable templates, which is critical for building reader trust. Vellum is only Mac compatible, so if you don't own a Mac, you can use Atticus, another amazing book formatting program. Both can be bought online as a one-off purchase. Don't worry if you're not that tech-savvy or have time obligations, you can also hire someone to format your book for you on Fiverr for a small fee.

Step 4: Create your Book Cover

You have a couple of options to create a book cover. You can design it yourself using Canva with provided templates. It's the least costly option, with only a monthly subscription, and it gives you full design control. OR, if you don't want to do it yourself, you can hire a professional on Fiverr, who will design the cover for you for a fee. However, in my opinion, the best option would be Ideogram.

Ideogram is an AI-powered design tool that makes book cover creation easy, even if you're not a professional designer. It requires a small subscription fee and allows you to create as many book covers as you desire, making it the most cost-effective option. To create a stunning book cover, begin by inputting a clear prompt that describes your book's theme, style, and key elements. For example, if your book is about AI and entrepreneurship, you can specify a futuristic design with sleek typography and digitally inspired visuals. Ideogram's AI will generate multiple design variations, allowing you to pick the best one or refine it further by adjusting colors, fonts, and compositions. Once you are satisfied, download the high-quality image and add any final touches using a tool like Canva or Photoshop. You can also use Canva to format the book cover to Jpeg or PDF option just by uploading the book cover image, selecting the format, and downloading it. This will be very important in the next step of publishing your book in Amazon KDP or other platforms.

Step 5: Publishing your Book on AMAZON KDP

To publish your book, Amazon Kindle Direct Publishing (KDP), IngramSpark, and Draft2Digital are some of the most accessible platforms available, and the best part is, they're free to use. By simply creating an account, you can start uploading your manuscript and cover with ease. Amazon KDP is particularly user-friendly and allows you to publish your book in both ebook and paperback formats.

To get started with **Amazon KDP,** follow these simple steps:

Step 1: Create Your KDP Account

If you don't already have an Amazon account, you'll need to create one. Once you've logged in, go to Amazon KDP and sign in using your Amazon account details. If you don't have an account, just click on "Sign up" to create one.

Step 2: Start a New Title

Once logged in, you'll be directed to your KDP dashboard. Click the "+ Kindle eBook" or "+ Paperback" button to start a new book project. KDP will prompt you to enter book details, including the title, author name, and a brief description of the book.

Step 3: Upload Your Manuscript

Here, you'll need to upload your manuscript file in a compatible format (such as DOC, DOCX, or PDF). Amazon provides formatting guidelines to ensure your book looks great in both eBook and paperback formats. If you're unsure, KDP also offers a free downloadable eBook and paperback templates to help you format your manuscript properly.

Step 4: Add Your Book Cover

KDP gives you two options for adding a book cover:

1. **Upload your own cover:** If you've already created a cover using a tool like Canva or a professional designer, you can upload it here.

2. **Use KDP's Cover Creator:** If you don't have a cover yet, KDP offers a free tool to help you design a cover using pre-made templates.

Step 5: Set Your Keywords and Categories

When uploading your manuscript, KDP will ask you to enter keywords that best describe your book. This is where tools like Publisher

Rocket come in handy. By analyzing profitable niches, Publisher Rocket helps you find high-demand, low-competition keywords that improve your SEO, making your book more discoverable. Use this research to identify relevant and strategic keywords that target your ideal audience. Additionally, you'll need to select the appropriate categories (such as "Science Fiction," "Self-Help," or "Romance") that best represent your book.

Step 6: Set Pricing and Royalties

Decide on your book's price and select your royalty rate. Amazon offers two royalty options for eBooks:

- **35% royalty** for books priced between $0.99 and $2.98.

- **70% royalty** for books priced between $2.99 and $9.99.

You can also choose to enroll your book in KDP Select, which allows you to reach Amazon's exclusive audience in exchange for making your book available only through KDP for 90 days.

Step 7: Preview and Publish

Once everything is filled out and you've uploaded your manuscript and cover, KDP gives you the option to preview your book. This is your chance to ensure everything looks perfect—check the formatting, layout, and cover alignment. Once satisfied, hit the "Publish" button!

FYI: Important details you must not ignore

When creating a book, I cannot stress enough how important it is to ensure your book is of the highest quality, free of spelling or grammar mistakes, and represents the title and topic you are writing about. It must look professional and well-formatted. Any work produced using AI tools should always be double-checked and reworded if it needs to sound more natural or more in theme with your book. To protect your work, include a copyright page at the beginning of your book followed by the content page. All work must be referenced, and resources must be provided at the back of the book.

From Pen to Profit: How to Monetize Writing and Publishing

Self-publishing is one of the most accessible and profitable ways to monetize your writing. Thanks to platforms like Amazon Kindle Direct

Publishing (KDP) and IngramSpark, you can publish both eBooks and print-on-demand paperbacks without any upfront printing costs. This low-risk, high-reward model has opened the doors for writers everywhere to turn their passion into profit.

To boost your success, it's smart to write in high-demand genres such as self-help, romance, thrillers, historical fiction, or fantasy. These categories consistently attract large, loyal audiences that are always hungry for fresh content. But don't just guess—use AI-powered research tools like Publisher Rocket to uncover profitable sub-niches and low-competition keywords. Instead of writing a generic self-help book, why not tap into a more targeted niche like *"Mindfulness for Busy Entrepreneurs"* or *"Time Management Hacks for Remote Workers"*?

Once you've found your niche, AI writing assistants like ChatGPT, Sudowrite, and Jasper can help with brainstorming, outlining, and drafting. This means you can publish faster and more consistently—an essential key to long-term success in self-publishing. Imagine building a catalog of 5 to 10 books over the course of a year. With each new release, your previous titles gain visibility and boost your overall royalties.

One particularly effective strategy is to create a series. For fiction writers, this could be something like a *"Small Town Detective"* mystery series, with each book solving a new case. Once readers are hooked on Book 1, they'll eagerly follow through the rest of the series—turning one customer into multiple sales. For nonfiction, a multi-part series on *personal productivity*—covering topics like goal setting, habit building, and work-life balance—can appeal to the same effect.

In terms of revenue potential, many self-published authors earn $200 to $1,000+ per month per book, especially in well-researched niches. A growing library of quality content can compound your earnings, especially if you layer in other opportunities like audiobook versions or international translations—both of which AI can assist with.

By leveraging AI tools to streamline the creative process, optimize your positioning, and build a loyal reader base, you're not just publishing books—you're creating a scalable, sustainable writing business that pays you while you sleep.

1. Write and Publish Short E-books for Niche Markets
Tapping into niche markets—like DIY crafts, plant-based recipes,

or minimalist home organization—can be a powerful strategy for writers looking to stand out and earn from highly targeted audiences. These micro-niches often have passionate, engaged readers actively searching for practical, specific solutions. This is where short e-books shine.

With the help of AI tools like ChatGPT or Sudowrite, you can quickly create concise, valuable e-books ranging from 20 to 50 pages that solve real problems or teach a focused skill. For instance, a quick guide titled "10 Easy Plant-Based Meal Preps for Busy Beginners" or "Declutter Your Closet in One Weekend" can be written, formatted, and published in just a few days with the right tools.

Once your book is ready, promote it through social media groups, niche forums, Pinterest boards, or targeted blogs where your ideal readers are already spending time. These communities are often overlooked by mainstream marketers, which gives you an edge and less competition.

Because these short e-books are easy to consume and offer quick wins, they're perfect for casual readers who may not commit to a full-length book. Pricing them between $2.99 and $6.99 makes them attractive impulse buys—especially when positioned as practical, time-saving resources.

Even better? Once you've written and published a few, the income becomes scalable. Just five niche e-books earning $100–$300 per month each can generate an extra $500–$1,500 per month in passive income—all while building your brand and authority in your chosen niche.

By combining focused content, smart AI-powered writing, and niche-targeted promotion, these short, specific e-books can become an efficient and reliable income stream—all from home.

2. Create Content for Subscription Platforms (e.g., Kindle Unlimited)
Amazon's Kindle Unlimited (KU) program offers another powerful way to monetize your writing, especially if you're building a series or writing multiple related titles. For a monthly fee, subscribers gain access to a vast library of books—yours included. As a writer, you're paid based on pages read, not just sales, meaning that the longer readers stay immersed in your books, the more you earn.

This makes series writing incredibly lucrative. When readers enjoy your first book, they're likely to continue with the next installment—and that binge-reading behavior can lead to hundreds or even thousands of pages read per reader. Imagine having a three-part cozy mystery series, each book around 200 pages. If one reader finishes the full trilogy, that's 600 pages read—and you get compensated for every single one.

Some authors using KU report earnings of $2,000 to $10,000+ per month, depending on how many books they have and how well they market them. While these numbers take time and consistency to reach, even new authors can earn a few hundred dollars per month with just a handful of well-written, engaging titles in popular genres like romance, thriller, or sci-fi.

In short, Kindle Unlimited rewards consistency and binge-worthy content—and with AI in your creative corner, building a profitable book series from home has never been more achievable.

Amazon's Kindle Unlimited program allows readers to access a library of books for a monthly fee, and writers are compensated based on pages read. If you have a series or several related titles, publish them through Kindle Unlimited, encouraging readers to read multiple titles and increasing your page-read revenue. AI tools can speed up the process of building a series, and tools like Sudowrite can even help you maintain continuity across books (important for character consistency in fiction series). By keeping readers engaged across multiple volumes, you enhance your earning potential from the program.

3. Sell Serialized Fiction on Digital Platforms (e.g., Radish, Wattpad, or Substack)
Serialized fiction offers a compelling way for writers to generate income by releasing stories chapter-by-chapter, with readers paying for each part of the story as it unfolds. Platforms like Radish, Wattpad, and Substack make it easy for authors to monetize their stories, offering options like pay-per-chapter or subscription-based models.

This model works particularly well for genres that rely on suspense and ongoing narratives, such as romance, thriller, or fantasy. Readers are often eager to follow along with each new installment, which keeps them coming back and ready to pay for the next chapter. By incorporating cliffhangers at the end of each chapter, you can further encourage this anticipation, ensuring a steady flow of readers throughout the series.

With the help of AI tools like ChatGPT, you can efficiently outline story arcs, develop characters, and generate plot ideas, speeding up the writing process without sacrificing creativity. AI can even assist with drafting chapter summaries or suggesting twists to keep the story engaging. The ease of content creation allows you to release chapters more frequently, which can help build a larger, more dedicated readership.

As for revenue, serialized fiction authors on platforms like Radish can earn around $0.05 to $0.10 per page read, which can add up quickly with a highly engaged audience. For example, if a chapter is about 5,000 words (roughly 20 pages), and you gain 1,000 readers, you could potentially earn $50 to $100 per chapter. Over time, as you release more chapters, build your following, and develop a series, these figures can grow exponentially.

Once the serialized story is complete, consider packaging the chapters into a single eBook for additional income. The "complete edition" can attract readers who prefer binge-reading the entire story or who missed earlier chapters. Depending on the pricing model, you could earn $5 to $10 per sale for the eBook, and if your story has a strong following, it could sell thousands of copies. For example, a well-received serialized romance series could easily generate $1,000 to $5,000 or more per month once it gains traction and a loyal reader base.

Ultimately, serialized fiction combined with AI tools provides a scalable, high-revenue opportunity for writers. As your following grows and you continue to release more chapters or series, you can create a consistent income stream while tapping into a passionate and loyal audience that eagerly awaits the next chapter of your story.

4. Ghostwriting and Freelance Writing Services

Ghostwriting is a profitable niche in the self-publishing world, where many individuals and businesses seek skilled writers to bring their ideas to life in the form of books, articles, or blogs. This is where your ability to write compelling content can be turned into a consistent revenue stream. If you have expertise in a specific field, you can offer ghostwriting services on platforms like **Upwork, Fiverr,** or even through personal referrals.

The demand for ghostwriters is substantial across various industries—business, health, self-help, and even fiction. With the rise of content marketing, many companies need high-quality articles, blog posts, or eBooks to fuel their digital presence, and they're often willing to pay top dollar for well-written material that engages their audience.

To stand out in the competitive ghostwriting market, it's crucial to build a strong portfolio that showcases your ability to write in various styles and genres. This will demonstrate your versatility and help attract clients with different writing needs. Be transparent about using AI tools to improve efficiency but emphasize that the final product is crafted with care, attention to detail, and expertise. The combination of your skills and AI-powered speed will allow you to deliver high-quality content at a faster rate, increasing your productivity and earning potential.

As you build a reputation, collect positive reviews, and nurture long-term relationships with clients, you'll be able to command higher rates for your services. You may even expand your clientele, taking on larger projects or working with businesses on an ongoing basis, providing steady work and income.

Depending on the complexity of the project, ghostwriters can charge anywhere from $50 to $100 per hour, or $500 to $5,000 per book or eBook, with rates increasing as your experience and reputation grow. If you're working on shorter projects like articles or blogs, expect to earn $100 to $500 per piece, while larger projects (e.g., full-length novels or business guides) can easily bring in $3,000 to $10,000 per project or more. With consistent work, ghostwriting can turn into a sustainable and lucrative income stream, especially if you focus on long-term client relationships and expand your services to include high-demand niches.

5. Create and Sell Educational E-books and Workbooks
Educational content is in demand across various fields, from language learning and business skills to creative writing and personal development. Write educational e-books or interactive workbooks that offer valuable lessons or exercises. Platforms like **Gumroad** or **Teachable** allow you to sell digital downloads directly to customers. Use AI tools to develop in-depth content and accompanying exercises. Grammarly can help refine instructional clarity, while Jasper can suggest topics based on industry trends. Promote these e-books on LinkedIn, social media, or through partnerships with online courses to target readers looking for specialized knowledge.

The earning potential in this space can vary widely depending on the niche and the value of your content. Here are some rough estimates:

- E-books: Depending on the length and subject, educational e-books typically sell for $10 to $50. If your book gains traction, it can generate $500 to $5,000 per month in revenue, especially if you have multiple titles or a series.

- Interactive Workbooks: These can be priced similarly, but with added value for the exercises and interactive content, you might charge between $20 and $100 per workbook. A strong marketing strategy could earn you $1,000 to $10,000 per month.

- Online Courses: If you decide to create a more comprehensive offering (like a course on Teachable or Udemy), you can charge $50 to $500 per course. With proper marketing and quality content, you could earn $2,000 to $20,000+ per month depending on the scale of your course and the demand for your expertise.

By offering educational content, you not only create a valuable resource for your audience but also tap into an evergreen income model. With AI tools, you can expedite the creation process while still delivering high-quality, professional materials. Over time, as you expand your offerings and grow your audience, the potential to turn this into a sustainable and profitable business is significant.

6. Launch a Blog to Build an Audience and Sell Self-Published Works
Blogging is an effective strategy for writers looking to build a loyal audience. Write blog posts on topics related to your books, creating an engaged reader base. You can then promote your e-books and paid content directly to this audience, encouraging them to explore your published works. Use AI tools to generate blog posts, research trending keywords, and maintain a consistent publishing schedule. By building credibility and authority in a particular field, you'll foster a group of followers likely to purchase your books. Additionally, SEO-optimized blogs bring in organic traffic, expanding your reach without a large marketing budget.

Final thoughts: Maximizing Your Self-Publishing Success

Publishing a book is an incredible achievement, but the journey doesn't end once you hit "publish." In today's digital world, it's about reaching your audience, ensuring your book is discoverable, and continuously optimizing for better visibility. With the power of AI tools like Publisher Rocket, KDP's easy-to-follow platform, and strategic keyword research, you're equipped to not only write your book but also set it up for success in the competitive world of self-publishing.

Monetizing from home through your book can open up a world of opportunities. By leveraging platforms like Amazon KDP, you can start earning passive income from your book sales, royalties, and even affiliate marketing if you include relevant links in your content. Many self-published authors make anywhere from a few hundred to several thousand dollars per month, depending on their marketing efforts, niche, and the quality of their work. Some have even turned their books into full-time businesses, earning six figures annually from book sales, digital products, and coaching or consulting gigs.

The beauty of self-publishing is the flexibility it offers—you can write, market, and monetize from the comfort of your own home. While it may take time to build a steady income, with the right strategy and persistence, your book can be a powerful tool in generating multiple streams of income. Remember, this process may take time, patience, and a willingness to refine your work, but the rewards of sharing your knowledge, creativity, and passion with the world are well worth the effort.

With each step, from drafting to marketing, you're making progress toward turning your book into a successful venture. Keep learning, stay persistent, and never lose sight of your vision. Your book is the start of something big, and the world is waiting to hear your story. The best part? You're doing it all from home, and the earning potential is limitless.

CHAPTER 3

Monetizing AI Freelancing Opportunities of Today

As you may have learned already, AI is the tool that gives freelancers the edge they need to stay competitive and build a solid income stream. From creating eye-catching videos to handling repetitive tasks more efficiently, AI can simplify and supercharge your freelance work.

In this chapter, we'll explore more freelance opportunities where AI can help you not only save time but also deliver quality work. The goal is to work smarter, not harder, and AI offers the perfect way to expand your freelancing options while enhancing the value you bring to clients.

Harnessing AI for Profitable Video Creation

Video creation has become a powerhouse in digital marketing, entertainment, and education, with platforms like YouTube, TikTok, and Instagram driving massive audiences and revenue. AI tools simplify every aspect of video production, from scripting and editing to visuals and distribution. By harnessing AI, creators can not only streamline their workflows but also unlock multiple profitable revenue streams. With AI-driven tools optimizing content for SEO, ensuring consistency, and helping with cross-platform distribution, creators can increase their chances of building a successful, sustainable income stream. Whether you're just starting out or looking to take your video content to the next level, AI is the key to turning your passion into profit and tapping into the substantial earning potential that digital video creation offers.

Top AI Tools for Effortless Video Creation

In today's fast-paced digital world, video content is king—whether it's for marketing, education, or entertainment. However, creating high-quality videos can be time-consuming, requiring extensive research, editing, and post-production work. This is where AI comes in. From generating scripts and voiceovers to editing and enhancing video quality, AI tools can significantly reduce the effort and time required, making professional-grade video production more accessible. In this section, we'll explore the top essential AI tools you need to succeed in video creation, helping you craft compelling content with ease and efficiency.

Let's begin with **Synthesia,** a powerful yet super user-friendly AI video tool that lets you create high-quality videos featuring lifelike avatars— no need to be on camera yourself. It's a favorite among businesses, educators, and content creators who want to make engaging content without the hassle of filming. You can choose from a range of avatars, type in your script, and Synthesia will handle the rest, including realistic voiceovers and automatic lip-syncing. It even supports multiple languages, making it great for global audiences. Whether you're creating explainer videos, training materials, or marketing content, Synthesia helps you get it done quickly and professionally, all from your laptop.

InVideo, on the other hand, is a versatile AI-powered platform designed for marketers, entrepreneurs, and social media creators. It offers a vast library of templates for formats like YouTube intros, Instagram Reels, and Facebook ads, along with stock footage, animations, and AI-assisted editing features such as text-to-video conversion and smart scene transitions. With additional tools like AI voiceovers, background music, and auto-captioning, InVideo simplifies high-quality video production for both beginners and professionals.

Descript is a versatile, all-in-one tool that streamlines video and audio editing, transcription, and screen recording, making content creation more accessible than ever. Its intuitive interface allows users to edit videos and podcasts as easily as editing a text document, with features like drag-and-drop editing and automatic transcription. One of its most powerful tools, **Overdub,** enables voice cloning, allowing creators to fix audio mistakes without the need for re-recording.

Pictory, another AI-driven platform, excels at transforming text-based content into engaging videos by incorporating AI-powered visuals, voiceovers, and dynamic transitions. This makes it ideal for repurposing blog posts, summarizing articles, or producing short-form social media content with minimal effort.

Similarly, **Lumen5** specializes in converting long-form written content into compelling video narratives, automatically pairing relevant visuals with key text highlights. For content marketers, educators, and entrepreneurs, these AI-powered tools offer a seamless way to enhance storytelling, boost engagement, and expand audience reach with visually rich, high-quality video content.

From Idea to Viral Video: Leveraging AI for Seamless Production

As digital content continues to dominate online platforms, the ability to create polished videos quickly and effectively has become a huge advantage. Thanks to AI, the entire video creation process—from scriptwriting to editing—is now more streamlined and accessible than ever. You no longer need to be a seasoned video editor or invest in pricey gear to produce professional-quality content. Whether you're a small business owner, a content creator, or just someone with a message to share, AI tools make it easier to turn your ideas into compelling videos. Let's walk through a step-by-step process to create a high-quality, potentially viral video with minimal hassle.

Step 1: Video Scriptwriting with AI

The first step in video creation is developing a compelling script, which sets the tone for the entire video. AI-powered scriptwriting tools like **Jasper** and **Copy.ai** can generate engaging scripts based on simple prompts. For example, if you're creating a video to promote a new product, you might input a prompt like:

"Write a 60-second script for a promotional video for a new eco-friendly water bottle aimed at millennials."

The AI tool will provide a well-structured script with an attention-grabbing opening, a description of the product's benefits, and a persuasive call to action.

To make the script more personalized, you can further refine the language, adjusting the tone and style to suit your brand voice. With AI tools, you can quickly produce scripts for multiple videos, which is essential for high-volume content creators or businesses looking to streamline their video production process.

Step 2: AI-Generated Video Editing

Once the script is ready, AI tools can assist with video editing, cutting down on time spent in post-production. **Pictory** and **Synthesia** are excellent tools that can take your script and automatically generate a video by selecting relevant visuals and animations based on the script's content. These tools can convert written content into engaging video clips by adding images, voiceovers, and transitions.

For example, if you have a script about the benefits of using eco-friendly products, AI can help you automatically generate a video with clips of nature, sustainability, and product shots, while providing a voiceover that aligns with the tone of the script. The AI analyzes the keywords from the script and matches them with appropriate media from its library, creating a polished video without manual editing.

Additionally, tools like **Adobe Premiere Pro's** AI features or **Magisto** can assist in automatically editing footage by analyzing the video's content and applying smart edits, like cutting out unnecessary segments, adjusting pacing, or adding transitions. This makes video editing faster and more accessible for creators without extensive technical skills.

Step 3: Enhancing Video Quality with AI-Generated Visuals and Effects

AI tools can also enhance the visual quality of your videos by adding elements like animations, graphics, or even virtual effects. Tools like **Runway ML** allow you to generate high-quality animations from static images or create special effects using AI algorithms. This means that even if you don't have professional animation skills, you can still create stunning, dynamic visuals to enhance your video content.

For example, if you're making a product demo video and want to show how your product interacts in different environments, AI-powered tools can generate 3D animations or overlay effects to visualize the product in action. These features can add depth to your videos, making them more engaging and helping you stand out in a crowded content landscape.

Step 4: Automated Voiceovers with AI

Narration and voiceovers are key components of many video formats, and AI can assist in this process as well. Tools like **Descript** and **Murf. ai** allow you to create realistic, human-like voiceovers for your videos. Instead of hiring a professional voice actor, you can input your script into the tool, choose a voice, and generate a voiceover in a matter of minutes.

For instance, if you're creating an explainer video on how to use your product, you can use AI to generate a clear, professional voiceover that matches the tone and style of your script. AI tools can also adjust the pacing and tone of the voiceover to ensure it fits seamlessly with your video's visuals, adding a personal touch that might otherwise require professional recording equipment.

Step 5: AI for Video Marketing and Optimization

Creating the video is just one part of the process. To ensure your video reaches its target audience and performs well, you can also leverage AI tools for video marketing. Platforms like **TubeBuddy** and **VidIQ** use AI to analyze video performance metrics on YouTube and recommend keyword optimizations, video tags, and titles that will help your video rank higher and attract more views.

Additionally, AI can assist with video SEO by generating optimized descriptions, titles, and tags. For example, if you're uploading a video on YouTube, AI can suggest the best keywords and phrases to include in your title and description to ensure your video is discoverable by your audience. AI tools can also track viewer engagement and provide recommendations on how to improve future videos, allowing you to continuously optimize your content strategy.

Step 6: Monetization and Scaling

Once you've mastered using AI for video creation, you can explore various monetization strategies to turn your video content into a revenue-generating asset. Some options include:

• *Ad Revenue:* Platforms like YouTube and TikTok offer monetization through ads. Once your videos gain traction and build an audience, you can earn money through ad views and engagement.

• *Affiliate Marketing:* You can incorporate affiliate links into your videos and earn commissions when viewers make purchases through those links. AI tools can help you track and optimize these links to maximize your earnings.

• *Sponsored Content:* As you build a following, brands may approach you for sponsored video content. AI can help streamline the creation of sponsored content by assisting with scriptwriting, video editing, and social media promotion.

• *Selling Video Products or Services:* If you're offering educational content, consider selling courses, e-books, or consulting services within your videos. You can use AI tools to create high-quality, engaging promotional videos for your products.

Example Scenario: Creating a YouTube Product Review Video

Imagine you're reviewing a new camera for YouTube. You can start by inputting your product review script into an AI tool like **Jasper** to craft a compelling intro, key features, and a closing statement that encourages viewers to purchase. Next, you use **Pictory** to turn the script into a video, with AI selecting relevant product images and video clips from its library. You generate a voiceover using **Murf**.ai and use **Runway ML** to add dynamic effects that highlight key features of the camera. Once the video is edited, you optimize it for YouTube using **VidIQ**, ensuring it ranks well for search terms like "best budget camera for vloggers."

Harnessing AI for video creation allows you to efficiently produce high-quality, engaging videos while saving time and resources. Whether you're creating promotional videos, explainer videos, tutorials, or social media content, AI tools can help streamline the entire process, from scripting and editing to marketing and monetization. By incorporating AI into your video creation workflow, you can scale your content production, enhance the quality of your videos, and unlock new revenue streams.

How to Monetize AI Video Creation: From Concept to Cash

Here are the most effective ways to monetize AI-powered video creation:

1. Create and Monetize a YouTube Channel

Start a YouTube channel focused on a popular or niche topic like DIY crafts, tech tutorials, or travel guides. Produce consistent, high-quality videos using tools like Pictory and Descript to streamline editing and enhance visuals. Monetization on YouTube kicks in once you hit 1,000 subscribers and 4,000 watch hours, allowing you to earn from ad revenue. To increase engagement and watch time, use Synthesia to create unique avatars or animations that make your videos stand out. Consider uploading short-form content too, which YouTube promotes heavily through Shorts.

Once you've built a following, expand monetization by enabling

Super Chats for live streams, creating memberships, or directing viewers to affiliate links and sponsored content. With consistent effort, creative use of AI tools, and strategic monetization methods, you could potentially earn anywhere from $500 to $5,000+ per month in ad revenue, Super Chats, memberships, and affiliate commissions. As your channel grows, so does your income potential, offering a sustainable and scalable way to profit from your videos.

2. Offer Video Creation Services on Freelance Platforms

Offering video creation services on freelance platforms is an excellent way to monetize your skills and AI-powered tools. Platforms like Upwork, Fiverr, and Freelancer allow you to reach a broad audience of clients seeking professional video content at competitive prices. As a video creator, you can offer services like explainer videos, tutorial videos, promotional ads, and more. By leveraging AI tools like Synthesia, InVideo, and Pictory, you can streamline your production process, turning around high-quality videos quickly and efficiently. This not only allows you to handle multiple clients at once but also ensures that you can deliver polished results at a faster pace, which is a huge selling point for clients.

To successfully monetize on freelance platforms, start by building a strong profile that showcases your AI-driven video creation skills. Highlight the services you offer, such as explainer videos, ads, or product demos, and demonstrate how your use of AI tools allows for fast turnaround times and top-notch production quality. Initially, offer competitive rates to attract clients and build your reputation. Over time, as you accumulate positive reviews and experience, you can increase your rates and target higher-paying projects. Specializing in niches like real estate, e-commerce, or SaaS (Software as a Service) products can also help you stand out and command higher fees.

Freelance video creation offers substantial income potential, especially when you specialize in high-demand services. You can expect to earn anywhere from $500 to $5,000+ per month, depending on the number of clients, the complexity of the projects, and your experience level. For example, creating an explainer video for a small business could bring in $100 to $1,000, while producing a high-quality commercial or product video could earn you $1,500 to $5,000 per project. By combining AI tools with consistent effort and expanding your client base, you can develop a lucrative income stream through freelance video services.

3. Develop Educational or Training Courses

Use video to create educational or training courses in fields where you have expertise, such as language learning, business skills, or personal finance. Platforms like Teachable, Udemy, and Skillshare are great for course distribution. AI tools like Synthesia can create avatar-based instructors for courses, making it easy to produce professional, engaging lessons without appearing on screen. To stand out, design a curriculum that incorporates quizzes, practice exercises, and bonus materials. Promote your course on social media, and use LinkedIn to reach professional audiences looking to upskill.

To monetize these courses, you can charge a one-time fee, offer a subscription model, or provide tiered pricing for premium content. Platforms like Teachable allow you to set up automated sales funnels, so once your course is created, it can continue generating revenue with little ongoing effort. If you're able to build a reputation as a reliable instructor, you could even offer consulting or coaching sessions as additional services, significantly increasing your income potential.

In terms of revenue, creating a high-quality online course can earn you anywhere from $500 to $10,000+ per month, depending on the niche, the demand for your course, and the platform you choose. Some top creators on platforms like Udemy or Skillshare have reported making $50,000+ annually from course sales alone. If you leverage AI tools to streamline content creation and improve your course's reach, your income could increase significantly over time.

4. Sell Subscription-Based Content on Patreon or Ko-fi

Selling subscription-based content on platforms like Patreon or Ko-fi offers a fantastic way to monetize your video creation efforts, especially if you have a dedicated following or niche expertise. These platforms allow you to build a community of paying subscribers who are eager to support your content in exchange for exclusive access. Whether you're an artist, gamer, musician, or personal development coach, offering premium video content can create a steady stream of income and deeper connections with your audience.

To get started, think about the type of content your audience would value most. This could be behind-the-scenes footage, exclusive tutorials, Q&A sessions, or early access to new projects. The key to success on subscription-based platforms is offering high-quality content that your audience can't easily find elsewhere. For example, you could offer in-depth video lessons on a particular subject, exclusive mini-documentaries about your creative process, or special content like personalized video shout-outs or private one-on-one chats.

One effective strategy is to offer tiered subscription levels, where subscribers at different levels gain access to varying degrees of content. For example, a basic tier might offer early access to your content, while higher tiers could include personalized shout-outs, behind-the-scenes footage, or even private one-on-one chats. This tiered approach allows you to cater to different levels of support while incentivizing more people to upgrade for exclusive perks.

Once you start gaining subscribers, the potential for passive income grows. If you consistently produce quality content and engage with your subscribers, you can create a community that supports your creative work long-term. Platforms like Patreon also make it easy to manage your subscribers, track their engagement, and set up automated billing and communication.

In terms of revenue, Patreon creators can earn anywhere from $500 to $10,000 per month, depending on the size of their audience and the value of the content they provide. Some creators even make six figures annually by offering exclusive content on Patreon. A strong, engaged fan base is crucial, but with AI tools streamlining content creation, you can focus more on growing your audience and offering more value, leading to higher earnings over time.

5. Create Videos for Social Media and Run Ads for Small Businesses

Creating videos for social media and running ads for small businesses is a lucrative way to leverage your video creation skills while helping local or smaller brands grow their online presence. Many small businesses lack the resources to hire a full-time videographer or social media manager, creating a perfect opportunity for you to step in and offer your expertise.

As a video creator, you can help businesses enhance their online visibility by producing high-quality, engaging videos tailored to their target audience. Using tools like InVideo, you can easily create visually appealing, high-converting social media ads designed for platforms like Instagram, Facebook, and TikTok—where content is fast-paced and needs to capture attention within the first few seconds. With

InVideo's vast library of templates and pre-made elements, you can craft attention-grabbing videos even if you don't have extensive editing experience. Whether it's a promotional ad, behind-the-scenes content, or product demonstrations, you'll be able to deliver effective social media content that drives engagement and conversions for businesses.

The key to success in this model is positioning yourself as a content expert. Many small businesses need more than just someone who can make a video; they need someone who understands how to create content that resonates with their audience and leads to measurable results. By offering valuable insights on the types of videos that perform well on different platforms, you'll build a reputation as a go-to expert for social media content.

As you gain experience and build a portfolio, you can start offering monthly retainers, where clients pay a fixed fee for consistent video production. This provides a reliable stream of income, allowing you to focus on nurturing client relationships and creating content that helps their businesses succeed. Many small businesses are willing to invest in regular content that boosts their brand presence and attracts customers, which makes this a highly sustainable and scalable income model.

For example, a local coffee shop might hire you to create engaging Instagram videos that showcase their unique products, special promotions, or behind-the-scenes looks into how their coffee is made. With AI tools like Pictory or Descript, you can streamline the process of creating these videos by auto-generating captions, adding transitions, and enhancing visuals to match the brand's identity. Offering these services on a consistent basis would allow you to build long-term client relationships and ensure a steady income.

In terms of revenue, video creation for small businesses can be quite profitable. On platforms like Fiverr or Upwork, freelance video creators typically charge anywhere from $300 to $2,000 per video, depending on the complexity and client requirements. By securing monthly retainer contracts, you could easily earn $2,000 to $10,000 per month (or more) by working with multiple clients. As you refine your process and expand your client base, the potential for growth is substantial.

Ultimately, offering video creation services for social media and paid ads to small businesses provides a valuable solution to a common problem. It's a win-win: you get to apply your video production skills, leverage AI tools to streamline the process, and earn steady income while helping businesses boost their brand presence and drive more sales.

6. Launch a Subscription Channel or Membership Site

As niche video content continues to rise in popularity, launching your own subscription-based video platform offers an exciting opportunity to monetize your expertise and creativity. Platforms like Uscreen or Vimeo OTT allow content creators to build their own subscription-based sites, where audiences pay for access to exclusive, high-quality video content. Whether you specialize in advanced fitness routines, in-depth tech tutorials, or exclusive travel content, subscription-based platforms provide an effective way to generate recurring income from loyal followers.

A major benefit of this revenue model is the ability to control pricing and access. You can choose a subscription model that works best for your audience—whether that's a monthly, quarterly, or annual plan. With platforms like Uscreen or Vimeo OTT, you also have the flexibility to offer pay-per-view options or tiered memberships, where subscribers can pay more for premium content or one-on-one consultations.

To drive traffic to your platform, you can use a combination of social media, email marketing, and organic search strategies. AI tools like ConvertKit or Mailchimp can help you set up automated email campaigns, nurturing leads and encouraging sign-ups. Social media platforms like Instagram or TikTok are excellent for promoting teaser content, behind-the-scenes clips, or free samples of your premium offerings, helping potential subscribers get a taste of the value they'll receive on your platform. Offering free trials or samples of exclusive content can be a great way to attract new subscribers and convince them of the value your platform provides.

For example, if you're a fitness expert, you could launch a subscription-based platform on Uscreen, where subscribers pay to access advanced workout routines, nutrition guides, and weekly live workout sessions. By promoting these videos on your social media accounts and offering a few free workout tutorials, you'll attract a steady stream of fitness enthusiasts who are willing to pay for continued access to your expert-led content. With AI tools, you can automate much of the process, from video creation to content scheduling, making it easier to maintain consistency and engagement.

Monetary potential in this model can be significant. On average, creators on platforms like Uscreen earn anywhere from $500 to $5,000 per month based on their subscriber count and content offerings. If you gain a dedicated audience willing to pay for high-quality content, your earnings can grow even further. For instance, if you have 500 subscribers paying $10 per month, you could earn $5,000 in recurring revenue each month. As you grow your platform, the potential for scaling is immense, particularly when you offer tiered memberships or additional services such as one-on-one coaching or exclusive webinars.

7. Offer Custom Video Editing Services

AI-powered tools have revolutionized the way video editing services are offered, enabling creators to provide fast, customized video solutions with minimal effort. By leveraging tools like Descript, you can offer a variety of video editing services, including podcast video editing, YouTube thumbnail creation, and short-form content editing for platforms like TikTok and Instagram. These tools simplify the process of editing, adding captions, and even correcting audio, saving time while maintaining high-quality results. For instance, you can quickly convert a podcast episode into a polished video with dynamic captions, making it suitable for sharing across multiple platforms, or create eye-catching thumbnails for YouTube videos that drive higher click-through rates.

As you gain more clients, consider offering subscription packages for ongoing video editing needs. This model works particularly well for content creators and businesses that produce high volumes of video content. Regular content producers, such as YouTubers, influencers, and small businesses, often need reliable video editors to handle the continuous demand for fresh content. Subscription packages can help you secure a steady stream of income while allowing clients to enjoy a consistent level of service. For example, you might offer a package that includes editing a set number of videos each month, with added perks like priority turnaround times or custom graphics.

Additionally, AI tools can help you upsell value-added services that enhance the visibility and reach of your client's content. SEO optimization for video titles, descriptions, and tags is a great example. By using AI-driven tools to research trending keywords, you can help your clients optimize their video content for discoverability, leading to better ranking on platforms like YouTube and more engagement from their audience. You could also offer services like social media promotion, creating thumbnail templates, or incorporating engaging visuals to improve the overall presentation of their videos.

For example, imagine you're working with a client who creates fitness tutorials on YouTube. After editing their videos using Descript and creating custom thumbnails, you can go one step further by optimizing the video titles with popular, relevant keywords that will help the content appear in search results. As a result, your client's videos have a higher chance of being discovered, ultimately driving more views and engagement.

This business model is scalable and can be highly profitable as you continue to attract more clients. With AI-powered video tools, you can handle multiple clients simultaneously, even providing edits for clients in different time zones. For instance, a standard package might start at $300 per month for three videos, while premium packages offering faster turnaround times or extra services like SEO optimization can be priced higher, making it easy to increase your earnings as your reputation and client base grow.

8. Produce and Sell Stock Video Content

Stock footage is an evergreen market with constant demand, especially as businesses, marketers, and content creators rely heavily on high-quality videos for their campaigns. By leveraging AI tools, you can easily create stock videos that appeal to a wide range of industries, from advertising to social media marketing. Platforms like Shutterstock, Adobe Stock, and Pond5 provide a great avenue for monetization, allowing you to upload and license your videos for ongoing passive income.

AI-powered tools can streamline the process of creating high-quality footage, saving you time and effort. For example, AI software can help you produce animated graphics, aerial shots, and even complex time-lapse sequences, without requiring advanced video equipment or specialized skills. If you're creating an aerial shot, AI tools can enhance the footage with smooth transitions or even simulate complex visual effects. Additionally, using AI tools like Runway or Pictory, you can automatically generate unique sequences or enhance raw footage to meet specific market needs. These tools enable you to generate professional-grade videos without requiring extensive technical knowledge or a hefty budget for equipment.

To increase your chances of success, focus on producing niche stock videos that target in-demand categories. Popular niches include urban landscapes, nature scenes, business environments, technology-focused footage, and even social interactions for commercial use. For instance, businesses often require video content featuring office settings or business meetings, while social media marketers look for trendy, dynamic clips that capture attention. AI can help you create and edit videos in these niche areas, making it easier to produce footage that will appeal to specific industries.

Once you've created your videos, be sure to tag them with relevant keywords to maximize their searchability on stock video platforms. Proper tagging ensures that potential buyers can easily discover your content when searching for specific types of footage. For instance, if you've created a video of a bustling cityscape, use tags like "urban," "city life," "downtown," or "nighttime skyline." By doing this, you increase your chances of attracting more views and sales.

Building a large portfolio of stock footage is crucial to creating a reliable source of residual income. The more videos you upload, the more opportunities you have for consistent sales. Stock footage typically generates passive income because once you upload your content, you continue to earn royalties each time someone purchases or downloads your videos. Depending on the platform and licensing model, you can expect to earn anywhere from $10 to $100 per download, with higher payouts for exclusive content or extended licenses.

For example, let's say you've uploaded a collection of nature footage to a platform like Shutterstock. Over time, if your videos are high quality and effectively tagged, you could generate sales on a regular basis—especially if your videos fill a niche that is underrepresented in the market. This can lead to residual income, with earnings increasing as your portfolio grows and more customers discover your work.

To maximize your potential earnings, focus on creating a diverse portfolio that caters to various industries and niches. Whether it's b-roll footage for use in corporate videos or cinematic landscapes for use in travel ads, the key to success in stock video sales is consistency, quality, and a broad selection. With AI tools helping to streamline production and enhance creativity, you can quickly scale up your portfolio and start generating passive income from your stock footage.

9. Monetize via Live Streaming

AI-enhanced video production can take your live-streaming content to the next level, making it more polished, professional, and engaging for your audience. Whether you're into gaming, cooking, or interactive Q&A sessions, live streaming offers an excellent opportunity to monetize in real-time through various platforms like YouTube, Twitch, or Facebook Live. The potential for income through Super Chats, Twitch subscriptions, or donations makes live streaming an attractive revenue model. However, the key to success lies in maintaining high-quality production and audience engagement.

AI tools play a significant role in enhancing your live-streaming setup by providing seamless transitions, interactive overlays, and dynamic filters that give your streams a professional look. For example, AI-powered overlays can automatically display your most recent subscriber, top donors, or live chat messages on screen, making the stream more interactive and visually appealing. Tools like Streamlabs or OBS Studio integrate AI-driven features that automate the process of adding animations, text overlays, and even interactive elements, so you can focus on engaging with your audience rather than spending hours manually editing your stream.

When you're live, audience engagement is everything. AI can help you respond to comments and track engagement during your streams, ensuring you're actively connecting with your viewers. For instance, AI tools like Chatbot integration can help automate responses to frequently asked questions or direct viewers to certain resources, while AI-based sentiment analysis can give you real-time feedback on how viewers are responding to your content. This interaction can lead to increased viewer loyalty and a more dedicated fanbase.

To further incentivize engagement, consider offering rewards for donations or super chats, like personalized shout-outs or exclusive access to future streams. AI can help you keep track of donations and organize special giveaways or milestones that encourage more contributions. Additionally, planning a regular streaming schedule helps build anticipation and fosters a dedicated community.

As your following grows, brand partnerships and sponsored content become lucrative options. AI tools can help you track trends and audience demographics to attract potential sponsors who are a good match for your content. For example, if you're a cooking streamer, you could partner with kitchenware brands or ingredient suppliers for sponsored streams. AI platforms can also assist in identifying lucrative partnership opportunities, reaching out to relevant brands, and creating data-driven proposals that demonstrate the value of collaborating with you.

In terms of monetization, once you've built a steady stream of viewers, you can earn through Twitch subscriptions (where viewers pay a monthly fee for exclusive perks) or Super Chats on YouTube (where viewers donate money to highlight their messages). If you expand to multiple platforms or collaborate with sponsors, your income streams can multiply. AI-driven video production tools make it easier to maintain high-quality streams, ensuring that your content remains appealing and professional as you scale.

Final Thoughts: Turning AI Video Creation Into Real Income

AI video creation isn't just a futuristic trend—it's one of the most powerful, accessible ways to generate income from home today. Whether you're making faceless YouTube videos, short-form content for TikTok, or marketing videos for small businesses, the tools at your fingertips make it easier than ever to go from idea to income with very little upfront investment.

The beauty of AI video creation is that you don't need a full film crew, expensive gear, or even to show your face on camera. You just need a story, a message, or a niche—and the right AI tools to help bring it to life. Platforms like Pictory, Synthesia, and RunwayML can turn a script or blog post into an engaging video in minutes. Pair that with voiceovers, subtitles, and some smart editing, and you've got professional content ready to monetize.

But here's the key: consistency and clarity of purpose. Whether you're creating content for a YouTube ad revenue stream, selling video creation services, or building a brand online, focus on creating content that solves problems, entertains, or educates. The more value you provide, the faster you'll build an audience—or client base—that pays off.

And remember, it's okay if it feels a little overwhelming at first. You're learning something new, and with every video you create, you're sharpening your skills. The cool part? AI is here to support you every step of the way. So take the pressure off—experiment, explore different video styles, test platforms, and most importantly, keep going.

The opportunity is massive, and it's only growing. You don't need to be a tech genius or a video pro to succeed in this space—you just need curiosity, a bit of patience, and the willingness to try. With the knowledge you've gained here and the right tools in your corner, you're more than capable of turning your video ideas into real, lasting income.

You've got this. Let's turn those video concepts into cash.

Revolutionizing Graphic Design with AI

Graphic design remains a high-demand field, from digital marketing visuals to branded social media posts and website layouts. Traditionally, design skills required years of practice with software, but AI tools now enable even beginners to create polished visuals quickly. Leveraging AI for graphic design can open multiple revenue streams, allowing you to produce quality designs, streamline workflows, and attract more clients with impressive turnaround times.

Top AI Tools for Graphic Design: Streamline Your Creative Process

The world of graphic design has been revolutionized by AI-powered tools, making it easier than ever to create stunning visuals that captivate your audience. Whether you're a beginner or a seasoned designer, these innovative tools can help you produce professional-quality work in less time and with greater ease. Here are some of the top AI tools that can enhance your creative process:

Canva is a go-to tool for anyone looking to design beautiful graphics without a steep learning curve. Whether you're crafting social media posts, marketing assets, or presentations, Canva's vast library of templates makes it easy to get started. But what sets it apart is its smart AI features—offering layout suggestions, color harmonies, and design variations tailored to your project. It's perfect for those who want to create eye-catching designs quickly, without sacrificing quality. From beginners to professionals, Canva's simplicity and versatility make it a favorite among creators worldwide.

For those looking to take their design game up a notch, **Adobe Firefly** brings Adobe's cutting-edge AI capabilities into the mix. With features like quick image generation, text-to-image transformation, background removal, and style transfer, Firefly offers complete control over your designs. It's an ideal choice for designers who want more customization and precision in their creations, whether you're enhancing photos, building complex visuals, or experimenting with new artistic styles.

When it comes to branding, **Looka** is the ultimate AI-powered logo maker. Simply enter your brand's name and style preferences, and Looka will generate professional logos that perfectly capture your vision. But it doesn't stop there—Looka also provides brand kits to help maintain a consistent look across all your platforms. If you're an entrepreneur or a small business owner in need of a logo that stands out and represents your brand, Looka makes the entire process simple and efficient, delivering stunning results in minutes.

For those who need to transform raw data into visually compelling graphics, **Visme** shines as the perfect tool for creating infographics, business presentations, and educational content. Visme's AI-driven templates, icons, and graphs make it easy to convey complex information in a visually appealing way. It's an invaluable resource for professionals who want to engage their audience with clear, impactful designs that make data come to life.

Lastly, **Remove.bg** is a must-have tool for anyone working with images. It specializes in quickly and seamlessly removing backgrounds from photos, giving you high-quality, transparent images ready for use in any design. Whether you're working on product photos, marketing materials, or social media content, Remove.bg helps you create polished visuals in seconds, allowing you to focus on the bigger picture of your design work.

By incorporating these AI tools into your design workflow, you can streamline your creative process, save valuable time, and produce work that's both professional and polished. From logo creation to data visualization, these tools offer powerful features that elevate your designs and help you stand out in today's competitive digital landscape

Mastering AI Tools for Graphic Design

By leveraging AI-powered platforms, you can streamline the design process and produce high-quality visuals much faster and with more precision than traditional methods. These tools, such as Canva, Adobe Firefly, DALL·E, and MidJourney, are equipped with pre-built templates and intelligent algorithms that allow users to generate stunning visuals by simply providing a few inputs.

For example, when creating a brand logo, you could start by using Looka or Canva's AI-powered logo generator. These tools analyze design preferences, style, and the business's target audience to provide a range of logo options. Once the AI suggests a few concepts, you can easily tweak colors, fonts, and layout to make the logo unique to your brand. This process eliminates the guesswork and time-consuming manual adjustments designers used to face. Similarly, Adobe Firefly allows designers to experiment with graphic design elements and adjust compositions, from icons to complete branding kits, with the help of AI's real-time feedback.

Let's consider a scenario: you're hired to create a set of promotional social media graphics for a boutique coffee shop. Using Canva, you can quickly choose a template based on the platform's optimal size (Instagram post, story, or Facebook cover). Then, you can input your client's brand colors and logo into the design tool. Canva's AI will suggest text styles that fit the tone of the business, such as cozy, trendy, or minimalist, based on the customer's input. The tool also auto-suggests relevant imagery, such as photos of coffee beans or steaming mugs. You can adjust these further to create eye-catching visuals in minutes. Moreover, using AI, you can quickly create variations of the post for different social media platforms, adapting the design to each platform's specifications.

Another scenario could involve designing a custom illustration for an event like a wedding or festival. You could use DALL·E or MidJourney to generate unique, detailed art based on specific prompts. For instance, for a summer wedding, you could prompt the AI with "a whimsical botanical design featuring soft pink and green florals, with a vintage feel." The AI would generate a series of images based on your description, and you could choose the one that best fits your vision. This approach is particularly useful for creating one-of-a-kind designs without needing to start from scratch, allowing you to refine the design to perfection.

These AI tools are transforming how graphic designers approach projects, allowing them to automate tedious parts of the creative process, like resizing images, suggesting color palettes, or generating multiple design variations in minutes. By mastering these tools, designers can focus on the strategic and creative aspects of their work, elevating their efficiency while also producing designs that are innovative and high-quality.

In addition to social media graphics, logos, and illustrations, AI tools can be used to design entire websites, presentations, or marketing materials. Whether you're creating a sleek website layout using Figma's AI-assisted design suggestions or designing compelling ad copy in seconds with ChatGPT, AI tools provide you with the resources to streamline every step of the creative process. The result is not just faster turnaround times but also a higher level of creativity, as AI often suggests ideas or techniques you might not have initially considered. The ability to easily manipulate elements, generate variations, and access libraries of pre-designed assets means the creative possibilities are endless.

Monetizing AI-Powered Graphic Design: Unlock New Revenue Streams

Platforms like Upwork, Fiverr, and 99designs are full of clients looking for everything from social media graphics to complete branding packages. To attract these clients, you can use tools like Canva and Adobe Firefly to create standout portfolio pieces that show off your design skills and ability to produce high-quality work quickly. For example, you could design a brand logo or a complete branding kit (including fonts, colors, and templates) using Canva and showcase it in your profile to demonstrate your expertise.

To draw in more clients, you can set up design packages like "Custom Logo Design", "Complete Branding Kit", or "Social Media Graphic Bundle". These packages can be marketed to a wide range of clients, from small businesses to influencers, and they help clients understand exactly what they're getting for their investment.

To really stand out, offer specialized services like custom infographics or e-commerce product images using tools like Visme for creating sleek, data-driven graphics and Remove.bg for removing backgrounds from product photos. For example, you could help a fashion e-commerce store by providing them with professional product images for their website and social media, ensuring each image pops and is consistent with their branding.

As you gain more experience and positive reviews, you can raise your rates and offer more comprehensive packages. You might start offering ongoing design support, where you manage the client's social media graphics every month or provide retainer services where clients can get a set number of designs per month. These ongoing services create a reliable income stream and give you the chance to build long-term relationships with clients.

Beginner freelance designers can start by earning $100–$300 per project, especially for simple logo or branding tasks. As your portfolio and client base grow, your income can increase significantly. Intermediate-level designers often earn $1,000–$3,000/month, especially when offering bundled packages or working on multiple projects at once. Designers who secure retainer clients or specialize in high-demand niches (such as e-commerce or SaaS branding) can bring in $5,000–$10,000+ per month, particularly when leveraging AI tools to boost productivity and scale efficiently.

By showcasing your creativity and leveraging AI-powered tools to increase efficiency and output, you can build a thriving freelance design business that scales with demand. Whether you're creating visuals for a one-off project or managing full-scale branding efforts for multiple businesses, AI helps you deliver consistent, professional work that keeps clients coming back.

Launch a Social Media Graphics Service

Social media requires a constant flow of fresh visuals, making it a prime market for design services. Offer branded social media content packages where clients receive a set number of posts, stories, or ads each month. Use Canva's templates to streamline production, allowing for faster turnaround and easier bulk creation. Tailor your packages to different platforms (e.g., Instagram, LinkedIn, TikTok) to attract a diverse client base. Once you have a few clients, propose retainer packages for consistent income. Retainers can include monthly social media designs, seasonal campaigns, or branded templates for client use.

For social media content services, you can start by charging $150–$500/month per client for a basic package (e.g., 10–15 branded posts or stories). As your quality and client relationships improve, retainer packages can range from $750 to $2,000+ per month, depending on volume, turnaround speed, and whether you offer additional services like copywriting or content planning. Designers working with multiple clients at once—especially in high-traffic niches like e-commerce, wellness, or coaching—can comfortably scale to $5,000–$10,000/month or more, especially when using AI tools to increase output and efficiency.

By combining your design skills with AI-powered tools and packaging your services strategically, you can create a profitable, scalable social media design business from home.

Create and Sell Print-on-Demand Products

Designing products like T-shirts, posters, mugs, or tote bags has become a super popular and low-risk way to earn passive income—especially thanks to print-on-demand (POD) platforms like Printful, Redbubble, Society6, and TeePublic. The best part? You don't need to worry about inventory, shipping, or upfront costs. You just focus on the fun stuff—creating awesome designs and building a brand that people love.

With tools like Adobe Firefly, you can whip up eye-catching graphics, quirky illustrations, or cool typography that really stands out in these busy marketplaces. Maybe you design a fun "Cat Yoga" T-shirt series or go for a clean, minimalist botanical theme for home decor. Pair that with Canva to make polished mockups and apply your designs across tons of products. One idea can turn into a whole collection—T-shirts, mugs, stickers, tote bags—you name it.

To get noticed and boost sales, make sure your product titles and descriptions are packed with SEO-friendly keywords, and promote your designs consistently on Pinterest, Instagram, or TikTok. You'll have the best luck if you focus on a niche or trending theme—like seasonal holidays, pop culture references, or something fun like introvert quotes or plant lover humor. These kinds of targeted collections attract the right audience—and those are the people most likely to buy.

As for earnings, most platforms give you a cut per sale, usually around 10–30%, depending on how you price your items. On average, you might earn $3–$10 per sale, but it adds up. A lot of creators report earning $300 to $1,000/month within just a few months, especially if they hit on a viral design or get good search rankings. With time, a solid collection, and some regular marketing, you can scale to $2,000–$5,000/month or even more—especially if you're selling across multiple platforms and riding those seasonal waves.

All in all, print-on-demand is a fun, creative, and scalable income stream—perfect for anyone looking to build a brand and make money from home using AI-powered design tools.

Develop Digital Design Assets for Passive Income

Selling digital assets like templates, icons, fonts, or illustrations can be a great way to earn money online—especially if you enjoy being creative. With platforms like Etsy, Creative Market, or Envato Elements, you can upload your designs and make them available to buyers around the world. Using AI tools like Canva and Adobe Firefly, it's easier than ever to create original, high-quality assets that people can customize and use for their own projects.

Think of things like wedding invitation templates, resume layouts, Instagram story packs—these are always in demand. The cool part? Once your items are listed, they can sell over and over again, creating a nice stream of passive income.

Earnings per product usually range from $5 to $50+, depending on how detailed or valuable your asset is. Many creators with just 10 to 20 items in their shop report making around $200 to $500 a month. But once you build a bigger portfolio and start offering bundles or themed collections, you can easily scale up to $1,000 to $5,000 a month—or more. Some top sellers on marketplaces like Etsy make over $10,000 per month, especially when they combine good SEO, seasonal launches, and email list marketing.

If you're someone who enjoys designing and wants to build a semi-passive business, this is a fun and flexible way to do it. Plus, with AI speeding up your creative process, growing your digital shop from home has never been more doable.

Offer Branding Packages to Small Businesses

Small businesses crave great branding—but not everyone can afford a big design agency. That's where you come in. By offering affordable, ready-to-use branding kits, you can help startups and solopreneurs build a professional presence without blowing their budget.

Start with the essentials: a clean logo, business card design, branded social media templates, and a cohesive color scheme. Tools like Looka make it super easy to generate a full brand kit in minutes, and you can customize and expand on it using Canva—think Instagram post templates, email signature graphics, and even a few banner ads to get them rolling.

Once you've got your kit down, market your services in the right places. LinkedIn, Facebook groups for entrepreneurs, and small business forums are full of people looking for affordable branding help. You don't need to pitch like a sales rep—just showcase some examples, share a few tips, and let your value speak for itself.

As your client base grows, you can start offering add-ons like branded email templates, highlight covers, or web banners for an extra fee. These small upsells not only increase your earnings per project but also give your clients a more complete and polished look.

In terms of monetization, for a basic branding kit (logo, business card, and a few social media templates), you can charge $300–$800 per client, depending on complexity and the package you offer. As your reputation grows, and you add more services like custom email templates or website banners, you can increase your rates to $1,000–$2,500 per project.

With a steady stream of clients, you could realistically earn $3,000–$5,000 per month after a few months of consistent marketing and outreach. Top-tier designers working with established small businesses, especially those offering ongoing branding support, can scale up to $7,000–$10,000+ per month as their client base expands.

By focusing on quality, affordability, and fast turnaround—with the help of AI tools—you can build a solid income stream by helping small businesses look big.

Create Educational Design Courses

If you're comfortable with design concepts and AI tools, creating courses that teach others how to use AI in graphic design can be a highly rewarding venture. Platforms like Udemy, Skillshare, and Teachable provide a great space for launching and selling courses. You could create a course on topics like "Social Media Design with Canva" or "Creating Digital Products Using Adobe Firefly."

Start by designing a clear, structured curriculum. Begin with the basics: choosing templates, customizing layouts, and understanding design principles. Then, dive deeper into the magic of AI tools, like using Canva's AI-powered features or Adobe Firefly to generate unique graphics. These tools can drastically reduce production time while enhancing the creativity of students, so showing your learners how to harness that power will be a major draw.

Supplement your courses with practice assignments to help students solidify their understanding. You can create projects where learners need to design logos, social media posts, or branded assets, using both AI tools and traditional design techniques.

Course pricing on platforms like Udemy and Skillshare can range from $20 to $100+ per course. If you create a $50 course and attract 200 students in the first few months, you could earn around $10,000. With more complex or higher-value courses, such as those including additional resources or personalized support, you could charge higher rates—up to $200–$500 per course.

As you build a portfolio of courses and earn positive reviews, it's possible to scale your income. Experienced instructors on these platforms can earn anywhere from $1,000 to $5,000/month once their courses gain traction. More successful courses and instructors, especially with a growing reputation, can scale up to $10,000+/month with multiple courses, memberships, or bundled offerings.

By leveraging AI tools to enhance the learning experience and providing real-world, actionable skills, you can build a profitable and scalable online education business—helping others become design pros while making a steady income from home.

Sell Merch with On-Demand Production Partners

To make money with AI-powered design tools, consider collaborating with local or online print-on-demand suppliers to create custom merchandise. This can include products like T-shirts, bags, hats, and more. AI tools like Adobe Firefly help you design eye-catching visuals quickly and easily adapt those designs across multiple items. This is a great way to target small businesses looking for branded merchandise or individuals who want custom designs for special events like weddings or parties. You can promote these services to a broad audience by leveraging social media and online marketplaces, making it an accessible and scalable income opportunity

Your income will depend on the number of products sold and the pricing, but here's an estimate:

- On average, for a custom T-shirt design, you could earn $5 to $15 per item in profit, depending on the platform and product.
- For bulk orders, such as from a business or for an event, you could see larger profits. For instance, if a business orders 50–100 custom items, your earnings would increase accordingly.

If you sell about 50 items per month, with a profit of $10 per item, you'd make around $500/month. For larger orders or collaborations with businesses or influencers, your earnings could climb to $2,000 to $5,000/month, depending on the volume of orders and pricing.

By combining your design skills with POD services, you can establish a reliable, scalable income stream while helping others with their custom merchandise needs.

Offer AI-Powered Design Workshops for Businesses

With AI becoming a game-changer in marketing, why not jump on the bandwagon and offer workshops that teach businesses how to create killer graphics using AI tools? You could tailor your sessions to focus on things like social media design, building brand consistency, or even making presentations that pop. Whether you host these workshops online through Zoom or go local with in-person sessions, it's a solid way to provide value.

You can charge per participant—usually around $50 to $200 per person—or offer a flat rate for bigger teams, which could range from $500 to $2,000 depending on the company size and session length. For added engagement, use Canva or Adobe Firefly to create hands-on exercises and real-time demos, giving attendees a practical feel for using AI in their design work. With a few well-marketed workshops each month, you could easily pull in $1,000 to $5,000 a month, especially if you offer ongoing sessions or corporate packages.

Final thought: Monetizing AI-Powered Graphic Design

AI-powered graphic design is transforming the creative world—and the best part is, you don't need to be a professional designer to profit from it. Whether you're creating logos, Instagram posts, product packaging, or marketing materials, tools like Canva, Adobe Firefly, Looka, and Kittl allow you to produce stunning visuals in just minutes. The time-consuming, technical barriers of traditional design work? Gone. Now, anyone with a laptop and an idea can step into the design world and start building an income from home.

From selling pre-made templates on marketplaces like Etsy and Creative Market, to offering personalized design services to influencers or small businesses, the earning opportunities are endless. You can also use your AI-generated designs to launch your own print-on-demand store—turning your creations into T-shirts, posters, mugs, and more, with zero upfront inventory. Some creators even use tools like Midjourney to build unique branding kits or mood boards for businesses and charge premium rates.

But it's not just about the tools—it's about how you use them. Success in this space comes down to creativity, consistency, and knowing your audience. Keep experimenting, develop a unique style, and start small if you need to. One well-designed logo or template pack could be the start of a thriving passive income stream. And as you grow more confident, you'll be able to scale—offering higher-ticket services, monthly retainers, or exclusive design bundles.

The playing field has been leveled. AI gives you a seat at the table, even if you're just starting out. So whether you want to design full-time or just earn a side income from your home, AI-powered graphic design is one of the most exciting and accessible opportunities out there. Lean into it. Learn the tools, build your portfolio, and start offering value today. Your creative eye—supercharged by AI—might just be the thing that unlocks your next income stream.

AI-Powered Data Entry: A New Way to Earn from Home

In today's fast-paced, tech-driven world, AI-powered data entry offers a fresh and efficient way to work from home. Artificial intelligence tools can automate repetitive and time-consuming tasks, such as organizing, cleaning, and transferring data across platforms, which makes it easier than ever for anyone to get started. Whether you're entering information from forms, updating CRM systems, or extracting data from documents, AI-powered tools can speed up these processes, allowing you to focus on higher-level tasks while earning from home.

Top AI Tools for Fast and Efficient Data Entry Automation

With the rise of AI-powered automation tools, managing and inputting large amounts of information is now faster, smarter, and more accurate than ever. Whether you're organizing customer data, processing invoices, or updating spreadsheets, AI tools can help eliminate manual errors, save hours of work, and boost productivity. In this section, we'll explore the top AI tools designed to streamline data entry and show how you can use them to automate your workflow, cut costs, and scale your business operations effortlessly.

Let's begin with **Microsoft Power Automate**, a powerful automation tool that simplifies repetitive tasks across Microsoft 365 apps and external software. Whether you need to extract data, fill out forms, or automate entire workflows, Power Automate can handle it with ease. It helps users streamline processes without manual intervention, making routine tasks faster and more efficient.

Zapier is another popular automation platform that connects over 2,000 apps, allowing you to set up workflows between different platforms. It's especially useful for tasks like transferring data from one spreadsheet to another or moving information from online forms to databases. By automating these processes, Zapier saves time and ensures data is transferred quickly and accurately.

For larger-scale data entry tasks, **UiPath** provides advanced robotic process automation (RPA) capabilities. It's ideal for complex workflows such as invoice processing, form completion, and data migration. With UiPath, businesses can automate these processes with high accuracy, reducing the need for manual intervention and minimizing errors, especially in data-heavy environments.

Docparser is an AI-powered tool that specializes in extracting data from PDFs and scanned documents. It converts unstructured information into structured formats, which can then be easily imported into spreadsheets or databases. This tool is particularly helpful when dealing with large volumes of documents, such as invoices or contracts, and ensures that the data is organized and accessible for further use.

Lastly, **Google Sheets** with **AI Add-ons** offers a variety of tools, such as the **Machine Learning for Sheets** add-on, that can help with data cleaning, organization, and even predictive analysis. These AI features make Google Sheets a versatile and accessible option for simple data entry and management tasks, helping users ensure their data is accurate, well-organized, and ready for decision-making.

How to Use These AI Tools for Data Entry

Here are practical steps for applying AI tools to streamline data entry:

The first step in optimizing data entry is automating the collection of information from various sources. AI tools such as **Microsoft Power Automate** and **Zapier** allow users to create workflows that automatically pull data from sources like forms, emails, and surveys. For instance, by connecting **Google Forms** with **Google**

Sheets through Zapier, form responses are automatically added to a spreadsheet in real-time. This eliminates the need for manual data entry, ensuring that information is captured instantly and accurately, saving time and reducing human error.

Once the data has been collected, the next challenge is extracting useful information from unstructured documents. Tools like **Docparser** are designed to tackle this issue. Docparser uses machine learning to scan documents such as PDFs, invoices, and forms, extracting key data fields like names, dates, and transaction amounts. The extracted data is then structured into rows and columns, ready for seamless import into databases or spreadsheets. By configuring Docparser to recognize the layout of specific documents, users can ensure that only relevant data is extracted, reducing the time spent manually sorting through documents and improving overall accuracy.

After data has been extracted, the next step is cleaning and formatting it to ensure consistency and accuracy. **This is where Google Sheets' AI add-ons** and **Power Automate** come into play. These tools can automate tasks like detecting and removing duplicates, identifying missing values, and applying consistent formatting across columns of data. For example, Power Automate can automatically flag data entries that don't match the expected format, ensuring that only accurate and consistent data is processed. This AI-driven data cleaning ensures that your data is reliable and ready for further analysis or reporting.

To further enhance efficiency, tools like **UiPath** and **Power Automate** allow users to automate routine, repetitive tasks. Whether it's transferring data between spreadsheets, updating customer relationship management (CRM) systems, or generating reports, these AI tools can automate virtually any data entry task. By creating custom workflows, users can ensure that data entry processes are triggered automatically, reducing manual intervention and saving time. For example, a workflow can be set up to transfer new customer data from a spreadsheet to a CRM system or to generate weekly sales reports based on updated data. This automation not only saves time but also reduces the risk of human error, increasing productivity across teams.

Another useful feature offered by AI tools like **Zapier** is scheduling. Many AI tools allow users to schedule tasks, ensuring that data entry processes are performed at regular intervals without manual input. For example, Zapier can be set to pull daily sales data from your eCommerce platform and automatically update your reports. This functionality ensures that your data is always up to date, without needing to remember to manually update reports or databases. Scheduling updates in this way allows you to maintain a continuous flow of accurate data, helping you stay on top of business operations without the need for constant oversight.

In addition to streamlining data entry, AI tools also provide built-in validation features that further enhance data accuracy. AI-powered validation can flag inconsistencies, discrepancies, or errors in data entries. For instance, AI systems can identify outliers or entries that don't match historical patterns, providing users with alerts to review specific data points. This added layer of validation ensures that data is not only entered quickly but also remains reliable and accurate, which is essential for informed decision-making.

Finally, once data entry and validation are completed, it's often beneficial to integrate the processed data with business intelligence platforms like **Tableau** or **Power BI**. These platforms can automatically generate reports, dashboards, and visualizations from your cleaned and structured data, allowing you to gain actionable insights. By integrating AI into the data entry process, teams can shift their focus from manual input and data cleaning to analyzing trends and making informed decisions that drive business growth.

Monetizing AI-Powered Data Entry: A Step-by-Step Guide

Here's a comprehensive guide to monetizing data entry with AI tools

Freelance Data Entry Services

If you're looking for an easy way to get started with freelance work, offering data entry services on platforms like Upwork, Fiverr, or Freelancer is a great option. Businesses are constantly in need of help with tasks like data input, document processing, and database updates. To really stand out from the crowd, highlight your AI skills in your profile, especially tools like Power Automate and Zapier. These tools help automate the boring, repetitive stuff, making your work faster, more accurate, and way more efficient—something clients will absolutely appreciate.

Start by offering simple tasks, like updating spreadsheets or extracting data from PDFs. For example, you could offer a service where you take survey responses from a Google Form and automatically add them to a Google Sheets doc using Zapier—saving your client time and effort. It's an easy way to build trust and get some great reviews under your belt.

Once you've earned some positive feedback, you can start pitching for bigger jobs, like managing and organizing databases or processing large batches of data. For example, you could offer services to update thousands of records in a CRM system, with Power Automate doing all the heavy lifting in the background.

As you gain more experience, you could level up your offerings by providing premium services like data cleaning and validation. These are highly valued services where you can use AI tools to spot duplicates, fix errors, or standardize data, making it easier for clients to keep their records accurate and reliable.

Revenue Estimate

For data entry gigs, rates typically range from $10 to $25 per hour, depending on the complexity of the task. Starting out, you could expect to earn around $500 to $1,500 per month with simple projects. As you gain more experience and offer premium services, you could scale that up to $3,000 to $5,000 per month, especially if you're working with larger clients or offering AI-powered automation services. It's a flexible, scalable way to build a solid income stream with just a laptop and an internet connection!

Specialized Document Processing Service

Many businesses struggle with converting paper records or unstructured documents (like invoices) into digital formats. If you're looking to offer document processing services, AI tools like Docparser and UiPath can help you extract data from documents and organize it into usable, digital formats efficiently. For example, using Docparser, you can pull invoice details—such as dates, amounts, and client names—and automatically input that data into a spreadsheet or accounting software.

You could offer services like invoice digitization, where you take physical invoices or PDF files and convert the data into a digital format. This is especially helpful for businesses that need to keep their records organized and easily accessible. Another option is customer form processing, where you help businesses extract data from forms and securely store it in their systems. For e-commerce businesses, this could mean helping them update inventory records from paper logs or scanned documents into their digital inventory system.

To get started, promote your services on business forums and LinkedIn, where small businesses are constantly looking for ways to digitize their data. For instance, you could join a LinkedIn group for small business owners and offer your document processing services, highlighting how Docparser and UiPath save time and reduce human error when dealing with piles of paper.

As you gain experience, you can start offering premium services, such as data validation to ensure the accuracy of the extracted information or secure document storage, where you help clients manage and store their digital documents, ensuring compliance with data protection regulations. These additional services can justify a higher fee and make your offerings even more attractive to businesses looking for comprehensive solutions.

Revenue Estimate

For document processing services, rates typically range from $15 to $40 per hour, depending on the complexity of the task. Starting out with basic services, you could expect to earn around $500 to $2,000 per month. As you build your portfolio and expand to premium services like data validation and secure document storage, you could scale your income to $3,000 to $6,000 per month. Experienced professionals offering full-service solutions to larger businesses can potentially earn $8,000 to $10,000 per month or more, especially if you automate many processes with AI tools to increase efficiency and reduce manual effort..

Data Cleaning and Organization for Small Businesses

Small businesses often struggle with messy, unorganized data, making it hard to make informed decisions. If you offer data cleaning and structuring services, you can help businesses get their data in shape by removing duplicates, correcting formatting issues, and standardizing entries so everything is consistent and easy to use. For example, if a client has a customer list with different phone number formats (some with dashes, some without), you can standardize them all to one consistent format.

To automate parts of the cleaning process, you can use tools like Google Sheets or Microsoft Excel with AI add-ons. For instance, you can use Google Sheets' Machine Learning add-on to automatically flag duplicates or use Excel's Power Query feature to format and clean data in bulk, which saves time and reduces human error.

You can market this service as a way for businesses to save time and ensure their data is accurate, which is crucial for making good decisions. For example, you could offer a one-time data cleaning project where you take a business's messy spreadsheet of customer orders and clean it up—removing duplicates, fixing spelling errors, and organizing it by category, making it much easier for the client to analyze and act on.

Once you've built a relationship with clients, you could offer recurring maintenance packages where you check and clean their data on a regular basis. For instance, you might offer a monthly data review and cleanup service, where you go through their records, ensuring everything is accurate and up to date. You could charge on a project basis for the initial cleanup or offer ongoing monthly packages for regular maintenance.

This is a great way to offer valuable, time-saving services while creating a steady stream of work for yourself.

Automate E-commerce Data Entry

E-commerce businesses frequently need to update product listings, process orders, and manage inventory. Offer an automated data entry service using tools like UiPath and Power Automate to streamline these processes. For instance, automate data entry from order forms into inventory systems or create workflows that pull product data into spreadsheets for bulk upload. Target online businesses on e-commerce forums, LinkedIn, or specialized freelancing sites like PeoplePerHour. Offer your services as a way to reduce errors and save time, appealing to business owners looking to scale efficiently.

Run Data Entry and Automation Workshops

Many companies want to train their staff on using AI tools for data entry. Offer workshops on popular tools like Zapier, Microsoft Power Automate, or Google Sheets for data management. Tailor your workshops to industry-specific needs, like automating customer data entry for retail or invoice processing for finance teams. You can run workshops remotely or offer pre-recorded courses on platforms like Udemy and Skillshare, where students pay a fee to access lessons on demand. Charge per participant or offer customized packages for businesses needing team training.

Subscription-Based Data Management for Businesses

Offer a subscription model where businesses pay you a monthly fee to handle their data entry needs, such as daily sales reporting, CRM updates, or invoice processing. Use Power Automate to set up recurring workflows, ensuring data is consistently updated without daily intervention. Set up tiered plans, with basic packages covering core data entry tasks and higher plans including data cleaning, organization, and validation. Market this service to small to medium-sized enterprises on LinkedIn and relevant industry networks as a convenient, time-saving solution.

Develop and Sell Data Entry Templates

Create customizable templates for data entry tasks like CRM updates, inventory tracking, or customer survey analysis, and sell them on marketplaces like Etsy, Creative Market, or your own website. Use Zapier and Google Sheets to make these templates easy to integrate with popular apps. Promote your templates to small business owners and entrepreneurs looking for ready-made solutions for organizing data. By updating your templates periodically and offering customization services, you can generate a steady income from template sales.

Automated Data Collection and Reporting Service

Set up automated data collection and reporting services, ideal for clients needing regular insights but lacking the time for manual entry. Offer a package where you collect data (such as social media engagement or sales data) and generate automated reports using Power Automate or Zapier to connect with analytics platforms. Market this service to small businesses and entrepreneurs as a way to make data-driven decisions without dedicating hours to manual entry. As you build your expertise, expand your offerings to include advanced data visualization and trend analysis for a premium rate.

Data Entry and Cleanup for Real Estate Agents

Real estate agents often need help with organizing leads, updating property listings, and maintaining client databases. Offer a specialized data entry service targeting real estate professionals, using Power Automate and Zapier to streamline tasks like CRM updates and lead tracking. Promote this niche service through real estate forums, LinkedIn, and local business networks. Highlight your ability to improve their productivity and help them focus on client relationships by handling routine data tasks.

AI-Powered Form Processing for Healthcare

Healthcare providers handle vast amounts of paperwork daily, from patient forms to billing data. Offer an AI-powered data entry service using Docparser or UiPath to digitize these documents and automate data input into their systems. Target smaller clinics or healthcare providers looking for efficient solutions to handle patient intake and billing without extra staff. Approach clinics through healthcare networks, conferences, or LinkedIn, and emphasize the time-saving and accuracy benefits of using AI for document processing. As you build client relationships, consider offering long-term support packages for consistent income.

Final thought Monetizing AI-Powered Data Entry

If you're just getting started and looking for an easy entry point into the world of AI-powered income, data entry is actually one of the better beginner options. Why? Because it doesn't require deep technical skills, expensive software, or a steep learning curve. Most people already have some familiarity with spreadsheets or basic admin tasks. By pairing that knowledge with AI tools, you instantly level up what you can offer—making your service more attractive to businesses and more efficient to deliver.

That said, let's be honest—data entry isn't the most glamorous or highest-paying path in the AI world. Especially in the beginning, you might find yourself doing lower-paying gigs just to build credibility. But here's the upside: AI tools allow you to complete tasks in a fraction of the time it would take manually. That means you can take on more clients or projects without working longer hours. For example, if a task that used to take four hours now takes one thanks to automation, you've just freed up three hours to earn more money elsewhere.

Platforms like Upwork, Freelancer, and Fiverr have a growing demand for virtual assistants and data entry freelancers who know how to use AI tools like ChatGPT, Excel's Power Query, or Zapier. And because AI makes you faster and more accurate, clients are more likely to keep you on retainer once they see how efficient you are. Some freelancers even scale this into small virtual assistant agencies—outsourcing the manual parts and focusing on client management and automation setup.

Of course, not everything is smooth sailing. Success doesn't happen overnight. You'll still need to put in time to learn the tools, create your gig listings, respond to clients, and deliver results that build your reputation. Some clients may not understand the value of AI automation at first, so part of your job is educating them on why your service is faster and more effective than traditional data entry.

The reality? If you're consistent, responsive, and reliable, this path can absolutely grow into a steady stream of income. Some freelancers earn $500–$2,000 per month just from AI-assisted data entry services, depending on their niche and client base. And once you've mastered the workflow, you can turn it into a side hustle, a full-time income, or even use your skills as a stepping stone into more advanced fields like automation consulting, virtual assistance, or data analysis.

In short, if you're looking for a simple, low-barrier way to earn from home with AI, this is a great place to begin. It won't make you rich overnight, but it can definitely help you build the foundation of a sustainable, scalable income stream.

Revolutionizing Digital Marketing with AI

Digital marketing is the key to getting your brand noticed, bringing in customers, and making sales. The best part? AI tools make it easier than ever. From targeting the right audience to creating content faster and tracking what's working, AI helps marketers work smarter, not harder.

And this isn't just some passing trend—AI is a game-changer that can help anyone, whether you're just starting out or already running multiple campaigns. With the right tools, you can automate tasks, fine-tune your ads, and grow your income streams without spending hours on manual work.

Simply put, AI takes the guesswork out of digital marketing, helping you focus on what actually moves the needle.

Essential AI Tools for Digital Marketing Success

Digital marketing today is all about being strategic—knowing what to say, when to say it, and how to say it in a way that drives engagement. AI tools like **ChatGPT** and **GPT-4** aren't just here to write content fast—they're here to help you *think smarter* about your marketing. Whether you're brainstorming campaign angles, analyzing customer feedback, or A/B testing email subject lines, these tools can support every stage of the marketing journey. They help reduce the guesswork, spark new ideas, and give you data-backed insights that make your campaigns more effective. Instead of focusing just on the speed of content creation, think of AI as your marketing co-pilot—helping you plan, create, and optimize with ease.

HubSpot makes marketing easier with its AI-powered tools. It helps you automate emails, social media, and customer segmentation so you can focus on the bigger picture. Whether it's sending the right message at the right time or tracking customer interactions, HubSpot does a lot of the heavy lifting for you, helping you connect with your audience on a deeper level

For advertising, **AdCreative.ai** leverages artificial intelligence to create high-converting ad creatives for platforms like Facebook, Instagram, and Google. By analyzing past performance data, the AI generates compelling visuals and copy, ensuring your ads are optimized for maximum engagement and conversions.

When it comes to search engine optimization (SEO) and performance tracking, **Semrush** stands out as an all-in-one suite for keyword research, competitor analysis, and content optimization. With its AI-driven insights, Semrush helps marketers uncover valuable keywords, monitor competitors' strategies, and refine content to drive traffic and improve search engine rankings.

Lastly, **Canva Pro with AI** is an invaluable tool for creating visually appealing social media graphics, infographics, and presentations. With its AI features, users can generate professional-quality designs quickly, even without a graphic design background. Whether you're creating eye-catching posts for Instagram or detailed reports for presentations, Canva Pro simplifies the design process while maintaining a high standard of visual quality.

How to Leverage AI for Smarter, More Effective Digital Marketing

Use ChatGPT to draft blog posts, email newsletters, and ad copy, then go over it with a human touch for authenticity and character. For instance you can use ChatGPT to write engaging captions or email campaigns. Simply prompt it with:

"Write a catchy Instagram caption for a new fitness product launch. The tone should be motivating and fun."

You can then use AdCreative.ai to generate compelling ad visuals and copy for Facebook or Instagram ads, saving you hours of work while ensuring your ads are optimized for higher conversions. For example, you could upload the client's brand elements and let the AI create polished ad creatives that match their style and messaging.

Once created, schedule your posts using HubSpot or a similar tool, which also tracks engagement metrics. With AdCreative.ai, upload brand elements (like logo, colors, etc.), and it will create engaging ad visuals and copy. This is perfect for generating high-quality Facebook and Instagram ads without spending hours on design.

Use Semrush to identify high-ranking keywords related to your niche or industry. This data will guide blog posts, social media content, and ad targeting. For each piece, incorporate these keywords in titles, headings, and descriptions for SEO-optimized content.

HubSpot really shines when it comes to audience segmentation. It lets you break down your audience into specific groups based on things like their behavior, demographics, or how they've interacted with your brand in the past. This helps you create super targeted, personalized marketing content that speaks directly to each group's needs and interests. Plus, you can set up automated email campaigns or retargeting ads tailored to these segments, which can lead to higher engagement and better conversion rates—essentially, you're making sure the right people get the right message at the right time!

For visual content creation, Canva's AI tools make it quick and easy to design eye-catching social media posts, banners, and infographics. With a wide variety of templates to choose from, Canva's AI suggests layouts and graphics tailored to the type of content you're creating. Whether you're designing promotional posts for Instagram, Twitter, or LinkedIn, Canva helps you maintain a consistent, professional aesthetic without the need for a graphic design background.

How to Monetize from AI-Powered Digital Marketing

Offer freelance digital marketing services on platforms like Upwork, Fiverr, or LinkedIn to kickstart your career. You can start with specific services like social media management, email marketing, or ad copywriting, using AI tools like ChatGPT and AdCreative.ai to deliver high-quality results quickly.

As you position yourself as a time-efficient marketer using AI tools to optimize output, you'll stand out to clients who need fast, high-quality work. Highlight how AI tools help you save time, allowing you to deliver better results in less time. Here are a few examples hoe you might want to advertise your services:

Social Media Growth and Engagement example:

"With AI tools like ChatGPT and Canva, I offer a Social Media Growth Package where I'll create and schedule 20 posts per month tailored to your brand. I'll also handle daily engagement, from commenting to sharing relevant content, to build a dedicated following. Using AI, I'll track analytics and adjust strategies for even higher engagement."

AI-Enhanced Email Marketing example:
"Struggling with creating email campaigns that convert? I'll design and schedule a Monthly Email Marketing Campaign using AI tools to create personalized subject lines, engaging copy, and segment your list for optimal open rates. Plus, I'll analyze the results and optimize each campaign to get even better results next month."

As you gain experience and build your client base, you can expand into larger, more complex projects or even offer retainer-based services where you handle all aspects of a business's digital presence. For example, you could offer a comprehensive service where you manage everything from content creation to paid ad campaigns, along with analytics tracking—all powered by AI. Many businesses prefer freelancers for flexible marketing support, and by emphasizing how AI helps you deliver faster results, you can show clients that you're an invaluable asset to their marketing efforts.

Once you've built a trusting relationship with a client, you can pitch long-term retainer agreements, where you provide ongoing marketing strategy and support. With AI tools like Hootsuite, Canva, and Google Analytics, you can efficiently monitor campaigns and optimize strategies to keep clients ahead in the competitive digital space.

As for earnings, freelance digital marketers can charge anywhere from $20 to $75 per hour, depending on experience and the complexity of the service offered. When starting out, you might earn around $1,000 to $3,000 per month by offering specific services like social media management or ad copywriting. As you build a portfolio and gain more clients, your monthly earnings can rise to $5,000 to $8,000, especially if you offer retainer services or larger projects. Experienced digital marketers who manage full campaigns or multiple clients at once can make upwards of $10,000 to $15,000 per month. By consistently delivering high-quality results with the help of AI tools, you'll position yourself for sustainable growth in the competitive digital marketing space.

Niche-Specific Digital Marketing

Specializing in a niche allows you to build a reputation and charge higher rates. For example, if you focus on digital marketing for real estate agents, you can use Semrush to conduct targeted keyword research for terms like "best real estate SEO tips" or "homes for sale near me." This helps you create SEO-optimized content that will rank well for keywords specific to the real estate market.

You can also use AdCreative.ai to generate highly targeted ad creatives for your niche. Let's say you're working with a fitness brand. You can upload the brand's logo and color scheme, and AdCreative.ai will create ad visuals and copy that are specifically tailored to fitness enthusiasts, increasing the likelihood of higher engagement.

Once you've carved out your niche, promote your services on LinkedIn, Reddit, and niche-specific forums where businesses in your chosen industry gather. For example, if you're targeting the e-commerce sector, join forums like Shopify Community or e-commerce subreddits, where business owners are actively looking for ways to improve their marketing. By positioning yourself as the go-to person for digital marketing in e-commerce, you'll attract businesses willing to invest in high-quality, tailored services.

Affiliate Marketing with Content Creation

Create a blog or YouTube channel centered on a profitable niche like tech, fashion, or health. Use ChatGPT for blog content and Canva for visual elements like thumbnails and social media graphics. Once established, join affiliate programs (e.g., Amazon Associates or ShareASale) and embed affiliate links in your content. Use AI to streamline the content creation process, allowing you to post consistently and optimize for search engines. Semrush can help with SEO to increase visibility, while HubSpot's analytics can track what content performs best, guiding your strategy for more affiliate income.

Manage Ad Campaigns for Small Businesses

Small businesses often lack the resources to handle ad campaigns effectively. Offer to manage their Facebook, Instagram, or Google ads, leveraging tools like AdCreative.ai to produce engaging ad content that converts. Many businesses are open to monthly retainer agreements for ongoing ad management, providing a steady income stream. Target small business owners in your local area or online business communities, explaining how AI can make their ad campaigns more effective at a lower cost than traditional agencies. Provide case studies or performance metrics to back up your services and justify your rates.

Offer Social Media Content Packages

AI tools make creating and scheduling content faster, enabling you to offer affordable social media content packages to clients. Use Canva and ChatGPT to prepare graphics and captions, then schedule content with HubSpot or other social media management tools. Examples of packages include "10 social media posts for $X" or monthly social media management. Market these packages to solopreneurs, small businesses, or local influencers who need a consistent social media presence. Offering affordable starter packages allows clients to test your services, and if they're happy, you can upsell them on additional services like ad management or SEO.

Launch and Monetize a Marketing Blog

Use ChatGPT and Semrush to help generate valuable, SEO-optimized blog posts focused on digital marketing tips, trends, and case studies. Once your blog attracts a steady audience, monetize through ads, sponsored content, and affiliate marketing. Offer e-books, courses, or templates as digital products. Regularly update your blog using ChatGPT to quickly produce fresh content and Semrush for continuous keyword optimization. As your audience grows, partner with brands for sponsored posts or become an affiliate for marketing tools, creating multiple revenue streams.

Run Online Digital Marketing Workshops

Many businesses want to learn digital marketing but don't have the resources to hire agencies. Offer workshops on specific topics, such as "SEO for Beginners" or "Creating Social Media Ads with AI." Use Zoom or Google Meet to host live sessions, or record sessions and sell them as courses on platforms like Teachable or Udemy. Promote your workshops to small business networks or online communities, emphasizing the value of AI tools in making digital marketing accessible to non-experts. Charge per participant or offer group rates for businesses, creating recurring income from new participants or corporate clients.

Develop and Sell Digital Marketing Templates

Use Canva and HubSpot to create templates for common digital marketing needs, such as social media calendars, email sequences, and ad templates. Sell these on marketplaces like Etsy, Creative Market, or your own website. Provide packages for different levels (Basic, Standard, and Premium) and promote your products on

LinkedIn, Instagram, and within small business communities. For example, create a content calendar template for social media marketers or an email sequence template for e-commerce brands. AI helps you produce these templates faster and customize them as needed for clients.

Automated Email Marketing for E-Commerce

Many e-commerce stores require automated email campaigns for promotions, abandoned cart reminders, and customer follow-ups. Use HubSpot or a similar tool to set up automated email flows. You can offer this service as a one-time setup or as a monthly management service, where you update and optimize campaigns based on performance. Market this service to e-commerce business owners and emphasize the revenue-boosting potential of well-crafted automated email sequences. AI tools like GPT-4 can generate engaging, brand-aligned email copy, allowing you to deliver quality content quickly.

SEO and Content Optimization Services

With tools like Semrush and ChatGPT, offer SEO audits and content optimization for websites and blogs. Use Semrush to find keyword opportunities and ChatGPT to rewrite existing content with improved keyword targeting. As clients see improvements in their search rankings, you can pitch ongoing SEO services. Approach website owners, bloggers, and small business owners through LinkedIn or relevant online communities. Offering initial audits for a reduced fee can attract clients, after which you can propose long-term optimization packages for steady revenue.

Final thought Monetizing from AI-powered Digital Marketing

So, is AI-powered digital marketing really for you? Honestly, that depends on what you're looking for—but if you're reading this book, chances are you're curious about building something real from home, whether it's a side hustle or a full-blown income stream. The good news is: you don't need a marketing degree or a huge budget to get started. What you do need is a little patience, a willingness to learn, and the drive to apply what you discover.

AI tools like ChatGPT, Jasper, Copy.ai, and Surfer SEO aren't just shiny gadgets—they're real, functional tools that are already helping freelancers, small business owners, and even complete beginners build brands, sell products, and grow audiences online. From generating content to automating ad campaigns, these tools can cut your workload in half and boost your output tenfold. Sounds great, right?

But let's keep it real: it's not some instant get-rich formula. You're not going to push a button and wake up to thousands in your bank account. Like anything worth doing, it takes time to learn the ropes, test what works, make a few mistakes, and adapt. AI will help you speed up the process and give you an edge—but it's your consistency, your creativity, and your strategy that will ultimately bring in results.

If you're someone who loves experimenting, learning new tech, or creating value through content and strategy, this space can be incredibly rewarding. You might start out helping small businesses with their social media captions or blog content, then scale to managing full digital campaigns for multiple clients—or even your own brand. With low overhead and high flexibility, it's a perfect fit for anyone who wants to build income from home.

And if you're still unsure? That's completely normal. You don't have to have it all figured out right now. Start small. Explore the tools. Offer one service. See how it feels. As you keep reading this book, we'll walk through different ways to put these tools to work and help you find the approach that fits you. Digital marketing with AI isn't just a skill—it's a doorway. And if you're willing to step through, there's a world of opportunity waiting on the other side.

Unlocking the Potential of AI for Tutoring and Teaching Success

AI is transforming tutoring and teaching, making personalized education more accessible and manageable. By using AI tools, you can streamline lesson planning, tailor material to students' needs, and even automate some administrative tasks. This allows you to focus on creating impactful learning experiences and gives you the opportunity to turn tutoring into a profitable venture.

Essential AI Tools for Transforming Tutoring and Teaching

AI tools are revolutionizing the world of tutoring and teaching, providing educators with innovative solutions to create personalized, efficient, and engaging learning experiences. Khan Academy, with its AI-powered features, allows students to learn at their own pace, offering tailored lessons and exercises in subjects like math, science, and economics. This personalized approach ensures that every student receives the attention they need to master complex concepts. Socrative takes assessment to the next level by using AI to create real-time quizzes, surveys, and formative assessments, instantly analyzing student responses and offering valuable feedback. This feature helps instructors track individual progress and identify areas for improvement, ensuring that teaching methods remain adaptive and responsive.

For language and writing tutors, Grammarly is an indispensable AI tool. It goes beyond simple grammar checking by providing detailed explanations for corrections, helping students understand why changes are needed and empowering them to become better writers over time. Quizlet enhances memorization and learning with AI-driven flashcards, quizzes, and study sets that adapt to each student's learning style and pace. This ensures efficient study sessions and greater retention of material. For those teaching languages, Duolingo uses AI to personalize language learning, adjusting lessons based on each learner's strengths and weaknesses, making language acquisition more effective and engaging.

Brainly is another powerful AI tool, facilitating collaborative learning by connecting students with a community of experts who assist in solving homework problems. The AI technology behind Brainly ensures that students get the right guidance quickly, making it a go-to resource for self-directed learning. Moodle, an open-source learning management system (LMS), enhances the learning experience by integrating AI plugins that analyze student behavior, predict performance, and provide real-time, personalized feedback, giving educators the tools they need to fine-tune their teaching strategies. For creating personalized learning materials, Content Technologies, Inc. uses AI to generate customized textbooks, study guides, and assignments based on a student's individual learning needs, ensuring that resources are always relevant and tailored.

To further improve teacher-student engagement, TeachFX uses AI to analyze classroom conversations, offering feedback on how to optimize interactions and increase student involvement. This tool provides actionable insights that help instructors adjust their teaching methods for better communication and understanding. Finally, Classcraft takes an innovative approach to teaching by gamifying learning through AI-driven experiences. By turning lessons into interactive challenges, Classcraft keeps students motivated and engaged, making learning fun while reinforcing essential academic skills. These AI tools are transforming traditional education, allowing tutors and teachers to provide more dynamic, efficient, and personalized learning experiences that cater to each student's unique needs and learning style..

How to Leverage AI for Tutoring and Teaching

AI tools can make tutoring more efficient, engaging, and personalized by helping you create structured lessons, interactive quizzes, and targeted practice materials.

Use ChatGPT to outline lesson plans and generate practice questions based on your subject. This is especially helpful for topics students typically struggle with, ensuring that you always have relevant material ready. For example, if you're tutoring high school physics, you can prompt ChatGPT with:

"Create a step-by-step lesson plan on Newton's laws of motion, including practice problems and real-world examples."

Interactive learning tools like Quizlet and Kahoot! make studying more engaging by allowing you to create custom quizzes, flashcards, and interactive challenges. For example, you could create a Kahoot! quiz on historical events or a Quizlet set for SAT vocabulary, making learning feel more like a game while assessing students' knowledge.

If you're managing multiple students, Google Classroom and Microsoft Teams help you assign, track, and grade work efficiently. For example, you can set up a weekly homework schedule where students submit assignments digitally, and you provide feedback in real-time. This helps keep everything organized while allowing you to focus on teaching.

For writing-based subjects, tools like Grammarly and LanguageTool provide real-time grammar and style suggestions, making it easier for students to refine their essays and reports. Instead of spending extra time correcting small errors, you can focus on bigger-picture improvements, such as argument structure and critical thinking.

For math tutoring, AI-driven platforms like MATHia and ALEKS analyze student progress and identify weak areas, allowing for personalized practice. For example, if a student struggles with algebraic equations, ALEKS can generate step-by-step practice problems tailored to their specific needs.

Lastly, Socratic can be a great tool for independent learning. This AI-powered app allows students to take a picture of a problem or question, and it provides explanations, related articles, and even video tutorials. As a tutor, you can use it to guide students toward helpful resources outside of sessions, reinforcing key concepts and encouraging self-paced learning.

By integrating these AI-powered tools, you can make tutoring more efficient, interactive, and tailored to each student's needs—helping them succeed while saving time on lesson prep.

How to Monetize Tutoring and Teaching with AI

Offering tutoring services online through platforms like Wyzant, Chegg Tutors, or Tutor.com can be a great way to monetize your expertise, especially when paired with AI tools. These platforms make it easy to connect with students who need help in a variety of subjects, and with AI-powered tools like ChatGPT and Quizlet, you can efficiently create high-quality learning materials to enhance your lessons.

For example, if you're tutoring in a subject like history, you can use Quizlet to generate custom flashcards covering key events, dates, and figures, allowing your students to review and memorize the material quickly. This reduces your prep time while providing value to your students with resources they can access anytime.

Once you've had a few successful sessions and received positive feedback, use those testimonials to build your reputation. A great review from a student after a challenging calculus session could help you attract more students seeking help in similar subjects.

As you gain more experience and build your client base, consider offering service packages for consistent income. You could create packages like "Weekly Math Tutoring" or "Essay Writing Assistance," which offer a set number of sessions each week along with follow-up support, like homework help. These recurring packages ensure a steady stream of income while helping you establish long-term relationships with students.

By leveraging AI to create customized practice quizzes, study guides, or flashcards, you can deliver higher-value tutoring in less time. This allows you to charge competitive rates. For example, after creating a tailored set of SAT practice materials using AI, you can confidently explain to your students that this helps you deliver personalized, effective tutoring sessions quickly, making your services even more valuable.

Starting out, you can typically charge $20–$50 per hour depending on your expertise and the subject. For a weekly tutoring package, students may pay anywhere from $100–$300/month for consistent support. Experienced tutors offering specialized services or prep for exams like SAT/ACT can charge $75–$150 per hour, and you could scale your income to $2,000–$5,000/month or more as you build a steady base of recurring clients and reputation on these platforms.

Create Specialized Courses on Platforms like Udemy and Teachable
Another great way to monetize your tutoring skills is by creating online courses in a subject you're passionate about and have expertise in, such as "Basics of Algebra" or "Introduction to Creative Writing." AI tools can help streamline the creation process and make your courses engaging for students.

You can start by using ChatGPT to outline your course structure and generate ideas for each module. For example, you could ask ChatGPT to help break down complex topics into easy-to-understand sections and suggest key learning outcomes for each module. Quizlet can be used to create quizzes and flashcards that reinforce what students learn in each lesson, and Canva is great for designing professional-looking slides, handouts, and course materials.

Once your course is ready, you can upload it to platforms like Udemy, Teachable, or Skillshare. These platforms handle the technical side of things (like hosting and payment processing), allowing you to focus on marketing and improving your content. With every new student who enrolls, you'll earn passive income, especially if your course gains traction over time.

To maximize your course's reach, consider adding interactive elements like quizzes, assignments, or practice exercises to keep students engaged. Periodically updating the course with new content ensures that it stays relevant and valuable. If new concepts or resources emerge in your field, use ChatGPT to help generate new topics or create additional materials that reflect these changes.

By making your course interactive, visually appealing, and easy to digest, you can increase student retention and encourage positive reviews, which, in turn, can attract more students.

Course prices vary, but most instructors charge anywhere from $30 to $200 per course, depending on the depth of the material. As a new course creator, you might start with a few sales per month, earning anywhere from $100–$500/month. Once your course gains momentum, you could earn anywhere from $1,000–$5,000/month, or more, especially if you consistently update the content, market your course through social media, and tap into niche audiences. Top-selling courses can even bring in $10,000+ per month.

Develop and Sell Digital Study Guides or E-Books
One great way to generate income from your tutoring expertise is by creating and selling digital study guides or e-books. You can compile comprehensive study materials, practice questions, and summaries on subjects you're passionate about. For example, if you specialize in SAT prep, you can create detailed guides or e-books with practice tests, study strategies, and tips to help students succeed. Tools like ChatGPT and Grammarly can assist in generating and refining content, while Canva or Google Slides can be used to design visually appealing layouts that make your guides more engaging.

These digital products can be sold on platforms like your own website, Etsy, or educational marketplaces like Teachers Pay Teachers. Popular subjects like math, science, and language arts, or focused test prep guides for the SAT, ACT, or even advanced topics like calculus, will likely attract a broad audience. By offering high-quality, easy-to-use resources, you're building a valuable asset that works for you even while you're not actively teaching.

As for income, depending on the depth and quality of the content, you can charge anywhere from $10 to $50 for a study guide or e-book. If you focus on test prep guides or subject-specific content that's in high demand, it's not unusual to generate between $300 to $1,000 per month in passive income, especially once you establish a reputation and increase the number of guides in your portfolio. With consistent updates and smart marketing, your digital products could potentially scale beyond that, allowing for an even larger, more passive income stream.

Offer Homework Help Subscription Services
Many parents are willing to pay for ongoing homework support. Offer a monthly subscription where students can reach out for help on specific assignments. Use AI tools to quickly produce explanations, practice problems, or examples during study sessions. Market this service to parents on social media, local community boards, or school parent-teacher associations. As students gain confidence and parents see improvement, you may expand the service to include more subjects or even small group sessions.

Become a Test Prep Specialist
Use AI to create specialized test prep services, such as for SAT, ACT, or GRE exams. Platforms like Quizlet and Kahoot! allow you to create practice quizzes and mock tests. ChatGPT can help generate explanations for complex questions, saving time and providing students with effective study tools. Advertise your services on tutoring platforms, in school communities, or through social media. Over time, you can develop complete test prep packages that cover all sections of an exam, potentially creating recurring income from each new test season.

Launch a YouTube Channel for Teaching Content
With ChatGPT and Canva, create scripts, visuals, and study guides for YouTube videos on topics you teach. Post regular videos covering popular subjects, exam tips, or homework help. Monetize through YouTube ads once you build a following, and promote additional resources, like study guides or tutoring services, in your videos. To gain more views, use SEO tools to identify popular search terms in your subject area. Once you reach a larger audience, consider collaborations or sponsorships to increase your income streams.

Create and Sell Monthly Memberships for Subject-Specific Study Groups
Host online study groups for students in specific subjects, such as calculus or English literature. Use tools like Google Classroom and Kahoot! to create a structured learning experience. Charge a monthly fee, and use AI to keep the content fresh and interactive for students. Market the study group on social media, in local schools, or even to homeschooling networks. Many parents appreciate a group setting where students can collaborate, and the monthly membership offers you a steady income.

Offer Corporate or Professional Skill Courses
Many professionals seek to upgrade skills in areas like data analysis, communication, or business writing. Use ChatGPT to create course outlines and content on these topics and offer workshops or online courses. Tools like Kahoot! and Quizlet are great for corporate training, as they make learning interactive. Promote your services on LinkedIn, targeting companies looking for professional development options. You can sell individual sessions or corporate packages and offer add-ons, such as one-on-one coaching.

Develop and Sell Customized Lesson Plans for Teachers
Use ChatGPT and Canva to create customizable lesson plans that

teachers can download and adapt for their classrooms. Popular sites like Teachers Pay Teachers are excellent platforms to sell these resources, and AI allows you to quickly generate new plans for various subjects and grade levels. Include lesson plans on current topics, holiday themes, or curriculum-aligned guides for subjects like history, language arts, or science. By consistently adding new materials, you can develop a following among teachers seeking time-saving, high-quality resources.

Host Virtual Workshops on Educational Techniques
Educators and parents are often interested in learning about effective teaching strategies. Host virtual workshops on topics like "Using AI to Enhance Learning" or "Interactive Math Lessons." Charge a fee for attendance and provide participants with takeaway resources. Use platforms like Zoom or Google Meet to conduct the workshop, and market the event on education forums, social media, and LinkedIn. Record sessions and sell them as standalone digital products afterward for additional revenue.

Final thoughts
AI tools are reshaping the tutoring and teaching landscape, making it easier than ever to earn from home. With platforms like Wyzant and Chegg Tutors, combined with AI-powered tools like Quizlet for flashcards or ChatGPT for lesson plans, you can create a personalized learning experience for students, all while managing your schedule from the comfort of your home. Whether you're offering one-on-one tutoring sessions, creating e-learning materials, or building online courses, the possibilities are endless.

By leveraging AI, you can not only work smarter but also expand your reach and increase your earning potential. Imagine having a steady stream of students, building your own brand, and getting paid for what you love to do—all while working from home. As more people embrace online learning, the demand for tutors and educators with specialized skills is only going to grow. The best part? You get to set your own rates, choose your hours, and create a flexible business that fits your lifestyle. So, if you're passionate about teaching and ready to tap into the power of AI, the future of your business is brighter than ever!

CHAPTER 4

AI for Social Media and Customer Service

AI is changing the game when it comes to managing social media and customer interactions, making things faster, smarter, and more personalized. Whether it's handling customer questions with chatbots, scheduling posts at the perfect time, or getting AI-generated content ideas, these tools make life a whole lot easier.

In this chapter, we'll explore how AI can take the stress out of customer service, from automated replies to real-time problem-solving. Plus, we'll dive into how AI can boost your social media game, helping with everything from content creation to analytics and post-scheduling.

So, whether you're a business owner wanting to connect with customers more efficiently or a content creator trying to grow your online presence, AI has your back. Let's explore how you can use these tools to save time, stay ahead of the game, and level up your digital strategy.

Social Media Management

Social media isn't just about posting—it's about strategy, engagement, and results. AI-powered tools make it easier to create, schedule, and analyze content, helping businesses stay visible online while allowing you to manage multiple accounts with less effort and more impact.

What AI Tools to Use for Social Media Management

Running social media doesn't have to be overwhelming. **Hootsuite** and **Buffer** are two of the best AI-powered scheduling tools for managing social media like a pro. Instead of manually posting every day, you can batch-create your content to perfection, schedule it ahead of time, and let AI handle the rest. Plus, their AI-driven insights help you post at the best times by analyzing audience activity so your content reaches more people when they're most likely to engage.

For example, if you're running a promo or launching a new product, you can set up an entire month's worth of posts across Instagram, Facebook, and Twitter in just a few clicks. AI helps by picking the best times to post when your audience is most active, so you get more likes, shares, and comments without constantly being online. If a post is performing well, these tools can even suggest reposting it or creating similar content to keep the momentum going.

By using Hootsuite or Buffer, you can focus less on when to post and more on engaging with your audience, creating fresh content, and growing your brand—all while saving a ton of time.

For content creation, **Canva's AI tools** make designing eye-catching graphics and templates incredibly simple. Whether you need Instagram posts, Pinterest pins, or Facebook banners, Canva's AI suggests layouts, fonts, and color schemes to match your brand—no professional design skills required. To repurpose existing content, **Lately.ai** converts long-form materials like blog posts and podcasts into bite-sized social media snippets, making it easy to maximize content reach across platforms without constantly creating new material from scratch.

For writing compelling captions, ad copy, and social media posts, **ChatGPT** and **Jasper AI** generate engaging, on-brand text tailored to different tones and audiences. Whether you're creating fun, trendy TikTok captions or professional LinkedIn posts, these tools can adjust to match your brand's voice. On the analytics side, **Sprout Social** and **Brandwatch** use AI to monitor trends, track brand mentions, and analyze audience sentiment, giving businesses valuable insights into content performance and engagement strategies.

To further optimize social media performance, **Predis.ai** provides AI-powered post ideas, hashtag recommendations, and engagement predictions, helping businesses craft high-performing content that resonates with their target audience. For video-based content, **InVideo** and **Pictory AI** help turn text-based scripts, blog posts, or raw footage into polished, engaging videos perfect for platforms like TikTok, Instagram Reels, and YouTube Shorts.

How to Use These AI Tools for Social Media Management

Use ChatGPT or Jasper to generate engaging captions, brainstorm creative post ideas, and craft content tailored to your brand's voice. These AI tools allow you to fine-tune messaging by specifying the audience, tone, and platform, making it easy to create content that truly resonates. For example, if you're managing social media for a fitness brand, you can prompt ChatGPT with:

"Generate 10 Instagram post captions for a fitness brand promoting a new high-protein smoothie. The tone should be energetic, engaging, and motivational."

For brainstorming post ideas, you might use:

"Give me 5 unique social media post ideas for a beauty brand launching an organic skincare line. The tone should be friendly, educational, and engaging."

If you're crafting a LinkedIn post for a corporate client, you could refine the AI output by specifying the level of professionalism, such as:

"Write a LinkedIn post for a tech startup announcing a new AI-powered customer support chatbot. The tone should be professional, yet approachable, highlighting the key benefits for businesses."

To optimize post reach, always provide AI with details about the target audience and tone. For instance, if you're promoting a luxury fashion brand, your prompt could be:

"Create 5 Instagram captions for a luxury handbag launch, targeting fashion-forward women aged 25-40. The tone should be elegant, sophisticated, and aspirational."

For brands targeting Gen Z on TikTok, you might use:

"Generate 3 TikTok caption ideas for a trending dance challenge promoting a new sneaker line. The tone should be fun, trendy, and engaging."

By tailoring AI-generated content using specific prompts, you can ensure that social media posts align with the brand's voice and effectively resonate with the intended audience. This strategic approach not only saves time but also enhances engagement and brand consistency across different platforms.

Another AI tool that makes designing social media posts a breeze is Canva. With tons of templates, graphics, and AI-powered design suggestions, you can create eye-catching posts, stories, and banners in minutes. If you're managing social media for a client, you can also set up reusable templates so they can easily keep their branding consistent without starting from scratch every time. Whether it's Instagram stories, Pinterest pins, or Facebook ads, Canva helps make everything look polished and professional with minimal effort.

When it comes to actually getting your content out there, tools like

Hootsuite and Buffer make life easier by letting you plan and schedule posts in advance. No more last-minute scrambling to post at the right time! These platforms also give you insights into the best times to post, so you can hit peak engagement hours and get the most eyes on your content while freeing up time to actually interact with your audience.

If you've got long-form content like blog posts, podcasts, or videos, Lately.ai is a game-changer. It can break down a single piece of content into multiple social media posts, turning key points into short clips, captions, or bite-sized highlights. That means less effort spent creating new content from scratch and more mileage out of what you already have. For example, a single podcast episode can be turned into Instagram quote posts, TikTok clips, and Twitter threads, giving you content for days.

Want to know what's working and what's flopping? Sprout Social and Later give you all the juicy analytics, tracking engagement, clicks, and audience demographics so you can tweak your strategy for better results. These AI-powered insights help you figure out what type of content your audience loves so you can double down on what works and ditch what doesn't.

By using these AI tools, managing social media becomes way less stressful and a whole lot more effective. You can save time, keep branding on point, and make smarter decisions based on real data—all while keeping your audience engaged and growing.

How to Monetize from AI-Powered Social Media Management

You can create profile listings on Upwork, Fiverr, or LinkedIn that highlight your social media management services like content creation, scheduling, and engagement tracking, powered by AI tools to make your workflow efficient and scalable. For example, you can offer a "Weekly Content Creation and Posting Package" on Fiverr, where you promise to create and schedule daily social media posts for clients. You can emphasize how AI tools like Hootsuite allow you to schedule posts ahead of time, optimizing timing for maximum engagement, while Canva's AI-driven design features help you create polished, on-brand graphics in a fraction of the time it would take manually. These kinds of packages can easily bring in $100–$200 per client per week, depending on the scope and platform

Let's say you're offering a service on Upwork that focuses on social media content strategy and engagement. You could list a service like "Instagram Growth Package", where you create a month's worth of posts, design branded graphics with Canva, and track engagement using Sprout Social or Buffer. You'd emphasize how using AI tools like Canva's content suggestion engine and Hootsuite's automated scheduling helps you deliver professional results quickly, which is exactly what busy business owners are looking for. A package like this can range from $300–$600 a month, and once you're established, charging higher rates for premium strategies becomes totally doable.

You can also start small to build trust—offering a "Branded Graphics Set" with 5-10 custom visuals for around $50–$100 or a weekly post package at $75–$150. These smaller gigs are a great way to rack up positive reviews, especially from solopreneurs and small business owners who need help but aren't quite ready for full service. This allows you to build trust with clients who want reliable, timely social media content but don't need full service yet. Once you've earned trust, you could offer bigger services, like a complete monthly content calendar or full social media account management, including content creation, post scheduling, and engagement analytics.

Once you've built momentum, offer bigger packages like a full monthly content calendar or full-service account management. On LinkedIn, for instance, you could list a "Full-Spectrum Social Media Management" package where you create, schedule, and monitor content performance, and deliver monthly reports. Services like this often go for $500–$1,500+ per month depending on how many platforms you're managing and the amount of content included.

As your portfolio grows, you can offer long-term retainer contracts, such as managing an entire brand's social media presence for a fixed monthly fee. These retainers often fall in the $1,000–$3,000/month range, especially if you're offering additional services like AI-powered ad campaigns using tools like AdCreative.ai. These types of gigs provide you with steady income and give clients the consistency they're after—especially when you back it up with performance reports and strong branding results.

1. Specialize in Niche Social Media Management Services

Focusing on a specific industry, like fitness, real estate, or e-commerce, helps you stand out and justifies higher rates. Research industry trends and create sample content using AI to showcase your expertise. AI tools make it easy to stay updated on each niche's trends, giving you an edge over generalist managers. Market your niche services through LinkedIn or niche-focused communities, emphasizing your understanding of the industry's unique demands. As your niche reputation grows, you can command higher fees and attract clients who appreciate your specialized expertise.

2. Create and Sell Branded Social Media Content Templates

Design customizable social media templates on Canva for businesses. These templates allow clients to produce content that aligns with their branding without starting from scratch each time. Focus on popular formats, such as Instagram stories, Facebook posts, and Pinterest pins. Sell these template bundles on Etsy, Gumroad, or your own website. By creating templates in various themes (e.g., "Fitness Launch" or "Holiday Season"), you can build a steady income as businesses purchase and reuse them.

3. Set Up Monthly Content Calendar Subscriptions

Create a subscription-based service where clients receive a monthly content calendar. This includes captioned posts, graphics, and hashtags that they can post independently. Use AI tools like ChatGPT for captions and Canva for graphics, allowing you to develop high-quality content quickly. Market this as a lower-cost option for clients who want content ideas without full management services. Promote this option on your website or social media, and offer different tiers based on the number of posts per month.

4. Run Social Media Strategy Consulting Sessions

Many businesses struggle with direction for their social media. Offer one-on-one strategy sessions to help clients identify their target audience, preferred platforms, and content types. Use AI analytics tools like Sprout Social to analyze current social media performance and identify areas for improvement. Charge a flat fee for each session and offer add-ons, such as a follow-up action plan or a mini content calendar. This service is valuable for smaller businesses that may not need ongoing management but want professional guidance.

5. Manage Influencer Partnerships and Sponsored Content

For clients looking to expand their reach, offer influencer management services. Use AI tools to identify influencers that align with your client's brand, and draft outreach emails or proposals for collaborations.

You can charge clients a fee for each influencer campaign, tracking performance with tools like Sprout Social to assess ROI. This service is particularly valuable for e-commerce and lifestyle brands looking to leverage influencer marketing.

6. Launch a YouTube Channel or Blog About Social Media Tips

Create content-sharing social media tips and strategies on platforms like YouTube, Medium, or LinkedIn. Use AI tools to plan video scripts or articles, sharing your expertise with a wider audience. Once you have a following, monetize through ad revenue, sponsorships, or affiliate marketing for tools like Canva or Buffer. Promote your services alongside these educational materials to attract clients who want professional management. As your reputation grows, you can charge higher fees and offer workshops or courses.

7. Develop and Sell Social Media Playbooks or eBooks

Write comprehensive playbooks or eBooks detailing strategies for different platforms, such as "Mastering Instagram Growth for Small Businesses." Use ChatGPT for drafting and Canva to design layouts. Sell these resources on your website or platforms like Amazon or Gumroad. They're a valuable passive income source, appealing to clients who want to DIY their social media but need a structured guide.

8. Offer Ongoing Engagement and Customer Support Services

Many brands need consistent engagement with their followers. Offer a service to respond to comments, answer questions, and engage with followers on behalf of clients. AI tools can help automate common responses and identify frequently asked questions, allowing you to handle a large volume of interactions. Charge a monthly fee for this service, with options for higher engagement levels or expanded hours. This is valuable for businesses that want to foster community without dedicating internal resources to constant engagement.

9. Run AI Social Media Training Workshops for Businesses

Educate business teams on how to use AI for their social media strategy by offering workshops or training sessions. Teach employees how to create content, track analytics, and optimize their posts using AI tools. This service appeals to companies that want to empower their marketing teams to manage social media independently. Offer online workshops, charging a flat fee per participant or a bulk rate for company-wide training. You can conduct sessions over Zoom, provide recorded materials, and create digital handouts.

Final Thought: Is AI-Powered Social Media Management Right for You?

If you've ever spent hours scrolling through Instagram, pinning boards on Pinterest, or curating the perfect TikTok vibe—congratulations, you already have a feel for the world of social media. The only difference now is you're learning to monetize those instincts using powerful AI tools that make the process faster, smoother, and more profitable. You don't need a degree in marketing or years of experience. You just need a willingness to learn, a creative mindset, and the courage to take that first step.

The truth is, AI-powered social media management is one of the most beginner-friendly online income streams out there. Why? Because every business, influencer, and brand wants a digital presence—but many don't have the time or expertise to manage it. That's where you come in. With tools like ChatGPT, Canva, Ocoya, and Buffer, you can create scroll-stopping content, schedule posts weeks in advance, and even analyze engagement data without being glued to your phone all day.

You can start small—maybe by managing posts for a local shop, your cousin's clothing brand, or your own growing brand. Then, as you build confidence and experience, you can scale up: offering full-service social media packages, monthly retainers, or even launching your own micro-agency from the comfort of your home.

But let's be real—this isn't a get-rich-overnight situation. Like anything worthwhile, it takes consistency, adaptability, and some trial and error. You might have slow months or clients that drop off. That's part of the process. But the upside? You're gaining real digital skills that are in high demand, and you're creating income opportunities that don't rely on punching a clock or commuting to an office.

So, if you're wondering whether this path is right for you—just remember: You don't have to be a tech expert or social media star. You just have to be curious, committed, and open to experimenting with new tools. The learning curve is manageable, and I'll guide you through the rest of it in this book.

This is your chance to turn your scroll into strategy, your content into currency, and your online time into real income. AI is the accelerator, but you are the engine.

Let's build this together.

Customer Service Solutions

Customer service is all about enhancing interactions and providing seamless support to your customers across different channels, whether through live chat, email, or over the phone. AI-powered customer support tools are making it easier than ever for you to handle customer inquiries, streamline service, and boost engagement. With the rise of AI-powered tools, you can now streamline operations, respond faster, and boost customer satisfaction like never before.

Essential AI Tools to Use for Customer Service Solutions

AI is revolutionizing customer service by streamlining inquiries, improving response times, and enhancing customer satisfaction. Businesses can now handle high volumes of customer interactions more efficiently without overwhelming human support teams. **ChatGPT** and **IBM Watson** are smart chatbots that can respond to customer questions in real-time, offering accurate answers based on past interactions and common queries. For example, an e-commerce store could use ChatGPT to automate responses to order status questions, reducing the need for manual support.

For managing customer support tickets, tools like **Zendesk** and **Freshdesk** keep everything organized and automated. They track issues, assign tickets, and even suggest automated responses, helping support teams respond faster and more efficiently. If you're running a small business, Freshdesk can help you prioritize urgent customer issues, ensuring no request goes unanswered.

If you want to engage website visitors and capture leads, tools like **Drift** and **Intercom** use chatbots to start conversations instantly. For example, if a visitor lands on your pricing page, Drift's chatbot can pop up with a personalized message, helping answer questions and nudging them toward a purchase.

For businesses looking for an all-in-one customer service solution, HubSpot Service Hub offers tools for managing interactions, collecting feedback, and automating support tasks. If you're scaling a business, this can help keep customer service running smoothly without hiring a huge team.

Zoho Desk takes things a step further with AI-powered ticket prioritization, predicting customer needs before they even reach out. For example, if a SaaS company notices a surge in similar support requests, Zoho Desk can flag the issue early, helping the team proactively fix problems before they escalate.

And for managing email support, **HelpScout** is a lifesaver. It provides a shared inbox so support teams can collaborate easily, along with reporting features to track response times and customer satisfaction.

By integrating AI-driven customer support tools, businesses can automate repetitive tasks, improve response times, and create a seamless support experience, keeping customers happy while saving time.

How to Apply AI Tools for Customer Service Solutions

When you're just starting your business, offering fast, reliable customer support can give you a huge edge—but doing it all manually is time-consuming. That's where AI-powered tools like ChatGPT, IBM Watson, and Intercom step in to help you scale smartly without sacrificing quality.

Step 1: Deploy a Smart Chatbot for Instant Help

Start by integrating a chatbot like ChatGPT or IBM Watson directly on your website or e-commerce platform. These tools can be trained to handle FAQs, product questions, and general support—all while you're sleeping. For instance, if you sell digital planners, your chatbot can answer questions like "Does this work with GoodNotes?" or "How do I download my files?" by pulling answers from your help center or knowledge base.

To get started:

- Create a list of common customer questions from past emails or messages.

- Feed these into your chatbot's knowledge base.

- Use conditional logic to guide conversations. For example, if someone asks about a refund, the bot can respond with your refund policy or route them to a form.

Example:

Imagine a customer visits your site at midnight with a question about shipping. Instead of waiting until morning, they get an instant reply from your chatbot:

"Hi! Standard shipping usually takes 5–7 business days. Need to track your order? Click here."

That's a great experience—and you didn't lift a finger.

Step 2: Centralize Everything with a Support Desk

As you grow, things can get messy fast—emails, DMs, and comments coming in from all directions. Tools like **Zendesk** and **Freshdesk** help keep it all in one place. These platforms automatically convert incoming messages into support tickets, categorize them by topic (billing, shipping, tech issue), and even assign priority levels.

For example, if a customer reports a payment issue, Zendesk can tag it as "urgent" and push it to the top of your to-do list. You can also create canned responses for common questions. So instead of writing out "Thanks for your message, your download link is here…" 50 times a day, you just click, send, done.

Step 3: Analyze the Conversations

Use **HubSpot Service Hub** or **Zoho Desk** to analyze your customer interactions. These platforms track everything—from response times to resolution rates—helping you understand what's working and what needs fixing.

Let's say you discover a pattern: a lot of people are confused about how to apply your digital product license. That's a signal to update your onboarding or FAQ page—or create a quick how-to video. HubSpot even lets you tag specific interactions and run reports, so you can see what types of questions are trending.

Step 4: Make It Personal with Data

One of the best parts of AI is personalization. With the right tools, you can tailor your communication based on behavior. Tools like Tidio, Drift, or ManyChat can access customer data (past purchases, browsing habits, etc.) and use it to personalize replies.

For instance, a returning customer who just bought an online course could be greeted with:

"Hey Sarah, ready to jump back into your course? Need help accessing Module 2?"

That kind of tailored support builds trust and loyalty.

Step 5: Use Automated Follow-Ups to Show You Care

Finally, automate follow-ups using tools like **Intercom, Tidio,** or **ChatBot.com.** After an issue is resolved, send a quick message a day or two later:

"Hi again! Just checking in—did everything work out with your download? Let us know if you need anything else."

These little touches go a long way in showing customers that you genuinely care, and they often lead to glowing reviews or repeat business.

When you start building your business, implement chatbots like ChatGPT or IBM Watson on your website or customer service platform to provide 24/7 support. Start by training the bot on common customer queries and integrating it with existing systems to pull relevant information. This ensures the chatbot can provide accurate and contextually relevant answers.

Use platforms like Zendesk or Freshdesk to centralize customer inquiries. Set up automated ticketing systems to categorize and prioritize issues, ensuring that urgent matters are addressed promptly. Create templates for common responses to save time and maintain consistency in messaging.

Use tools like HubSpot Service Hub to track and analyze customer interactions across various channels. Implement feedback loops to gather insights from customers, helping you to identify pain points and improve service quality.

Leverage customer data collected from previous interactions and purchasing behavior to tailor responses. Use AI tools to analyze this data, allowing for personalized communication that meets individual customer needs.

Set up automated follow-up messages using tools like Intercom or Drift. After resolving a customer issue, send an automated message to check in and ensure their satisfaction. This demonstrates commitment to customer care and helps foster long-term relationships.

How to Monetize AI-Powered Customer Service Solutions

One of the easiest and most scalable ways to earn from home is by offering AI-driven customer service as a freelancer on sites like Upwork, Fiverr, and Freelancer. You can start by offering simple chatbot setup services using tools like ChatGPT, Zendesk, or Freshdesk. Even if you're not super technical, these platforms are built for beginners and come with drag-and-drop options or setup wizards.

Start small with a "Basic Chatbot Setup" gig—design a bot that handles FAQs for a small business website. This can earn you around $50–$150 per project.

As you gain experience, upgrade your offer. A "Standard Automation Package" that sets up workflows, auto-responses, and chatbot scripts can fetch $300–$600 per client.

Then, go big with a "Premium AI Customer Service Suite" that includes setup, automation, chatbot training, and monthly reporting. These can bring in $1,000–$2,500 depending on the client and scope.

With 3–5 ongoing clients, that could mean $3,000–$8,000/month—all from your laptop.

Build and Sell Customer Service Training Programs
Companies are eager to learn how to implement AI but don't know where to start. That's your opportunity to build and sell training courses that teach them how to set up AI-powered support systems using platforms like Drift, Intercom, and HubSpot Service Hub.

Record video tutorials using screen recorders like Loom or OBS, create slide decks with Canva, and structure your course with Teachable or Udemy. You don't need to be camera-ready either—voiceovers or screen shares work just fine.

You could sell individual courses for $49–$199, depending on the depth.

If you package them for teams or small businesses, offer licenses or group access starting at $499+.

Some creators even bundle coaching and charge $1,000+ for live workshop packages.

With just 100 course buyers per year at $99 each, that's $9,900 in passive income. Not bad for a product you create once and sell forever.

Create Customer Feedback and Survey Solutions
Businesses need customer feedback, but analyzing it manually takes forever. You can offer a service that sets up feedback collection tools

and uses AI to analyze the results. Use Google Forms or Typeform to build surveys, then import the data into tools like MonkeyLearn or ChatGPT to auto-generate insights.

You can charge:

- $150–$300 for setting up basic feedback forms

- $400–$700/month for ongoing analysis and reporting

Offer a "Customer Insights Package" where you deliver a monthly feedback summary and improvement suggestions. A few retainer clients could bring in $2,000+/month.

Develop and Sell AI Chatbot Solutions
Design ready-made chatbot templates tailored to industries like e-commerce, real estate, or healthcare. Use tools like Botpress, ChatGPT API, or Tidio to create them. Once the bot is built, businesses just plug it into their website and it's good to go.

You could sell basic chatbots as one-time installs for $300–$500 each.

Custom bots with training data and full integration could command $1,000–$3,000+ per client.

You can also charge monthly support fees ($100–$300/month) for updates and fine-tuning.

Get 5 clients on recurring plans and you've got yourself a stable $1,500/month baseline.

Manage Customer Service Outsourcing with AI
Want to take it a step further? Position yourself as an AI-first customer support agency. Use AI tools to handle the bulk of inquiries while keeping a small team (or yourself) for escalations.

Set pricing as a monthly retainer:

- Small biz plan: $500/month

- Mid-size business: $1,000–$2,000/month

- Enterprise clients: $3,000+/month

With just 3–5 clients, you could hit $5,000–$10,000/month—and the best part is AI handles most of the heavy lifting.

Specialize in E-Commerce AI Support

E-commerce stores are flooded with questions about orders, returns, and shipping. Offer a done-for-you service where you set up automated e-commerce support using ChatGPT or Tidio bots. You can also integrate Shopify apps that work with AI to answer repetitive questions.

Offer packages like:

- $299 for basic setup (FAQ chatbot + email templates)

- $750 for chatbot + ticketing + autoresponders

- $1,500/month for full support management

The more stores you work with, the more income you can stack—plus they often need holiday support, so you can even offer seasonal upsells.

Host Workshops or Webinars on AI in Customer Service

Teaching is one of the most rewarding and scalable ways to earn. Host workshops on how AI transforms customer support—teach businesses how to implement it and avoid rookie mistakes.

Charge:

- $99–$299 per attendee for live webinars

- $500–$2,000 for private corporate workshops

Add a consulting upsell at the end and offer 1-on-1 help for $250/hour. You can run these monthly or quarterly, keeping your income flexible but predictable.

Monetize Content on Customer Service Best Practices

If you enjoy writing, blog about AI in customer support. Break down tools, offer tips, and review platforms. Monetize through:

- Affiliate links for platforms like HubSpot, Freshdesk, Intercom

- Sponsored posts from SaaS companies

- Selling e-books or templates (like a chatbot scripting guide for $29)

Even a small blog with 10,000 monthly views could earn $500–$1,000/month in affiliate commissions alone.

Launch a Full-Service Customer Support Agency

Once you're confident, take things to the next level by building a boutique AI-powered support agency. Recruit other freelancers to handle tickets while you manage the systems and client relationships.

Charge per-service or retainer style:

- Small biz: $1,500/month

- Large clients: $5,000+/month

With just 4–6 clients, you could be running a six-figure business from your living room.

Final Thought

AI-powered customer service is one of those golden opportunities where innovation meets real, everyday demand. More and more businesses are shifting online, and with that shift comes a huge need for responsive, efficient customer support. But not everyone has the time, team, or technical know-how to make it happen. That's where you come in. With AI tools like ChatGPT, Zendesk, or HubSpot, you're not just helping businesses run smoother—you're offering a smarter way to serve customers, and they'll pay for that peace of mind.

What's really exciting is how beginner-friendly this space has become. You don't need a tech degree or a full-fledged agency to get started. Most of these tools are plug-and-play, and with a bit of practice, you can learn to train bots, automate responses, and build workflows that look incredibly professional. It's the kind of skill that gets easier with each client—and it scales. You can start small, offering chatbot setups or FAQ automation, and as your confidence and client list grow, so can your income. Many freelancers in this space are pulling in anywhere from $500 to $3,000+ per month per client, depending on the level of service and automation involved. That means if you lock in just a few long-term clients, you could be earning a full-time income from home without ever needing to manage a physical team.

Of course, no opportunity is without its learning curve. You'll need to stay up to date with the tools, occasionally dive into troubleshooting, and learn to communicate clearly with business owners who might not understand AI—but all of that adds value to your service. It positions you as more than just a service provider. You become a trusted partner in making their operations smoother, faster, and more cost-effective.

At the end of the day, this isn't just about setting up bots—it's about solving real problems in a way that's fast, affordable, and genuinely helpful. And when you focus on delivering that kind of value, you'll find yourself not just making money—you'll be building long-term business relationships, gaining referrals, and creating a steady stream of income that grows with you. Whether you're looking for a flexible side hustle or a scalable business you can run from home, AI-powered customer service opens the door to both. The tools are ready. The demand is here. All that's left is for you to step in.

Consulting and Training

Businesses are constantly looking for expert guidance to navigate new technology, improve performance, and upskill employees. With industries evolving at a rapid pace, companies need specialists who can provide insights, training, and tailored solutions to help them stay competitive. If you have knowledge in a specialized field, whether it's AI implementation, digital marketing, business strategy, or leadership development, you can offer consulting and training services from home—turning your expertise into a profitable income stream without ever stepping into an office.

Essential AI Tools to Use for Consulting and Training

Running a successful consulting or training business from home has never been easier, thanks to AI-powered tools that streamline workflows, enhance client experiences, and even create new revenue opportunities. Whether you're developing training programs, coaching clients, or managing consulting projects, the right tools can help you work smarter while maximizing your earnings.

AI language models like ChatGPT and OpenAI's GPT-4 are invaluable for content creation, making it easy to generate training materials, draft consulting proposals, and provide quick, accurate responses to client inquiries. Instead of spending hours writing from scratch, consultants can use AI to outline detailed business strategies, create interactive lesson plans, or develop industry-specific reports in minutes. For example, a leadership coach could use ChatGPT to generate a step-by-step program on improving team communication, saving time while delivering high-value insights to clients. You'd simply input a prompt like: "Create a 6-week leadership coaching program focusing on communication skills, emotional intelligence, and conflict resolution. Include weekly exercises and key takeaways." Within seconds, you'd get a structured program complete with weekly goals, practical activities, and summary points—giving you a polished foundation you can tweak and personalize for each client. This not only speeds up your workflow but also allows you to consistently deliver quality content that feels tailor-made, without the heavy lift of starting from scratch every time.

For those looking to scale their knowledge into a passive income stream, **Teachable** and **Thinkific** provide user-friendly platforms for building and selling online training programs. These platforms allow trainers to upload video lessons, quizzes, and downloadable resources, creating a seamless learning experience for students. A digital marketing consultant, for example, could turn their expertise into an SEO training course, selling it as an evergreen product that generates revenue without requiring live sessions. By leveraging these platforms, experts can reach a global audience and earn consistent income from their knowledge.

Virtual collaboration is essential for delivering high-quality consulting and training services, and tools like **Zoom** and **Microsoft Teams** enable seamless communication. These platforms allow professionals to conduct live coaching sessions, team workshops, and corporate training without geographical limitations. A consultant specializing in AI implementation, for instance, could use Zoom to walk a company through the process of integrating chatbots into their customer service, sharing screens to provide hands-on guidance in real time. These tools help create a more interactive and engaging learning environment, even in a remote setting.

Collecting feedback and tracking the impact of consulting or training sessions is key to continuous improvement, and platforms like **SurveyMonkey** and **Google Forms** make it easy to gather insights from clients and students. A business coach could send out a Google Forms survey after a three-week productivity workshop, asking participants to rate their experience and suggest areas for improvement. This data not only helps refine future training programs but also provides testimonials that can be used for marketing and credibility building.

To stay organized and efficiently manage multiple clients, projects, and deadlines, consultants can rely on **Notion** and **Trello** for project management. These tools offer structured workspaces to track tasks, store client notes, and streamline workflows. A career coach, for example, could use Trello to organize client progress, setting up boards for each stage of the coaching process. Meanwhile, Notion could serve as a central hub for storing training materials, session notes, and long-term strategy documents, ensuring everything is easily accessible and well-structured.

By integrating these AI-powered tools into their businesses, consultants and trainers can operate more efficiently, deliver high-quality services, and create multiple income streams from home. Whether offering live consulting, corporate training, or digital courses, these platforms help professionals scale their expertise while maximizing productivity and profitability. The combination of AI automation, engaging content creation, and smart organization makes it possible to run a successful, home-based consulting business with global reach.

How to Use These AI Tools for Consulting and Training

Start by using ChatGPT or GPT-4 to create outlines and content for your training session. For instance, let's say you're creating a leadership development program. You can simply input a prompt like:

Prompt:

"Create a 4-week leadership training program for managers focusing on communication, decision-making, conflict resolution, and team motivation."

What AI Will Generate:

- **Week 1: Communication Skills** – How to deliver clear messages and listen effectively.

- **Week 2: Decision-Making & Problem Solving** – Teaching managers how to make informed, confident decisions.

- **Week 3: Conflict Resolution** – Approaches to resolving conflicts constructively within teams.

- **Week 4: Team Motivation & Coaching** – Building trust and inspiring team performance.

The AI will also generate talking points, activities, and even case studies to include, saving you hours of brainstorming and structuring the content.

Once you have your content, it's time to create visually appealing materials. Tools like Canva or Visme are fantastic for putting together professional-looking presentations, workbooks, and infographics. These tools come with templates that are easy to customize with your branding, charts, and images.

So for example, Let's say you're coaching clients on time management. You could use Canva to design a "Daily Productivity Planner" that outlines blocks of time for focused work, breaks, meetings, and priority tasks. Add motivational quotes, branded colors, and icons to make it visually appealing and easy to follow. This kind of resource is not only useful for your sessions but can also be offered as a downloadable freebie or bonus material for clients—adding value while reinforcing your brand in a professional, polished way.

In addition, Canva's AI-powered suggestions will help you optimize your layout and give you ideas for design elements, so you don't need to spend too much time trying to make everything look professional.

For live sessions or webinars, Zoom or Microsoft Teams are essential. These platforms allow you to share slides, interact with participants, and record the session for future use. So, for instance, based on the above example for your Week 2 training on decision-making, you might use Zoom's screen-sharing feature to walk participants through a real-time decision-making exercise, showing them how to weigh risks and make strategic decisions in a business scenario. After the session, you can send out the recorded session to attendees so they can revisit the content.

You can also create breakout rooms in Zoom for small group discussions, where participants can role-play conflict resolution scenarios or make decisions as a team. This interactive format keeps participants engaged and gives them hands-on practice.

After each training session, it's essential to gather feedback to assess the effectiveness of your program and make improvements. Tools like SurveyMonkey and Google Forms are perfect for this.

So after your Week 1 session on communication for instance, you might create a survey to gather feedback. Your survey could ask:

- *"Was the content clear and easy to understand?"*

- *"Did the exercises help you improve your communication skills?"*

- *"What topics would you like to explore further?"*

With this feedback, you'll gain insights into how your training is landing with participants and can make adjustments for future sessions.

AI tools like Notion and Trello can help you stay organized and on track. You can use these tools to create project boards, track deadlines, and keep all relevant information in one place.

If you're managing a leadership training program for multiple teams, you can set up a Trello board with lists like:

- **To Do:** Preparing training slides, scheduling sessions, drafting emails.

- **In Progress:** Sessions currently happening, materials being reviewed.

- **Completed:** Finished sessions, feedback collected, materials sent to clients.

In Notion, you can create a dedicated client workspace where you store all notes, meeting records, and resources for each project. You can even set up reminders and keep track of client-specific goals. For example, if you're working with a corporate client, you might create a separate page for their training program timeline, noting key milestones, deliverables, and meetings.

Once your program is up and running, don't forget that you can repurpose your content into a new income stream. By recording your sessions, gathering feedback, and packaging your materials, you can sell your training as an online course. For example, after completing your leadership training program, you could upload the recorded sessions to Teachable or Thinkific, turning them into a self-paced course that anyone can purchase. You can also offer additional resources like workbooks, quizzes, or exclusive coaching sessions for those who want more personalized help.

By doing this, you're creating a scalable business model that generates passive income while still offering high-quality value to clients.

How to Monetize from AI-Powered Consulting and Training

One of the smartest ways to turn your knowledge into income from home is by offering consulting services through freelance platforms like Upwork, Fiverr, or Freelancer. Don't worry if you're just starting out—clients are looking for practical problem-solvers who can get results. Whether your background is in business strategy, HR, or digital marketing, you can use AI tools to enhance what you already know. Let's say you're helping small businesses improve their online presence—you could use ChatGPT to draft tailored email campaigns or social media content in half the time, freeing you up to take on more clients. Many beginners start by charging $200 to $500 for simple projects, and as your skills and reviews grow, you can move up to $1,000+ for more advanced AI-powered services like workflow automation or market research insights.

Another great way to earn from home is by building and selling your own online training programs. If you're confident teaching something like leadership, digital marketing, productivity, or even how to use AI tools themselves, platforms like Teachable or Thinkific make it simple. You can use ChatGPT to write lesson scripts, Canva to design slide decks, and Loom or Zoom to record videos. Courses like these often sell between $99 and $399 depending on the value offered. Imagine enrolling just 50 people at $149 each—that's over $7,000 from one launch, and you don't even have to leave your home office.

If you prefer more personal interaction, one-on-one AI coaching is another path to explore. You could work directly with small business owners or solo entrepreneurs, helping them apply tools like ChatGPT or Canva to their specific goals—like writing blog posts, creating visuals, or automating repetitive tasks. You don't need to be a tech wizard, just someone who's a few steps ahead and willing to guide others. Many new coaches charge $100 to $250 per session, or offer bundles that earn them $1,000+ per client. With just a few steady clients each month, this can quickly turn into a reliable $3,000–$5,000/ month income stream from home.

Host Workshops and Webinars

Running online workshops or webinars is a fantastic way to share what you know while building your brand—and the best part is, you can do it all from your living room. Pick a topic you're confident in— maybe it's using AI for content creation, productivity hacks for remote workers, or social media strategy for beginners. Then use platforms like Zoom or Google Meet to host your sessions. You can charge anywhere from $25 to $100 per participant depending on the value you provide. Let's say you get 30 sign-ups at $49—that's $1,470 from one event. Sweet, right?

To make your workshops even more appealing, offer bonuses like downloadable workbooks, templates made in Canva, or exclusive access to a private Facebook or Discord community. Early bird discounts and bundle deals (like "bring a friend and save") can also help drive registrations. These live sessions are not only great for income—they also position you as an expert and can lead to ongoing coaching clients, collaborations, or course sales. If you run one workshop a month, you could easily earn $1,000–$3,000 consistently, depending on how you price and promote it.

Create a Subscription-Based Training Model

If you enjoy teaching and building community, starting a membership site is a solid way to turn your knowledge into recurring income—all from your laptop. You can create a private online hub where subscribers get exclusive access to training videos, downloadable resources, templates, and maybe even a support community through a Facebook group or Discord. Whether you're sharing AI tutorials, productivity strategies, or business-building blueprints, you're offering real value that people are happy to pay for.

Use tools like ChatGPT to help generate and update your content, keeping it fresh based on member feedback and trending topics. Platforms like Podia, Kajabi, or Thinkific make it easy to set everything up—even if you're not super techy.

Charge a monthly or yearly fee—something like $19 to $49/month is a sweet spot when you're starting out. Let's say you get just 100 members at $29/month—that's $2,900 a month in recurring income. As your membership grows, so does your earning potential, all without having to trade time for money every single day. And the best part? You're creating once and earning consistently, which is perfect for building sustainable income from home.

Write and Publish a Book on Your Expertise

As discussed in the previous chapter, you can establish yourself as an authority in your field by writing a book on your area of expertise. Use AI tools to help you draft, edit, and format your book, making the writing process more efficient. Publish your book through self-publishing platforms like Amazon Kindle Direct Publishing or traditional publishing houses. Promote your book through your website, social media, and during your training sessions or workshops.

Collaborate with Other Professionals

You don't have to do it all alone—collaborating with other professionals is a smart way to grow your business from home. Whether it's another coach, a content creator, or a tech-savvy consultant, teaming up for joint workshops, online courses, or webinars can double your reach and boost your credibility. Each person brings their own audience, skills, and ideas to the table, which means more exposure and more value for everyone involved.

Let's say you're great at AI content creation, and you team up with someone who specializes in branding. Together, you could run a course that teaches entrepreneurs how to build a brand and create AI-powered marketing content—something way more appealing than either topic on its own.

Revenue from these partnerships can vary depending on pricing and audience size. A successful joint webinar charging $50 per seat with 100 attendees can pull in $5,000—split between both parties. With recorded content or a bundled digital product, that income can keep flowing even after the event ends. So not only do you get new connections and skills, but you also create fresh income streams without burning out trying to do everything solo.

Build an Online Presence through Blogging or Vlogging

Lastly, one of the most effective ways to monetize your consulting and training expertise is by building a strong online presence through blogging or vlogging (video content creation). This not only helps establish credibility but also creates multiple income streams that supplement your consulting business. By consistently sharing valuable insights, strategies, and expert advice, you position yourself as a trusted authority in your field, making it easier to attract clients, partnerships, and business opportunities. With the rise of AI tools, content creation has become faster, more efficient, and more accessible than ever—allowing you to streamline the process while maximizing your reach and earnings.

If writing is your strength, starting a blog is a great way to showcase your expertise. Platforms like WordPress, Medium, or Substack provide a space to share in-depth content on topics relevant to your industry. For example, a business consultant could write a blog post on "5 AI Tools to Streamline Business Operations", explaining how entrepreneurs can use automation tools to boost productivity. AI tools like ChatGPT or Jasper can help generate blog ideas, structure outlines, and even refine your writing, making content production much easier and time-efficient. If video content is more your style, launching a YouTube channel allows you to connect with your audience through tutorials, behind-the-scenes insights, and expert breakdowns of industry trends. A career coach, for example, could create a YouTube video titled "How to Use AI to Write a Winning Resume", demonstrating AI-driven resume builders and optimization strategies. AI-powered video editing tools like Pictory and InVideo can help you create professional-looking videos without the need for advanced editing skills.

Once you've built an audience, there are several ways to monetize your content. One of the most common methods is affiliate marketing, where you earn commissions by recommending products or services, as discussed in the previous chapter. For instance, if you discuss AI writing tools like Jasper or Grammarly in your blog post or YouTube video, you can include affiliate links that generate revenue every time someone signs up through your referral. Many AI and business software platforms offer affiliate programs, turning your expertise into passive income. Another revenue stream is sponsored content, where companies pay you to feature their tools or services. A leadership consultant running a blog on corporate training might be approached by an AI-driven HR platform to write a post about "How AI is Changing Employee Training." Brands are willing to pay premium rates for content that reaches their target audience.

For those creating video content, YouTube's Partner Program provides opportunities to earn from ad revenue. Once your channel reaches 1,000 subscribers and 4,000 watch hours, you can start earning money through ads placed on your videos. A consultant sharing weekly AI-powered business growth tips could easily build a steady audience, leading to consistent income from ads. Beyond ads and sponsorships, the biggest benefit of blogging and vlogging is that your content acts as a lead generation tool for your consulting services. Every blog post or video should strategically link back to your one-on-one coaching, corporate training programs, or digital courses. For example, a social media strategist could offer paid consulting packages for businesses struggling with AI-driven content marketing.

Another lucrative way to monetize your expertise is by selling digital products or training courses. Once you have an engaged audience, you can create ebooks, templates, workbooks, or full online courses and sell them on platforms like Teachable, Gumroad, or Udemy. For instance, a productivity coach could develop a self-paced course on AI-powered time management, providing step-by-step strategies and tools to help clients automate daily tasks and optimize their work habits. Digital products allow you to earn passive income, as they can be sold repeatedly with minimal ongoing effort.

Beyond financial benefits, blogging and vlogging help build long-term credibility in your industry. Many professionals who discover your free content may eventually become paying clients, whether for consulting, coaching, or in-depth training programs. By continuously sharing valuable AI-driven insights, you create a sustainable, scalable business model that generates income while reinforcing your expertise.

CHAPTER 5

Becoming An AI Entrepreneur Through Digital Product Creation

In today's digital world, creating and selling digital products is one of the most accessible and lucrative ways to earn an income—especially for those looking to break free from the traditional 9-to-5 grind. Digital products—whether it's an online course, an eBook, design templates, stock photos, or even software—offer a world of possibilities. They can be created once and sold repeatedly, making them the perfect option for generating passive income from the comfort of your home.

The beauty of digital products lies in their scalability and low overhead costs. Unlike physical products that require manufacturing, storage, and shipping, digital products can be produced and distributed with minimal effort. With the right tools and a bit of creativity, you can turn your skills, knowledge, or passion into a product that can be marketed to a global audience.

Whether you're an expert in your field or simply passionate about a topic, the digital landscape offers endless opportunities to monetize your expertise. AI tools, platforms like Teachable and Udemy, design apps like Canva, and marketing strategies all work together to help you bring your ideas to life and start earning money from them.

Creating digital products isn't just about making money—it's about creating value. It's about packaging your knowledge or creativity in a way that helps others, educates, entertains, or solves a problem. In this section, we'll explore how you can harness your unique skills and knowledge to create digital products that not only generate income but also position you as an authority in your niche.

Whether you're looking for a side hustle or planning to build a full-fledged digital business, the potential of digital products is vast. All it takes is a little time, effort, and the right mindset. Let's dive in and explore how you can start creating digital products that will allow you to succeed from home.

This chapter will explore how you can go from zero to an AI

entrepreneur by creating AI-driven digital products. Whether you're a complete beginner or a seasoned business owner, you'll learn how to leverage existing AI tools and platforms to build products and services that people will pay for, setting you on the path to creating a business powered by innovation.

Creating Digital Products

Here, I'll walk through the essential steps for creating and selling digital products, whether you're looking to build an app, a website, or an AI-powered service. By following this roadmap, you can bring your idea to life and start monetizing AI quickly, even if you don't have a technical background.

Phase 1: Identify a Practical Market Need

The most successful products solve real-world problems or provide value in a way that's faster, cheaper, or more efficient than traditional methods. AI's ability to streamline workflows, automate tasks, and personalize experiences makes it a powerful tool for product creation. To get started, think about common frustrations or time-consuming tasks that people face daily. What do people struggle with? What are businesses willing to pay for? Identifying a practical need is the first step toward developing an AI-driven product that people will actually use.

For example, Grammarly recognized that millions of people struggle with writing professional and error-free content. Instead of hiring expensive editors or spending hours proofreading, users can now rely on Grammarly's AI-powered writing assistant to improve grammar, clarity, and tone in seconds. This tool has become essential for students, professionals, and businesses alike, proving that a simple AI-powered solution can have mass appeal.

Another example is, the growing demand for AI-generated printables and templates. Many small business owners, content creators, and influencers need high-quality designs for social media posts, marketing materials, or business branding but lack the time or expertise to create them. By using AI tools like Canva's AI-powered design features, you can quickly generate and sell custom templates for Instagram posts, business cards, or digital planners on platforms like Etsy, Gumroad, or Creative Market. These digital products require little ongoing effort, yet they can generate passive income as people continuously purchase and download them.

By focusing on a practical, in-demand niche, you can create AI-powered products that people already want and need. Whether it's AI-driven content tools, digital downloads, or print-on-demand merchandise, the key is to leverage AI to make something faster, smarter, or more convenient. You don't need to invent the next ChatGPT or build a complex AI model—you just need to apply existing AI technology in a way that adds value.

Phase 2: Develop Practical Digital Products

Once you've identified a practical market need, the next step is to bring your AI-powered product to life. Thanks to user-friendly AI tools, you don't need coding skills or advanced technical knowledge to create a product that sells. Whether you're building digital templates, AI-generated artwork, an online service, or a simple app, the key is to use AI to automate, enhance, or personalize the process.

If you're creating digital products, tools like Canva, Leonardo AI, and ChatGPT can help you generate high-quality assets quickly. For example, if you're selling social media templates, Canva's AI-powered design suggestions can speed up the creation process, ensuring your designs look polished and professional. If you're developing an AI-powered ebook or online course, ChatGPT can assist with generating chapter outlines, content drafts, and marketing descriptions in minutes. The goal is to leverage AI to reduce the time and effort needed to develop your product, so you can focus on refining and scaling your offerings.

For those interested in e-commerce, print-on-demand services make it easy to sell AI-generated designs without holding inventory. Platforms like Redbubble, Teespring, and Printful allow you to upload your designs and sell them on products like T-shirts, mugs, stickers, and home décor. Using tools like MidJourney or DALL·E, you can create custom, high-quality artwork that appeals to niche markets, such as retro gaming posters, aesthetic home prints, or anime-style clothing. Once the designs are uploaded, the platform handles production and shipping, allowing you to earn passive income with minimal ongoing work.

If you're considering building an AI-powered app or service, there are plenty of no-code and low-code platforms that make the process easier. Tools like Bubble, Adalo, or Glide allow you to develop AI-integrated applications without writing a single line of code. For example, if you want to create a resume-building tool that uses AI to generate professional resumes, you can integrate ChatGPT's API into a drag-and-drop app builder and launch a functional service in weeks rather than months. Similarly, if you want to create an AI chatbot to assist small businesses with customer inquiries, platforms like ManyChat or Tidio offer simple ways to set up AI-driven conversational bots.

Regardless of what you're creating, the most important step is to test your product before launching. Offer free samples or beta versions to friends, social media followers, or online communities to gather feedback. If you're selling AI-generated templates, offer a few free downloads in exchange for testimonials or reviews. If you're launching an AI-powered app, invite beta testers and refine the features based on their experience. Early feedback will help you identify gaps, improve usability, and create a more polished final product.

By using AI tools to simplify product creation, you can develop a high-quality, market-ready product quickly and efficiently. Whether it's a digital product, e-commerce item, or AI-powered service, the key is to focus on solving a problem, streamlining the user experience, and ensuring high value.

Phase 3: Marketing and Selling Your Product

Once your product is developed, the next step is to get it in front of the right audience and start making sales. No matter how innovative or useful your product is, it won't generate income unless people know about it. The key to successful marketing is a combination of strategic promotion, audience engagement, and leveraging AI tools to optimize your reach. Whether you're selling AI-generated digital products, an AI-powered service, or an automated tool, the goal is to create a scalable system that drives traffic and converts visitors into paying customers.

1. Build an Online Presence
Your marketing success starts with creating a strong online presence. Having a website or landing page dedicated to your product gives potential customers a place to learn more, purchase, and contact you. Platforms like Carrd, Wix, or Shopify make it easy to build a professional-looking site with minimal effort. AI tools like ChatGPT can help generate website copy, product descriptions, and even FAQs to answer common customer questions.

For example, if you're selling AI-generated social media templates, your website could showcase sample designs, offer a free downloadable sample, and include customer testimonials. If you're offering an AI-powered service, such as an automation consulting package, your site should clearly explain the benefits, pricing, and a simple way for clients to book a consultation.

2. Leverage Social Media and Content Marketing
Social media is one of the most effective ways to attract buyers and create brand awareness. Platforms like Instagram, TikTok, LinkedIn, and YouTube allow you to demonstrate your AI product in action. Short-form videos are particularly powerful—showing how your product works in under a minute can be more effective than a long sales page.

For instance, if you're selling AI-generated T-shirt designs, you could create Instagram Reels showcasing new collections or TikTok videos featuring customer reactions. If you're offering an AI-powered copywriting service, you can create LinkedIn posts or Twitter threads demonstrating how AI can improve business marketing. AI tools like Lumen5 and Pictory can turn blog posts into engaging videos that help drive traffic to your website.

Another powerful way to attract organic traffic is by blogging. If you've developed an AI-based budgeting app, writing blog posts on "How AI Can Help You Save Money" can bring in readers who may become potential users. AI tools like Surfer SEO and Jasper can optimize your blog posts for search engines, ensuring your content ranks higher on Google.

3. Use AI to Automate and Optimize Sales
AI tools don't just help with product creation—they can also streamline and optimize the sales process. Chatbots like Tidio or ManyChat can handle customer inquiries on your website, providing instant responses and reducing lost sales due to unanswered questions. AI-powered email marketing platforms like Mailchimp or ConvertKit allow you to send personalized email sequences to potential buyers.

For example, if someone downloads a free sample of your AI-generated ebook, an automated email can follow up with a special discount offer on the full version. If a visitor adds an item to their cart but doesn't complete the purchase, AI-driven abandoned cart emails can remind them and increase conversion rates.

4. Sell on Multiple Platforms

Expanding your reach by selling on multiple platforms increases your chances of success. If you're selling digital products like AI-generated templates, list them on Etsy, Gumroad, or Creative Market in addition to your own website. If you're offering AI-powered business services, platforms like Upwork, Fiverr, or LinkedIn can help attract clients actively looking for solutions.

If you've built an AI-integrated tool or app, consider launching on AppSumo or Product Hunt to gain early adopters and user feedback. Print-on-demand products, such as AI-generated artwork or T-shirt designs, can be sold through Redbubble, Teespring, or Printify, reaching customers without requiring inventory management.

5. Run AI-Powered Paid Ads

For faster results, paid advertising can help you scale quickly. AI-driven ad platforms like AdCreative.ai can generate high-converting ad visuals and copy for Facebook, Instagram, and Google Ads. If you're selling an AI-powered service, LinkedIn Ads can target professionals in specific industries who need your expertise.

For example, if you've developed an AI-powered resume review service, you can run Facebook ads targeting job seekers with messaging like "Struggling to land interviews? Let AI optimize your resume for success." AI tools like Google Performance Max can analyze your audience's behavior and adjust your ad campaigns automatically for better results with lower costs.

Phase 4: Scaling and Automating Your AI Business for Long-Term Success

Once you've successfully launched your AI-powered product and started generating sales, the next step is to scale your business and create long-term sustainability. The goal of this phase is to increase revenue, expand your reach, and automate as many processes as possible so that your business continues to grow—even when you're not actively working. AI tools make scaling easier by helping you optimize marketing, automate workflows, and generate passive income streams.

1. Expand Your Product Line

One of the easiest ways to scale is by adding new products or services that complement what you already offer. If you started with AI-generated social media templates, you could expand into

AI-powered marketing courses or one-on-one coaching for social media growth. If you created an AI-powered resume review service, you might introduce career coaching sessions or LinkedIn profile optimization packages. By diversifying your offerings, you increase the lifetime value of each customer, meaning they continue to buy from you instead of making a one-time purchase.

For those selling AI-generated digital products, consider bundling existing items to create premium offers. For example, if you sell AI-generated printable planners, create a "Business Growth Bundle" that includes templates for social media content, business goal tracking, and financial planning. This not only increases sales per customer but also adds perceived value, allowing you to charge higher prices.

2. Automate Customer Acquisition and Sales
To grow your business without constantly chasing new customers, automation is key. AI-powered email marketing tools like ConvertKit or Mailchimp can nurture potential buyers with automated email sequences. For example, if someone downloads a free AI-generated lead magnet, such as a checklist or guide, an automated email funnel can gradually introduce your products, share testimonials, and offer discounts—all without you lifting a finger.

Chatbots like Tidio, Drift, or ManyChat can handle customer inquiries and guide visitors toward making a purchase. Let's say you run an AI-powered content writing service—a chatbot on your website can ask visitors about their writing needs, suggest the best package, and even process payments automatically. By reducing the need for manual customer interactions, AI-powered automation lets you serve more clients with less effort.

3. License or White-Label Your AI Product
If you've developed an AI-powered tool, template, or service, you can license it to businesses or offer it as a white-label solution. For example, if you created an AI-powered chatbot for small businesses, you could sell customized versions to different industries, such as real estate agents, fitness coaches, or online retailers. White-labeling allows companies to rebrand your AI product as their own, giving you a consistent stream of passive income while they handle the marketing.

For digital product sellers, licensing your AI-generated templates or resources to other businesses can be an easy way to generate additional revenue without extra effort. A Canva template seller, for instance, could offer exclusive "agency licenses" where marketing firms can use the templates for their clients, charging a higher fee for unlimited use.

4. Implement Subscription or Membership Models
One of the most powerful ways to increase predictable income is by shifting to a subscription-based model. Instead of selling one-time digital products, offer a monthly membership where subscribers get exclusive AI-generated content, templates, or premium tools.

For example, if you run an AI-powered digital marketing platform, you can charge a monthly fee for members to access new social media templates, ad copy generators, or AI-powered content calendars every month. Platforms like Patreon, Gumroad Memberships, or Kajabi make it easy to set up recurring revenue models.

Another way to create passive income is by offering an AI-powered service as a subscription. If you provide AI-generated business reports, automated resume writing, or AI-enhanced video editing, you can set up tiered pricing plans where clients pay for ongoing access instead of a one-time purchase.

5. Expand to International Markets
AI tools can help you reach global audiences without requiring additional resources. AI-powered translation tools like DeepL and ChatGPT allow you to convert your content into multiple languages, opening the door to international customers. If you've created a course, ebook, or AI-driven service, translating it into Spanish, French, or German could dramatically expand your customer base.

For those selling AI-generated digital products, platforms like Etsy, Gumroad, or Amazon KDP allow you to sell globally, so optimizing your listings with multi-language descriptions can help boost international sales. Running Facebook or Google Ads in different languages can also help you target new customers in untapped markets.

6. Partner with Influencers and Affiliates
Scaling a business doesn't have to be a solo effort. Partnering with influencers, industry leaders, or affiliate marketers can help you reach a wider audience without spending huge amounts on advertising. Setting up an affiliate program where people earn a commission for promoting your AI-powered product is a great way to drive sales with zero upfront costs.

For instance, if you sell an AI-powered Instagram caption generator, you could collaborate with social media coaches or influencers who promote your tool to their audience in exchange for a commission. Platforms like Refersion and PartnerStack can help automate affiliate payments and tracking.

Another effective strategy is offering guest posts, podcast interviews, or YouTube collaborations where you discuss how your AI-powered product solves real problems. This positions you as an industry expert while tapping into other people's audiences for increased exposure.

7. Continue Optimizing and Innovating
As AI technology evolves, staying ahead of trends will keep your business relevant and competitive. Follow AI industry updates, test new tools, and listen to customer feedback to refine your offerings. Regularly updating your products—whether it's improving AI-generated templates, adding new features to your AI tool, or refreshing your online course content—helps retain customers and attract repeat buyers.

For example, if you run an AI-powered content creation service, consider integrating new AI voiceover tools, automated video editing software, or AI-driven ad optimization features to expand your service offerings. Keeping your products fresh keeps customers engaged and boosts long-term profitability.

Monetizing Your Digital Product Creations

AI-driven products are revolutionizing industries, and entrepreneurs everywhere are seizing the opportunity to generate income from AI-based apps, tools, and services.

Whether you're building a simple AI-powered app or launching a complex digital tool, you can use several key strategies to monetize your creations effectively. Here, we'll explore various ways to turn your AI innovations into profitable ventures.

Choose Your Sales Platform

Where you sell can make a big difference. Each platform has its unique advantages, depending on your product type and target audience.

Etsy is perfect for selling digital products like printable templates, custom graphics, and personalized designs. It's ideal for creators looking to market items that cater to a wide audience.

Gumroad is an excellent platform for selling digital downloads, eBooks, and online courses. It's easy to use, and you can set your own pricing or offer "pay what you want" options.

For writers and content creators, Amazon's KDP allows you to publish eBooks or paperback books and reach a global audience. Patreon is great for creators who want to offer exclusive content to subscribers. This is especially effective if you create digital art, tutorials, or ongoing content like videos or blog posts.

If you're selling physical items (T-shirts, mugs, posters) featuring AI-generated art, Shopify, Redbubble and Printful are print-on-demand platforms that you can use to create without needing inventory.

Set Up a Freemium Model or Subscription

Freemium and subscription models work well for many AI-driven products, particularly if you're offering updates or new content regularly. Grammarly offers a freemium version for basic grammar checks, with advanced writing suggestions available on a subscription plan.

Offer basic templates, graphics, or other resources for free, with premium versions available for purchase. This allows users to sample your work before they commit. Provide regular content updates, new design templates, or exclusive tips for a monthly fee. AI tools like Jasper and Canva use this model, which works well if your product lends itself to continuous value.

Offer Tiered Pricing and Bundles

Tiered pricing helps you cater to different customer segments, and bundles allow you to add value by packaging products together. Canva offers templates in bundled packages to boost user engagement, providing multiple options in one download. Canva offers templates in bundled packages to boost user engagement, providing multiple options in one download.

Offer different levels of service, with each tier offering additional features or resources. For instance, an AI-generated eBook series could have a "starter" book, a more detailed guide, and an expert version. Group related items together, like a set of social media templates, planners, or exclusive graphic packs. Bundling adds value and can be a great way to increase your average order value.

License Your Product

Licensing is a great way to make recurring income from your AI-driven products, especially if they're reusable digital assets. Shutterstock allows artists to earn royalties each time their image or digital product is downloaded, providing a steady income stream for creators.

Set a lower price for personal use (for customers who just want to use it themselves) and a higher price for commercial use (businesses or professionals looking to use your work for profit). In fields like stock photography or custom AI art, you can receive royalties for each time your product is used.

Monetize Through Affiliate Marketing

If your product or service pairs well with existing AI tools, you can promote these tools and earn commission through affiliate marketing. Many digital content creators write tutorials or offer online classes that show others how to use their preferred AI tools, providing affiliate links to earn additional income.

Develop content explaining how your product works in combination with an AI tool, such as how to optimize AI-generated art using Adobe Photoshop or how to enhance writing with Grammarly. Many AI companies, including Jasper and Canva, offer affiliate programs where you earn a commission when users sign up through your referral.

Utilize Social Media and Content Marketing

Social media and content marketing can drive significant traffic to your product while establishing your expertise. Canva promotes its platform with tutorials and blog content, showing users how to get the most out of the product.

Create short, engaging videos on platforms like TikTok or YouTube demonstrating how you create or use your AI products. Videos help to build interest and familiarity.

Writing helpful blog articles, case studies, or tutorials showcasing how your AI products solve real problems can boost your visibility on search engines.

Social Media Ads: Platforms like Instagram, Facebook, and Pinterest are ideal for targeting users interested in design, digital products, or unique tech solutions.

Gather Customer Feedback and Improve Your Offerings

Listening to your customers is one of the smartest moves you can make. Their feedback gives you the inside scoop on what's working, what's not, and what they'd love to see next—helping you fine-tune your products or services to better meet their needs.

Encourage happy customers to leave reviews and ratings. These testimonials not only build trust but also help new buyers feel more confident about making a purchase. A glowing review can be just as powerful as a personal recommendation.

To boost participation, consider offering a small thank-you—like a discount on their next purchase or a bonus item. It's a simple gesture that not only shows appreciation but also increases the chances of getting honest, useful insights. The more you know about your audience, the better you can serve them—and the more your business can grow.

The beauty of digital products is that they're infinitely scalable—once you create them, you can sell them over and over again with minimal ongoing costs. For example, let's say you create an online course teaching small business owners how to use AI tools like ChatGPT and Canva to streamline their content marketing. If you price the course at $79 and attract just 100 students in the first month through social media and email marketing, you'd earn $7,900. Now imagine this course continues to sell while you sleep, and you grow your audience over time to bring in 500–1,000 students per month—that's $39,500 to $79,000 in potential monthly revenue. It may take time to build, but it's a powerful long-term strategy.

Ebooks and digital guides are another low-cost, high-reward product. Suppose you write an ebook titled "AI-Powered Productivity: Tools and Tips for Working from Home" and sell it for $15. If you sell just 1,000 copies in a year through your blog, social media, and a few affiliate promotions, that's $15,000 in passive income. Many creators bundle ebooks with worksheets, templates, or access to private webinars to increase their value and justify a higher price point—sometimes earning $30–$50 per sale for a package.

Then there are digital templates and design assets, which are especially popular on platforms like Etsy, Gumroad, or Creative Market. You could design Canva templates for social media managers, invoice spreadsheets for freelancers, or branding kits for new businesses. These typically sell anywhere from $10 to $50 per product. If you create 10 high-quality templates and each sells 100 times at $25, that's $25,000 from a few weeks of design work. Once your products gain traction, it's easy to scale by adding new templates, offering bundles, or creating a digital shop.

Membership programs and subscription-based products can bring in even more predictable, recurring income. For instance, if you build a membership site offering exclusive tutorials, downloadable resources, and monthly Q&A sessions for $20/month, getting just 200 members would earn you $4,000/month, or $48,000/year. As your community grows, so does your revenue—and since members are paying for ongoing value, you can keep them engaged with new content powered by AI tools to reduce your workload.

In short, digital products have massive earning potential if you're consistent, creative, and strategic. They require upfront effort to build and market, but the payoff can be significant—especially when you combine AI tools with your personal knowledge or niche. Whether your goal is to bring in a few hundred extra dollars a month or build a six-figure business from your laptop, digital products can help you get there.

Final Thought on Creating an Income with Digital Creations

Creating and selling digital products from home is an exciting and highly rewarding way to earn income, especially in today's fast-paced digital world. The freedom that comes with building something once and letting it generate income passively is powerful. Whether it's an online course, a guidebook, stock photography, or design templates, digital products are a scalable and flexible way to monetize your knowledge and skills. You can create these products on your own time, from anywhere in the world, and without the overhead costs that come with physical products—no need for shipping, storage, or physical inventory.

The most attractive part? Once your digital product is created and launched, it's essentially "set and forget." It works for you, earning passive income while you focus on other projects or enjoy more free time. Plus, with digital products, there are minimal costs involved in terms of production and distribution, so the potential for profit is high.

However, it's important to remember that, like any business model, creating and selling digital products from home comes with its challenges. Building something of true value takes time, effort, and focus. If you're venturing into this space, you need to be patient and consistent, especially when you're just starting. Your first product may not be an instant success, and it may take some time to grow an audience and refine your offerings. You'll need to invest in marketing and continuously promote your digital products to reach a wider audience.

Another challenge is the constant need to adapt. Customer preferences change, and trends evolve, so you'll need to stay ahead of the curve and be open to feedback. Using tools like AI-powered analytics or customer surveys can help you understand what your audience wants and refine your products to meet their needs. This is where the work continues after you create your product—it's about listening, improving, and iterating.

Despite these challenges, the upside to creating digital products is undeniable. You can truly build a business that's flexible and sustainable, allowing you to earn from home without the constraints of a 9-to-5 job. With the right tools, platforms, and a bit of creativity, you can turn your skills into something that not only earns money but also positions you as an expert in your field. From creating valuable content to selling your creations globally, digital products allow you to break free from traditional work structures and make money on your terms.

So, is it worth it? Absolutely. If you're willing to invest the time upfront and stay adaptable, creating digital products from home can provide you with a steady stream of income and the freedom to work whenever and wherever you want. The key is consistency, continuous improvement, and using AI tools to help streamline the process. Whether you're aiming for passive income or creating a full-fledged online business, this model offers endless potential—and it's all within your reach, right from the comfort of your home.

CHAPTER 6

Turning Creativity into Cash Using AI

In a world where creativity meets cutting-edge technology, the opportunities for artists, writers, musicians, and entrepreneurs to turn their passion into profit have never been more abundant. AI is transforming the creative world, enabling individuals to monetize their skills in once unimaginable ways. From generating artwork to composing music, writing copy, or designing unique products, AI tools provide a new toolkit for creators to amplify their talents and reach wider audiences.

For instance, Beeple, the digital artist who shocked the art world when he sold a piece of AI-assisted digital art for over $69 million at Christie's. Using his artistic skills and AI-generated visuals, Beeple opened the doors to a new era of creativity where human ingenuity and artificial intelligence collaborate to create unique, valuable works.

Similarly, Amper Music, an AI-driven music creation platform, empowers musicians and content creators to generate royalty-free music in minutes. What once took hours of studio time can now be achieved with just a few clicks, providing YouTubers, podcasters, and advertisers a way to add high-quality custom soundtracks to their projects.

Or consider Jasper AI, which copywriters and entrepreneurs use to create compelling blog posts, social media content, and product descriptions at scale. This AI tool helps freelancers and marketers generate hundreds of pieces of content efficiently, allowing them to serve more clients and, in turn, increase their income.

This chapter explores how AI breaks down the barriers between creativity and commerce and how you can leverage these AI-driven innovations to turn your creative ideas into sustainable income streams. Whether you're an artist, musician, writer, or entrepreneur, AI tools can help you unlock your potential, amplify your work, and make money while doing what you love.

Music Production

AI is revolutionizing the music production and video editing industries, making it easier for creators to produce high-quality content without extensive technical skills. Whether you're a musician looking to compose tracks or a content creator aiming to edit professional videos, AI tools can streamline your workflow, enhance your creativity, and save time. This guide will walk you through the essential steps to get started with music production and video editing using AI-powered tools.

Essential AI Tools to Use for Music Production

Ableton Live is a powerful digital audio workstation (DAW) that is widely used for music production, live performance, and sound design. Its intuitive interface and extensive features make it suitable for beginners and professionals alike. **Logic Pro X** is a comprehensive DAW for Mac users, Logic Pro X offers advanced features for music production, including a vast library of sounds, virtual instruments, and audio effects. **FL Studio** is known for its user-friendly interface, FL Studio is a favorite among electronic music producers. It offers a range of features for creating beats, synthesizing sounds, and arranging tracks. **LANDR** is an AI-powered mastering service that can take your music tracks to the next level by automatically enhancing the sound quality and making them radio-ready.

Amper Music is an AI music composition tool that allows you to create original music tracks in various genres by simply selecting your preferences and adjusting parameters. AIVA is an AI composer that can help you create music for videos, games, or any other project. You can customize the style and mood, and AIVA will generate original compositions based on your input. **Soundtrap** is an online DAW that allows for real-time collaboration with other musicians. It's an excellent platform for creating music together with friends or other artists, regardless of location. Spotify for Artists is a platform that helps you manage your music presence on Spotify, providing tools for promotion, audience insights, and analytics to understand your listeners better.

How to Use These AI Tools for Music Production

Start by selecting a DAW that suits your style and needs. Ableton Live and FL Studio are great for electronic music, while Logic Pro X is ideal for a broader range of genres. Spend time exploring the features and tools available within your chosen DAW, as mastering its interface will streamline your production process.

Use your DAW to record your music or create beats using virtual instruments. Experiment with different sounds, loops, and effects. For instance, in Ableton Live, you can utilize MIDI clips to compose melodies and harmonies. Take advantage of the drag-and-drop functionality to easily arrange your tracks.

Once you have your tracks recorded, consider using LANDR for mastering. Upload your completed tracks, and the AI will analyze them to enhance the overall sound quality, ensuring your music is polished and ready for distribution. This can save you time and provide professional results, even if you're not a sound engineer.

Use Soundtrap or your DAW's collaboration features to work with other musicians. Share your project files and invite others to contribute remotely. This allows you to gain new perspectives on your music and incorporate diverse ideas and styles.

If you're looking to generate original music quickly, try Amper Music or AIVA. Input your preferences regarding genre, mood, and instrumentation, and these AI tools will create a unique track for you. This can be especially useful for background music or soundscapes for videos or presentations.

If you're feeling stuck, consider using AI tools to generate ideas. ChatGPT can help you brainstorm song themes, lyrics, or even melodies. Input prompts like "Give me a list of themes for a pop song" or "Create a catchy chorus for a love song" to get your creative juices flowing.

How to Monetize Music Production

Sell Your Music on Streaming Platforms
To get your music out there on platforms like Spotify, Apple Music, and Amazon Music, you'll first need to go through a digital distribution service. DistroKid, TuneCore, and CD Baby are some of the most popular options. They take care of the behind-the-scenes work like uploading your tracks, handling licensing, and pushing your music to all the major streaming services. Most of these platforms charge a yearly fee or take a percentage of your earnings—DistroKid, for example, offers unlimited uploads for around $20/year.

Once your music is live, it's important to claim your artist profiles—especially on Spotify for Artists. This lets you update your bio, add pictures, pin your latest release, and track your audience stats in real-time. A clean, well-branded profile helps new listeners take you seriously.

Now, let's talk revenue. Streaming doesn't pay much per play—Spotify pays around $0.003 to $0.005 per stream. That means for every 1,000 streams, you might make around $3 to $5. It's not life-changing at first, but it adds up as your fanbase grows. If you can hit 100,000 streams in a month across all platforms, you're looking at $300–$500 monthly just from plays. Hit a million streams in a year, and that's $3,000–$5,000 annually from streaming alone.

To increase your chances of reaching those numbers, promoting your music is key. Use Instagram Stories, TikTok, YouTube Shorts, and even Twitter/X to tease your songs and connect with fans. Share behind-the-scenes content, snippets of unreleased tracks, or your process in the studio—it builds curiosity and loyalty. Some artists have gone viral just by posting a catchy 10-second chorus on TikTok.

You can also run targeted ads on Facebook and Instagram to reach new listeners. A small ad budget (say $5–$10/day) focused on your genre and ideal audience can bring in hundreds of plays and followers over time. It's an investment, but it can pay off big when it leads to playlist placements or loyal fans.

And speaking of playlists—don't underestimate their power. Research and submit your songs to both algorithmic playlists and independent curators (you can find many on SubmitHub, Groover, or even Reddit threads). Landing on a single decent-sized playlist can give you thousands of streams in a week. Imagine getting picked up by multiple playlists—now we're talking serious traction and revenue momentum.

While streaming income might start small, the potential is huge when combined with strategic promotion, consistent releases, and a loyal audience. Many independent artists who release music regularly and promote smartly report earning $500–$2,000+ per month after a year or two of consistent effort.

Offer Music Production Services
If you've got a knack for music production, there's a real opportunity to turn that passion into income—right from your bedroom studio. First, decide which services you want to offer. You might be great

at mixing and mastering, or maybe you're a beat-making wizard. Some producers offer full-service packages, helping artists from the songwriting stage all the way to final mastering. Others focus on niche areas like podcast audio editing, film scoring, or even meditation music. The more specific your niche, the easier it is to attract the right kind of clients who are looking for exactly what you do.

To build trust and attract new business, you'll need a solid portfolio. If you've already worked with artists or clients, include clips that show the "before and after" of your mixing or production. If you're just starting out, don't worry—you can create a few polished demo tracks using AI tools like Boomy or Amper Music, and show off what you can do with beat creation, vocal enhancement, or sound layering. Add a few testimonials (even from friends or practice clients), and you're good to go.

Now it's time to get visible. Platforms like Fiverr, Upwork, and SoundBetter are packed with artists looking for affordable, reliable producers. Set up a strong profile, upload your best samples, and write descriptions that clearly explain what the client will get. Use relevant keywords like "affordable hip-hop mixing," "female vocal mastering," or "trap beat production" to boost your visibility in search results.

Start with lower, competitive pricing to build your client base—many new producers charge around $30–$75 per project when they're just getting started. Once you've got a few 5-star reviews under your belt, you can raise your rates significantly. Seasoned freelancers on these platforms often charge $150 to $500+ per project, especially when offering full-production or fast-turnaround services. If you're doing 4–5 small projects a week at $75 each, that's around $1,200–$1,500/month. If you scale up with higher-tier services or packages, you could easily push past $2,500/month.

Don't rely solely on platforms—promote yourself on social media, too. Post short videos of your workflow on TikTok or Instagram Reels, share sound snippets on Twitter or YouTube, and engage in music production forums and communities on Reddit or Facebook. These spaces are full of independent artists, podcasters, and YouTubers constantly looking for reliable production help. Sometimes a single connection in one of these groups can turn into a long-term client.

This route is perfect if you love working with audio and want flexible, creative work you can do entirely from home. And thanks to AI tools and easy-to-use DAWs, it's never been easier to produce professional-sounding work—even without expensive studio gear.

Create and Sell Sample Packs

If you've got a good ear and a passion for sound design, selling sample packs is a smart way to monetize your skills without constantly trading time for money. The beauty of this hustle? Once a sample pack is created, it can sell over and over again—making it a prime source of passive income.

Start by figuring out what kind of sounds you want to create. You could focus on punchy drum loops, atmospheric vocal chops, ambient textures, synth one-shots, or even full MIDI packs. Take time to research what's hot—genres like trap, drill, lo-fi, house, and cinematic scores always have a strong demand. Use software like Serum, Kontakt, or even AI-powered tools like AIVA or Boomy to craft original, polished sounds. And don't forget about your file organization—your pack should be easy to navigate, with clearly labeled folders and tempos, keys, or tags. You want other producers to love using your sounds without having to dig around.

Themed packs perform especially well. Think "Lo-Fi Rainy Day Loops," "Dark Trap Basslines," or "Cinematic Impacts." These titles help buyers understand exactly what they're getting and make your packs stand out on crowded marketplaces.

Once your pack is ready, you've got a few solid options for selling:

- Marketplaces like Splice, Loopmasters, or ADSR Sounds give you access to a large audience, but they do take a cut of your earnings.

- If you want more control and better margins, consider selling through your own website using platforms like Shopify, Gumroad, or Sellfy. These tools make it easy to set up a digital store and automate delivery.

Promoting your sample packs is just as important as creating them. Share demos on Instagram, TikTok, and YouTube—these platforms are full of beatmakers and bedroom producers looking for new inspiration. Create short videos showing how your samples can be flipped into full tracks. Consider giving away a small free sample pack to build an email list and attract loyal fans. You can also reach out to music production influencers and offer them a free copy in exchange for a shoutout or video using your sounds.

Now, let's talk about the money. Pricing typically ranges from $10 to $40 per pack, depending on the size and quality. If you're just starting out, even selling 100 packs at $15 each could bring in $1,500, and as your reputation grows, that number can scale significantly. Well-known creators can earn $5,000–$10,000+ per month, especially when they have multiple packs available and consistent marketing.

Best part? You're doing this from home, on your own schedule. It's a creative, scalable business that keeps working in the background while you focus on building the next big sound.

Monetize Your YouTube Channel
Start a YouTube channel focused on music production. You can share tutorials, gear reviews, song breakdowns, or even vlogs about your production process. Focus on creating high-quality content that provides value to your audience. Use relevant keywords in your video titles, descriptions, and tags to improve your visibility on YouTube. Research popular search terms related to music production to help attract more viewers. Once you meet YouTube's eligibility requirements (1,000 subscribers and 4,000 watch hours in the past year), apply for the YouTube Partner Program to start earning ad revenue. Additionally, you can include affiliate links in your video descriptions for products you recommend. Build a community by responding to comments, asking for feedback, and creating content based on viewer requests. Engaging with your audience can increase viewer loyalty and encourage subscriptions. Consider offering paid courses, selling merchandise, or providing one-on-one consulting services related to music production through your channel. This can create additional revenue streams beyond ad income.

Teach Music Production Online
Decide on the structure of your course. You could cover topics like basic music theory, sound design, mixing techniques, or using specific software. Ensure your content is well-organized and caters to different skill levels. Select a platform to host your course. Popular options include Udemy, Skillshare, or Teachable. These platforms provide built-in audiences and marketing tools to help you reach potential students. Use video, audio, and written materials to create engaging lessons. Consider including downloadable resources, such as project files or worksheets, to enhance the learning experience.

Promote your course through social media, email marketing, and online communities. Share snippets of your lessons or testimonials from previous students to build interest. Consider hosting free webinars or workshops to attract potential students. This allows them to experience your teaching style and content before committing to a paid course.

License Your Music for Commercial Use

Look for opportunities to license your music for films, commercials, and video games. Websites like AudioJungle, Pond5, and Music Vine are great places to start. Make sure you read their guidelines for submissions carefully. Ensure your tracks are high-quality and formatted correctly for licensing. Provide various versions of each track (e.g., instrumental, vocal, shorter edits) to increase their usability. Create a catalog of your licensed tracks, complete with descriptions and keywords to improve searchability. The more tracks you have available, the higher your chances of being licensed. Connect with filmmakers, video game developers, and advertisers who might need music for their projects. Attend industry events, engage in online forums, and utilize LinkedIn to expand your network.

Keep up with trends in media and advertising to understand what types of music are currently in demand. This knowledge can help you tailor your compositions to fit market needs.

Build a Brand Around Your Music

Determine what makes you unique as an artist. This includes your musical style, visuals, messaging, and target audience. Your brand should resonate with your audience and reflect your personality. Build a website that serves as a hub for your music, biography, tour dates, and merchandise. Use a website builder like Wix or Squarespace for easy customization. Ensure your website is mobile-friendly and visually appealing. Create profiles on platforms where your target audience spends their time. Regularly share updates about your music, upcoming releases, and personal insights into your creative process. Engaging content can help grow your audience.

Build an email list to communicate directly with your fans. Send out newsletters with updates, exclusive content, or early access to new releases. Email marketing is a powerful tool for maintaining a connection with your audience. Collaborate with other musicians to tap into their audiences and broaden your reach. This can be done through features on tracks, joint performances, or guest appearances on each other's platforms.

Final Thought: Turning Creativity into Income from Home

At the end of the day, using AI tools in music production is like having your own virtual studio assistant—one that helps you move faster, stay creative, and make professional-quality content without needing a full production team or fancy setup. Whether you're crafting beats, mixing tracks, selling sample packs, or composing background scores, you've now got the tech and platforms to do it all from your bedroom.

What's exciting is how accessible it's become. You don't need to be signed to a label or have a massive following to start earning. With some hustle, smart marketing, and quality sound, you can start making real income—whether it's a few hundred dollars a month from sample pack sales, or scaling up to thousands through streaming, freelancing, or licensing.

AI isn't here to replace your creativity—it's here to help you unlock it, package it, and profit from it. So if you've got a passion for music and a laptop at home, you've got everything you need to turn your sounds into income streams.

Video Editing

Video editing is another creative task that AI can significantly streamline, offering everything from automated scene editing to AI-generated transitions and effects. Let's dive into the steps to create high-quality videos using AI-powered video editing tools.

What AI Tools to Use for Video Editing

AI-powered video editing tools have made it easier than ever to create professional-quality videos, even for those with little to no editing experience. Whether you're producing content for social media, business marketing, YouTube, or online courses, AI helps streamline the editing process, automate tedious tasks, and enhance video quality. From automatic resizing and scene detection to AI-generated captions and templates, these tools save time while maintaining high production standards.

For professional-grade video editing, **Adobe Premiere Pro** remains an industry leader, offering AI-powered features such as auto-reframing, which automatically adjusts video dimensions for different platforms like YouTube, Instagram, and TikTok. It also includes scene edit detection, which quickly identifies cuts in raw footage, and color matching, which ensures consistent visuals across multiple clips. **Final Cut Pro**, designed for Mac users, provides similar AI-driven capabilities, such as Smart Conform, which adjusts aspect ratios, and automatic scene detection, making the editing process more efficient. Both tools are ideal for content creators who want to maintain full creative control while benefiting from AI-powered automation.

For a more text-based approach to video editing, **Descript** allows users to edit videos as if they were editing a document. Its AI-driven transcription automatically converts speech into text, enabling users to cut or rearrange video segments simply by editing the text. This is particularly useful for podcasters, educators, and business professionals who need a quick way to edit dialogue-heavy content. Descript also includes **Overdub**, an AI-powered voice-cloning feature that can replace or fix spoken words without requiring a new recording, making it a game-changer for those who want to correct mistakes effortlessly.

For marketers and social media creators who need fast, AI-assisted editing, platforms like **InVideo** and **Lumen5** are great options. InVideo provides thousands of customizable templates where users can input text, and the AI will automatically generate a video with matching visuals, animations, and music. This is ideal for business owners looking to create engaging ads or promotional videos without advanced editing skills. Lumen5, on the other hand, specializes in turning blog posts or written content into videos. It scans text, selects key sentences, and pairs them with relevant stock footage and animations, making it perfect for bloggers, educators, and brands looking to repurpose content into video format.

Another great AI-powered tool for content creation is Animoto, which simplifies slideshow-style video production. This tool is excellent for small businesses, e-commerce sellers, and social media influencers who want to create product showcases, testimonial videos, or branded content quickly. With AI-generated transitions, text overlays, and music selection, users can create polished videos with minimal effort.

For those seeking a balance between beginner-friendly and professional editing tools, **Pinnacle Studio** offers AI-powered features such as motion tracking, stabilization, and object detection. These features are particularly useful for sports videos, vlogs, and instructional content, where tracking movement and maintaining smooth visuals are essential.

How to Use AI Tools for Video Editing

Depending on your experience level and the type of video you want to create, select the video editing software that suits your needs. For beginners, tools like InVideo or Animoto are user-friendly, while professionals may prefer Adobe Premiere Pro or Final Cut Pro for their advanced capabilities. After selecting your tool, import your video footage. Organize your clips into folders or bins to streamline your editing process. Label each clip clearly to make it easier to locate specific footage later.

Take advantage of AI-driven features in your chosen software. For instance, use Adobe Premiere Pro's auto-reframing feature to quickly adapt your video for different social media formats. In Descript, utilize the transcription feature to generate captions automatically.

Start editing by cutting and trimming your clips to remove any unnecessary content. Use AI tools to enhance your video's quality, such as automatic color correction in Final Cut Pro. Experiment with transitions, effects, and audio adjustments to create a polished final product. Use text overlays, graphics, and animations to enhance your video. Tools like InVideo offer a variety of templates for adding engaging titles, lower thirds, and calls to action. Ensure that the text complements the video content and is easy to read.

Once you're satisfied with your edits, export your video in the desired format. Most video editing software will provide options for different resolutions and file types. Optimize your video settings based on where you plan to share or upload your content.

How to Monetize Video Editing

Video content is more in demand than ever, and businesses, influencers, and content creators are constantly looking for polished, engaging videos that grab attention. With the rise of AI-powered editing tools, you don't need to be a seasoned pro or invest in expensive software to start offering your services. All you really need is a decent computer, a stable internet connection, and the willingness to learn the tools that can make your workflow faster and smarter.

One of the easiest ways to start monetizing video editing is by offering freelance services. Platforms like Fiverr, Upwork, and PeoplePerHour are filled with clients searching for affordable and fast video editors to help with YouTube intros, TikTok videos, Reels, podcast edits, product demos, and more. Instead of spending hours manually cutting and arranging footage, AI-powered tools like Runway ML, Descript, or Pictory can help you automate time-consuming tasks. Descript, for example, turns audio into text and lets you edit video by simply editing the transcript—perfect for podcast or webinar edits. Runway ML can remove backgrounds, upscale videos, or add motion effects in just a few clicks.

To stand out, create a portfolio of sample edits using royalty-free footage. You can easily find free clips on sites like Pexels, Pixabay, or Mixkit. Use AI tools to add transitions, subtitles, and audio enhancements that showcase your ability to deliver polished results quickly. Clients love seeing examples of what you can do, even if you haven't worked with anyone professionally yet. Once you land your first few jobs and gather reviews, you can raise your rates and start offering more advanced packages like AI-enhanced color grading, motion graphics, or video repurposing.

Another great way to monetize is by helping businesses and creators repurpose long-form content into short, punchy clips for platforms like TikTok, Instagram Reels, and YouTube Shorts. Tools like Opus Clip use AI to automatically identify the most engaging moments in long videos and turn them into viral-ready shorts, complete with captions and optimized layouts. You could charge a flat fee or subscription service for this kind of repurposing—imagine earning $200–$500/ month per client just to convert their weekly YouTube content into social clips.

If you're more entrepreneurial, consider creating and selling your own video templates, transitions, or stock video effects using platforms like Envato Elements, Motion Array, or Gumroad. AI can help you design templates quickly—for example, you can use AI-generated text animations or transitions created in tools like Kaiber or Runway. Once uploaded, these assets can generate passive income over time as more creators download and use them.

For educators and content creators, creating a video editing course or tutorial series is another fantastic monetization strategy. You can record your screen using tools like Loom or OBS Studio, and then polish your videos using AI to clean up audio, enhance visuals, and add subtitles. Platforms like Teachable or Skillshare allow you to host your course and earn revenue from every student who signs up. If you're active on YouTube, you can even build an audience while promoting your editing services or products—once you hit monetization thresholds, ad revenue, affiliate links, and brand sponsorships can start rolling in too.

Finally, don't overlook the value of licensing your own edited content. If you enjoy creating aesthetic B-roll footage, travel montages, or music videos, you can sell them to stock video sites like Artgrid, Pond5, or Adobe Stock. AI tools can help you edit faster, sync music automatically, and even suggest visual changes that boost the commercial value of your footage.

YouTube

YouTube has become one of the most powerful platforms for earning money online, allowing creators to generate income from the comfort of their homes. Whether you're sharing educational content, entertainment, tutorials, product reviews, or lifestyle vlogs, YouTube offers multiple monetization opportunities beyond just ad revenue. With the right strategy, you can turn your passion into a profitable business through sponsorships, affiliate marketing, memberships, and digital product sales. Thanks to AI-powered tools, content creation is now easier than ever, helping you streamline video production, editing, and audience growth. Whether you're a beginner or an experienced creator, learning how to leverage AI and YouTube's monetization features can help you build a sustainable income stream from home—all while doing something you love.

Essential AI Tools to Use for YouTube

TubeBuddy is a must-have for any YouTube creator. This browser extension offers a suite of features that help optimize your videos for better visibility and engagement. TubeBuddy includes tools for keyword research, tag suggestions, and thumbnail generators—all designed to improve the SEO of your videos and ensure they reach the right audience. By analyzing trending keywords and suggesting the best tags, TubeBuddy helps you rank higher in search results and increase your channel's discoverability. Similarly, **VidIQ** provides in-depth video performance insights, including competitor analysis, keyword tracking, and real-time analytics. By using VidIQ, creators can track what's working, optimize their strategy, and grow their channels faster.

When it comes to creating visually engaging content, **Canva** is a powerful AI-driven graphic design platform. Canva simplifies the process of designing thumbnails, channel art, and social media posts.

With AI-powered templates, you can easily customize designs to match your brand, making it easier to create professional-looking visuals in minutes. For example, if you're launching a new YouTube video and want to make a standout thumbnail, Canva offers AI-generated design suggestions, helping you create eye-catching thumbnails that increase click-through rates.

For editing, **Descript** offers an innovative solution by allowing you to edit video content like text. With its AI-powered transcription feature, you can easily add subtitles, captions, or make edits to the video's content just by adjusting the text. If you have a talking-head video or a podcast, Descript's text-based editing makes it incredibly easy to cut out filler words or rearrange sections of the video. This is especially useful for content creators who need to produce subtitled videos quickly or want to fine-tune their content with minimal effort.

For professional-grade video editing, **Adobe Premiere Pro** stands out with its AI-driven tools that speed up the editing process. Features like auto-reframing, which automatically adjusts aspect ratios for different platforms, scene edit detection, and color matching make it ideal for editing content efficiently. These features ensure that you spend less time on manual adjustments and more time focusing on the creative aspects of your videos. If you're producing high-quality YouTube videos and want to maintain consistent video quality, Adobe Premiere Pro's AI tools help enhance the final product without sacrificing time.

Another excellent tool for video creation is **Lumen5**, which turns written content into videos. Perfect for repurposing blog posts or turning articles into engaging videos, Lumen5 uses AI to suggest images, video clips, and layouts based on your written content. This tool is especially useful for bloggers, marketers, or businesses who want to expand their content from text to video without a lengthy editing process.

Finally, if you need a quick and easy video editor for marketing videos or social media content, **InVideo** is a great choice. Offering AI-powered templates, InVideo lets you create high-quality videos without starting from scratch. It's especially useful for promotional content, product videos, or social media ads. InVideo's AI tools will suggest designs and layouts based on your content, making it easier to create polished videos in minutes. This can save you hours of editing time and ensure your content looks professional without requiring specialized editing skills.

How to Use AI Tools for YouTube

Use tools like TubeBuddy or VidIQ to conduct keyword research. Identify trending topics and keywords related to your niche. Plan your content around these insights to maximize visibility and attract your target audience. Design compelling thumbnails using Canva. A good thumbnail grabs viewers' attention and encourages clicks. Experiment with different colors, fonts, and imagery to see what resonates best with your audience.

Edit your videos using Adobe Premiere Pro or Descript. Utilize AI features to streamline your editing process. For instance, Descript allows you to edit audio and video by simply editing the text of the transcription, making it easier to refine your content. Use Descript or the built-in features in YouTube to generate captions automatically. Adding subtitles increases accessibility and can improve viewer retention, especially in sound-off environments.

After editing, optimize your video's title, description, and tags using insights from TubeBuddy or VidIQ. Incorporate relevant keywords to improve your video's searchability on YouTube. Regularly check your video performance using the analytics dashboard on YouTube and tools like VidIQ. Monitor metrics such as watch time, audience retention, and click-through rates to understand what works and what doesn't.

How to Monetize YouTube

Monetizing YouTube from the comfort of your home is one of the most exciting ways to earn money online in this generation while doing something you actually enjoy. Once you've built up a bit of momentum—posting videos consistently and starting to grow an audience—YouTube opens the door to several income streams. One of the first and most well-known options is joining the YouTube Partner Program (YPP), which allows you to earn ad revenue. To qualify, you'll need at least 1,000 subscribers and 4,000 watch hours in the past year. Once you're in, you start making money from the ads that run before, during, or alongside your videos. The revenue varies depending on your niche and audience, but creators can generally expect anywhere from $1 to $10 per 1,000 views. So, if you're pulling in 100,000 views per month, that could translate to around $500–$1,500 just from ads.

Affiliate marketing is another smart way to monetize your content, and it works great even if your channel is still growing. You simply promote products or services in your videos and include affiliate links in your descriptions. When viewers click those links and make a purchase, you earn a commission. This method is especially powerful if you're creating content around specific topics like tech, fitness, beauty, or digital tools—anything where people are already searching for recommendations. Some affiliates pay as little as 5%, while others, like software or high-ticket items, can pay 30–50% per sale. For example, if you're promoting a $200 software product and it pays 40% commission, that's $80 per sale. Even with a small, loyal audience, this can add up fast.

Sponsorships are where things can really start to take off. As your channel grows, brands might approach you (or you can reach out to them) to feature their products in your videos. They'll pay you a flat rate for a mention, shout-out, or full integration. Sponsorship deals can range from $100 for small channels to thousands of dollars per video for creators with a decent following. For a channel with 10,000–50,000 subscribers, you could realistically earn anywhere from $500 to $2,000 per sponsored video, depending on your niche and engagement. It's one of the highest-paying methods once you've built trust with your audience.

Then there are Super Chats and Channel Memberships, which are perfect if you enjoy going live or want to create a tighter-knit community. Super Chats let viewers donate money during livestreams to have their messages highlighted, which can be a fun and interactive income source. Channel memberships, on the other hand, allow fans to pay a monthly fee (typically $4.99 and up) for exclusive perks like badges, behind-the-scenes content, or members-only videos. If even 100 people sign up for a $5 monthly membership, that's $500 in recurring revenue—and it grows as your community does.

Selling your own digital products is another great way to monetize your channel while providing value to your audience. If you're a fitness coach, you could sell downloadable workout guides; if you teach business skills, you might offer an ebook or video course. Platforms like Teachable, Thinkific, and Gumroad make this super easy to set up. AI tools like Canva can help you create professional-looking product materials, and ChatGPT can help write the content. Digital products tend to have high profit margins since there's little overhead. A well-priced course at $99 could earn you $1,000 with just 10 sales, and this can keep earning for you long after you've created it. You can also offer one-on-one services directly through your channel. Maybe you're great at video editing, life coaching, or small business marketing. Whatever your area of expertise, you can book consultations, coaching calls, or personalized feedback sessions. Use tools like Calendly to manage bookings and Zoom for the actual calls. Pricing varies widely depending on your experience and niche, but even charging $75–$200 per session can quickly add up. With just five sessions a week, that's potentially $1,000 a week or more.

Don't forget about merch! YouTube lets eligible creators use the merchandise shelf to sell branded gear right from their channel. Sites like Printful or Teespring make it easy to design and sell T-shirts, mugs, tote bags—you name it—without handling inventory or shipping yourself. It's a fun way to build brand identity while adding another revenue stream. If you sell just 50 shirts a month at a $10 profit each, that's $500 right there.

To maximize all of these income streams, AI tools can give you a serious edge. TubeBuddy and VidIQ can help you find trending keywords, analyze competitors, and fine-tune your titles, tags, and descriptions to get more views. Descript lets you edit videos by editing the transcript—making the whole process way quicker. ChatGPT can help write scripts, video outlines, or clever responses to comments to keep your audience engaged.

So whether you're just starting your YouTube journey or ready to level up, these monetization options offer something for every kind of creator. And with the right combination of content strategy and AI tools, you can build a channel that not only reflects your passion but also provides a steady, scalable income from home.

TikTok

TikTok has rapidly become one of the most popular social media platforms, particularly among younger audiences. With its short-form video format, TikTok allows creators to express their creativity, share knowledge, and entertain users in a matter of seconds. The platform is not only a hub for viral trends and challenges but also a viable space for monetization. With the aid of AI tools, creators can streamline their content creation and optimize their strategies to maximize growth and income.

Essential AI Tools to Use for TikTok

InVideo, an online video editor offers templates specifically designed for TikTok videos. Its AI features help you quickly create engaging videos by providing pre-made layouts and stock footage, saving time in the editing process. CapCut is an all-in-one video editing app that provides various effects, filters, and music options. CapCut's user-friendly interface allows for quick editing and seamless integration with TikTok, making it easy to create eye-catching content. Canva is a versatile design platform that helps you create stunning graphics and thumbnails for your TikTok videos. Canva's templates and design tools make it easy to produce visually appealing content that stands out on the platform.

Tools like **Analisa.io** or TikTok's native analytics feature help you track your performance and audience engagement. These insights are crucial for understanding what content resonates with your viewers. Lumen5 is an AI-driven video creation tool that transforms text into engaging videos. It's useful for turning blog posts or other written content into short videos for TikTok, helping you repurpose content effectively. Synthesia is an AI platform that allows you to create professional videos with AI avatars. If you want to present information or tutorials without appearing on camera, Synthesia can generate realistic video content based on your script.

How to Use AI Tools for TikTok

Use InVideo or Lumen5 to create short videos based on your ideas or scripts. Choose templates that suit the TikTok style and add visuals, text, and music to make your content engaging. Edit your videos using CapCut to add effects, transitions, and audio. Utilize its features to ensure your videos are dynamic and visually appealing, capturing the attention of viewers quickly.

Use Canva to design eye-catching thumbnails and overlay graphics for your TikTok videos. Good visuals can help increase clicks and engagement on your posts. Regularly check your TikTok analytics to understand which videos perform best. Use tools like Analisa.io to gain deeper insights into your audience demographics and engagement patterns. If you have existing content (like blog posts), use Lumen5 to create videos that summarize or highlight key points. This can expand your reach and diversify your content offerings.

How to Monetize TikTok

TikTok has rapidly become a goldmine for creators looking to turn their passion into profit. Whether you're sharing funny skits, dancing videos, educational content, or lifestyle tips, there are plenty of ways to make money on this platform without ever leaving home. Here's a breakdown of how you can monetize your TikTok account effectively.

1. Join the TikTok Creator Fund

One of the simplest and most accessible ways to start earning money on TikTok is by joining the TikTok Creator Fund. This is a program designed to reward creators for producing engaging, original content. If you love making short videos and can consistently grab people's attention, this could be your first step into getting paid just for being creative on the app.

To be eligible, you'll need to meet a few basic requirements: you must be at least 18 years old, have 10,000 followers, and your videos must have received at least 100,000 views over the past 30 days. Once you hit these milestones, you can apply directly through the app under your Creator Tools tab. If accepted, you'll start earning money based on how many views and how much engagement your content gets.

Now, let's talk numbers—because that's what we all want to know. While the TikTok Creator Fund won't make you a millionaire overnight, it can be a decent source of passive income, especially as your following grows. On average, TikTok pays around $0.02 to $0.04 per 1,000 views. That means a video that racks up 1 million views could earn you between $20 to $40. It's not massive, but imagine putting out several high-performing videos a week—it can really add up. For example, if you consistently post viral or semi-viral content and get around 10 million views per month, you could make anywhere from $200 to $400 monthly just from the Creator Fund alone.

What's even better is that this income is just one piece of the puzzle. While the Creator Fund may offer modest earnings on its own, it often opens the door to even more lucrative opportunities like brand partnerships, affiliate marketing, product sales, and sponsored content—which can earn you much more.

The key to maximizing your earnings here is consistency and engagement. Use AI tools like CapCut or Adobe Premiere with AI features to make your editing process easier and your videos look polished. You can also use ChatGPT to come up with creative video ideas, write catchy hooks, or even script skits or voiceovers. The better your content, the more likely it is to get shared, go viral, and boost your visibility—not just on TikTok but across other platforms too.

In short, the TikTok Creator Fund is a great stepping stone. It gives you a way to start monetizing your content while you grow and refine your brand. And once you've got momentum, it can lead to multiple streams of income—all from posting short, entertaining videos from home.

2. Partner with Brands for Sponsored Content

As your TikTok account gains traction and your follower count starts to climb, one of the most exciting opportunities you'll encounter is sponsored content. This is when brands pay you to promote their products or services in your videos. It's one of the most lucrative ways to monetize your presence on the platform—and it all starts with building trust and engagement with your audience.

Whether you're posting about fashion, fitness, tech, parenting, or just daily life in a fun and relatable way, there's a brand out there looking for someone like you to help spread the word. Sponsored content is especially popular among companies trying to reach younger, highly engaged audiences—TikTok's sweet spot. These collaborations often come with creative freedom, allowing you to share the product in a way that feels natural and authentic to your style.

Here's how it usually works: a brand reaches out to you (or you pitch to them) to create a TikTok video that features their product or service. You might do a quick review, a how-to demo, or even a funny skit that includes the brand's item. The key to success is blending the brand into your content without making it feel forced—your followers should feel like they're discovering something cool from a trusted friend, not watching an ad.

If you're wondering how much you can make, it really depends on your niche, engagement rate, and audience size. Here's a rough breakdown to give you an idea:

- **Micro-influencers** (10,000–50,000 followers) can earn $100 to $500 per sponsored post

- **Mid-tier influencers** (50,000–250,000 followers) may charge $500 to $2,500 per post

- **Top-tier influencers** (250,000+ followers) can command $5,000 to $20,000 or more per post

Some creators even negotiate long-term deals, where they receive a monthly retainer for a series of sponsored videos. If you post consistently and deliver great engagement, brands will likely come back for more collaborations.

To get started, you can sign up for platforms like Upfluence, Grapevine, or Influence.co. These sites help match creators with brands and simplify the collaboration process. Make sure your TikTok bio clearly showcases what you're about, and consider linking to a media kit or a page with examples of your previous content and stats.

Let's say you're a fitness creator who posts home workout tips. A brand might approach you to promote a smart fitness tracker, protein powder, or resistance bands. You could film a "day in the life" video showing how the product fits into your routine. If done authentically, these kinds of partnerships not only earn you money but also enhance your content by introducing useful products to your followers.

AI tools can help you land and manage these deals, too. Use ChatGPT to draft your pitch emails or create a content proposal. Tools like Notion or Trello can help you organize your brand partnerships, deadlines, and deliverables, keeping you professional and on top of your game.

Ultimately, sponsored content allows you to get paid for doing what you love—creating. And as long as you stay true to your voice and maintain the trust of your audience, it's a win-win for both you and the brands you represent.

3. Use Affiliate Marketing
Affiliate marketing allows you to earn commissions by promoting other people's products. Platforms like Amazon Associates or ShareASale let you generate affiliate links for products. You can then promote these products in your TikTok videos, and whenever someone purchases through your link, you earn a commission. This is a great way to monetize your TikTok without needing to create your own products.

For example, if you're into fashion, you can link to clothing or accessories you wear in your videos and direct your followers to buy them through your affiliate links. You can use TikTok's bio or video descriptions to share your affiliate links.

4. Offer Digital Products or Services
Selling your own digital products is another great way to make money on TikTok. Whether it's an ebook, online course, or design templates, TikTok is an excellent platform to promote and sell your digital goods. You can showcase snippets or content from your digital products

in your TikTok videos to generate interest and drive traffic to your website or Etsy shop.

For example, if you're a photographer, you can sell preset filters, or if you're a fitness trainer, you could offer personalized workout plans. With TikTok's powerful short-form video format, you can generate interest in your products or services in just a few seconds.

5. Receive Tips from Fans via TikTok's Live Gifting Feature
Once you've built a loyal community on TikTok, going live can be a surprisingly effective way to earn income—thanks to TikTok's Live Gifting feature. This tool allows your viewers to send you virtual gifts during your livestreams, and those gifts translate into real money you can cash out. It's kind of like busking on the internet—except instead of tossing coins into a guitar case, your fans are sending you roses, fireworks, or even dragons.

To access Live Gifting, you'll need at least 1,000 followers and must be at least 16 years old (or 18 for cash withdrawals). Once you qualify, simply go live and interact with your audience. The more entertaining, helpful, or unique your content is, the more likely fans are to tip you with gifts. Whether you're hosting a Q&A, doing a live product review, teaching a dance, or just hanging out and chatting with your community, people love supporting creators they connect with in real time.

Now, let's talk about the potential revenue. TikTok gifts are purchased with coins (which users buy with real money), and the gifts you receive convert into Diamonds, which you can cash out. Typically, creators earn about $0.005 (half a cent) per coin, so if someone sends you 1,000 coins' worth of gifts during a live stream, that's about $5 in earnings. It may not seem like much at first, but it can add up quickly—especially during long or highly engaging sessions.

Here's an idea of what creators can make:

- **Casual streamers** (once or twice a week) might earn $20 to $100 per session, depending on engagement

- **Consistent streamers** (3–5 times a week) could bring in $300 to $1,000+ monthly, especially with a strong fanbase

- **Popular or niche creators** with highly engaged audiences can earn $1,000 to $5,000+ per month just from gifting

A great tip for boosting your income is to let viewers know what their support goes toward—maybe it's helping you upgrade your gear, support your music, fund your education, or continue making content. People love feeling like they're contributing to something meaningful.

You can also use tools like Streamlabs, OBS, or Restream to elevate your live streams by adding overlays, animations, or split-screen interviews. Even simple things like thanking every gifter by name or offering small shout-outs can go a long way in encouraging more tipping.

And don't forget—you can combine Live Gifting with other monetization strategies. Promote your merch, link your digital products, or even tease exclusive content on Patreon while you're live. It's all about creating an interactive experience where your fans feel seen, entertained, and appreciated.

At the end of the day, going live isn't just a way to make money—it's a way to build stronger connections with your community. And with AI tools like ChatGPT helping you brainstorm engaging live topics or Canva helping you create banners and visuals for your streams, it's easier than ever to host a professional, high-energy session right from your phone.

6. Launch Merchandising and Product Sales
If you've built a strong brand on TikTok, you can launch your own merchandise. Platforms like Printful, Teespring, and Redbubble allow you to design custom products (like T-shirts, mugs, and stickers) that are produced and shipped to your followers directly. Promote these items in your TikTok videos and link them to your online store.

For example, if you have a comedy TikTok channel, you could sell branded T-shirts with funny quotes or catchphrases from your videos. This allows you to monetize your personal brand by offering products that your followers are already familiar with.

7. Create and Sell Exclusive Content (Memberships)
Platforms like Patreon and Ko-fi allow creators to monetize their work by offering exclusive content to subscribers. By promoting your Patreon or Ko-fi page in your TikTok videos, you can offer fans access to exclusive behind-the-scenes content, tutorials, or even one-on-one interactions in exchange for a subscription fee.

This works well for creators who produce high-quality educational content (like cooking, DIY projects, or fitness tutorials). Fans who want to support you can pay a monthly subscription for access to your exclusive content, while you still make money from your free TikTok content.

8. Crowdfunding for Projects
Crowdfunding platforms like Kickstarter or GoFundMe can help you raise money for specific projects or ventures. If you have a creative or entrepreneurial idea, you can use TikTok to promote your crowdfunding campaign by showcasing your idea, progress, or product in videos.

For instance, if you're a musician raising funds to record an album, you could use TikTok to engage potential backers by sharing behind-the-scenes footage of your music-making process and linking them to your Kickstarter campaign.

9. Offer Online Workshops or Masterclasses
If you have expertise in a particular subject, you can host paid online workshops or masterclasses. Use TikTok to tease valuable insights from your class and link to the sign-up page. For example, a marketing expert could offer a class on social media marketing while promoting it on TikTok through tips and tricks that generate interest.

TikTok is an ideal platform for quick tips and teasers, and your followers may be eager to learn more from you in a paid course or workshop.

10. Collaborate with Other Creators and Cross-Promote
Partnering with other TikTok influencers or creators in your niche is a great way to reach a wider audience and increase your earning potential. Collaborations can lead to brand partnerships or joint ventures that provide additional opportunities for monetization.

For example, you can collaborate on sponsored content with another creator, split the revenue, and cross-promote each other's accounts to grow your followings. This increases your exposure and opens up opportunities for more monetization avenues.

Medium

Medium is a popular online publishing platform that allows writers to share their ideas and stories with a wide audience. It's a space where anyone can express their thoughts, insights, and expertise on various topics, from personal development to technology and beyond. With its unique combination of a blogging platform and a social network,

Medium provides writers with the opportunity to reach new readers and potentially monetize their content through various channels. By utilizing AI tools, writers can streamline their writing process, improve their content quality, and increase their chances of making money on the platform.

Essential AI Tools to Use for Medium

Grammarly is a writing assistant that uses AI to help you write error-free articles. It checks for grammar, punctuation, and style issues, ensuring that your writing is polished and professional. **ChatGPT** is a powerful language model that can assist in generating ideas, outlines, and even entire drafts. Use it to brainstorm topics or get suggestions on how to structure your articles.

Hemingway Editor helps you improve the readability of your writing by highlighting complex sentences, passive voice usage, and other issues. It's essential for ensuring your articles are accessible to a broad audience. **Copy.ai** is an AI content generator that can help create engaging headlines and introductions, ensuring your articles catch the reader's attention from the start. While primarily a graphic design tool, **Canva** can help you create eye-catching images and infographics to complement your Medium articles, enhancing their visual appeal.

Use Medium's native analytics to track your article's performance, audience engagement, and reading time. Understanding your audience's preferences is crucial for refining your content strategy.

How to Use AI Tools for Medium

1. Generate Article Ideas and Topics
AI tools like ChatGPT or Copy.ai can help you brainstorm article topics that resonate with your audience. Whether you're in a niche like self-improvement, technology, health, or business, these tools will help you create a list of relevant and trending topics based on keywords or themes you input.

Example:

Let's say you want to write for the self-improvement niche. You can use ChatGPT to generate article ideas. Simply type in a prompt like, "Give me 10 blog post ideas for self-improvement for Medium readers." It could generate ideas like:

• "10 Ways to Develop a Growth Mindset"

- "How to Overcome Procrastination and Stay Productive"

- "Why Morning Routines Matter and How to Build One"

This not only saves time but helps you focus on writing articles your audience is already searching for.

2. Write Articles Efficiently with AI

Once you have a topic, you can use ChatGPT, Jasper, or Frase to help you draft your articles quickly. These AI tools can write content that's relevant, engaging, and aligned with the tone you specify. You can also set up prompts for specific writing styles, like casual, professional, or inspirational, depending on what you want your articles to convey.

Example:

Let's say you decide to write about "How to Overcome Procrastination." You can ask ChatGPT to generate the first draft with specific instructions:

"Write an article in a friendly and motivational tone about overcoming procrastination. Include practical tips, quotes, and a step-by-step guide for readers."

ChatGPT might produce a draft with tips like:

- Breaking tasks into smaller chunks

- The Pomodoro technique

- Celebrating small wins

This allows you to start with a strong foundation, cutting down the time spent on research and drafting. You can then refine and personalize it for your voice.

3. Edit and Polish Your Content

Once you have your article, you can use Grammarly and Hemingway Editor to improve readability and grammar. These AI-powered tools help you polish your writing by checking for spelling mistakes, grammar errors, awkward phrasing, and improving readability. This is especially important for Medium, where clear and engaging writing is key to getting your articles noticed.

Example:

You've finished your article draft on overcoming procrastination, but you're unsure if it's clear enough for your audience. By pasting your content into Hemingway Editor, you may find long sentences or passive voice. The tool could suggest simplifying sentences like:

- **Before:** "In order to tackle procrastination, one must implement various methods to keep themselves on track."

- **After:** "To beat procrastination, try using simple methods to stay focused."

This helps make your article more readable and keeps your audience engaged throughout.

4. Optimize Your Content for SEO
SEO is essential for ensuring your articles get discovered on Medium. Tools like Surfer SEO and Frase can help you identify keywords, related topics, and even the ideal word count for your articles. These tools also analyze the top-performing articles in your niche and provide content suggestions to improve your chances of ranking higher.

Example:

For your article on overcoming procrastination, you can use Surfer SEO to analyze what keywords are ranking in other Medium articles on the topic. It might suggest adding terms like "focus techniques," "time management tools," or "habits for productivity" to your content. By optimizing your article for SEO, your content is more likely to appear in search results and attract readers.

5. Create Eye-catching Visuals
Visual content can significantly enhance the appeal of your article and keep readers engaged. Canva and Visme use AI-powered templates and design suggestions that make creating graphics, infographics, or featured images easy and professional-looking. These tools are especially helpful when you need to create visuals that complement your article and break up long blocks of text.

Example:

For your article on overcoming procrastination, you can use Canva to create an infographic summarizing key tips like:

- "Break Tasks Into Chunks"

- "Use Time-blocking"

- "Celebrate Small Wins"

This infographic can be added to your article, improving its visual appeal and increasing the likelihood that readers will share it.

How to Monetize Medium

Medium's Partner Program offers writers a unique opportunity to earn money by sharing their ideas and stories with the world. With its built-in audience of paying subscribers, the program rewards writers based on how many engaged members read and interact with their content. However, to make the most of it, you need to focus on creating high-quality, valuable content and building a loyal following.

Create High-Value Content
The cornerstone of earning money on Medium is creating content that delivers significant value to readers. Whether you're writing in-depth guides, tutorials, personal stories, or opinion pieces, the more value you provide, the more likely it is to be shared and engaged with. Content that offers fresh perspectives or deep dives into trending topics and niches typically performs better. Medium readers tend to gravitate toward thought-provoking and insightful articles, so consider topics that both resonate with the current interests and have lasting relevance.

For example, a well-researched guide about AI tools for home-based businesses could attract attention from both newcomers and seasoned entrepreneurs. If your article aligns with what readers are interested in, you'll increase your chances of higher engagement, which ultimately leads to higher earnings through the Partner Program.

Revenue Potential: As a writer on Medium, you earn based on the amount of time paying members spend reading your work. For high-performing articles, you might make anywhere from $20 to $300 per article in a month, depending on engagement. This could add up to anywhere between $1,000 to $5,000 per month if you publish consistently with high engagement.

Build a Following
Publishing consistently is key to growing your audience on Medium. The more articles you post, the more likely you are to develop a loyal following. To build this audience, you'll need to engage with readers by responding to comments and interacting with other writers in your niche. As you start to grow your base, your articles will begin to get more views and shares, further increasing engagement and

revenue potential.

Building relationships within the Medium community can also encourage other writers to share your work and promote your articles, creating a snowball effect that helps your audience expand.

A consistent publishing schedule combined with audience engagement could help you increase your earnings to $1,500 to $6,000 a month as your readership grows and more people subscribe to Medium through your content.

Repurpose Content

If you've already created content elsewhere (such as on your blog or in newsletters), you can repurpose it for Medium. This saves time while still providing valuable information to readers. When repurposing, make sure to tailor the content for Medium's audience by making it more engaging, breaking it into easily digestible sections, and making sure it meets Medium's editorial guidelines.

For instance, you could take a popular blog post and turn it into a more polished version for Medium, or you might take your email newsletter content and expand it into a more detailed piece that fits the platform's style. The goal is to reframe the content to suit Medium readers and enhance its quality without reinventing the wheel.

Revenue Potential: Repurposing can still generate significant earnings—especially if the content is already proven to be valuable. With well-repurposed content, you can expect to see $200 to $2,000 per article depending on how well it resonates with the Medium audience.

Offer Exclusive Content

One unique feature of Medium's Partner Program is the ability to offer exclusive content to paying members. By creating a series of in-depth articles or behind-the-scenes insights, you can entice readers to subscribe to Medium, knowing they'll get access to premium content. This could include exclusive how-to guides, expert interviews, or personal stories that only paying subscribers can access.

To make your exclusive content even more valuable, consider offering an ongoing series. For instance, if you're an expert in AI-driven business strategies, you could offer a multi-part series on how to integrate AI tools into daily workflows—something that your subscribers will find indispensable.

Revenue Potential: Offering exclusive content can increase your earnings as subscribers feel they are getting something valuable in exchange for their membership. You could expect to make $500 to $3,000 per month from exclusive content if you can get a consistent number of paying subscribers.

Collaborate with Other Writers

Medium is a community of writers, and collaboration can be a great way to increase your visibility and grow your audience. You can collaborate with other writers in your niche for guest posts or even co-author articles. These collaborations often lead to mutual cross-promotion, which helps both authors tap into each other's audiences.

Moreover, contributing to well-established Medium publications can be an excellent way to reach a wider audience. Publications like The Startup, Better Humans, and The Writing Cooperative already have large, dedicated followings, and writing for them can significantly boost your article's visibility and engagement.

Revenue Potential: Collaborations and publications can increase article views by up to 500%, leading to more engagement and higher earnings. By regularly contributing to these publications and collaborating, you could earn $1,000 to $4,000 per month from increased visibility and audience growth.

Leverage Social Media to Drive Traffic

One of the best ways to promote your Medium articles is by leveraging social media. Share snippets or key takeaways from your articles on platforms like Twitter, Instagram, or LinkedIn, encouraging followers to click through and read the full article. Tailor your promotional strategy to each platform—use visuals and hashtags on Instagram, concise teasers on Twitter, or long-form discussions on LinkedIn to drive traffic.

Additionally, promoting articles in relevant groups or forums—such as Facebook groups or Reddit communities—can help bring in new readers who are interested in your niche. The more traffic you generate, the more likely your articles are to be shared, read, and engaged with by Medium's paying members.

Revenue Potential: Consistently driving traffic through social media can significantly increase your article's performance. If done right, this could boost your earnings to $500 to $3,000 per month by attracting a wider audience.

Final thought

Medium is a powerful platform for monetizing your writing from home. By consistently creating high-value content, building a loyal following, and utilizing strategies like repurposing content and offering exclusive material, you can turn your Medium writing into a profitable business. Collaboration, leveraging publications, and social media can all increase your reach and engagement, ultimately leading to higher earnings through the Partner Program. With dedication, the right strategies, and continuous engagement, earning anywhere from **$1,000 to $5,000+ per month** on Medium is entirely possible, allowing you to monetize your passion for writing from the comfort of your home.

Medium offers a Partner Program that allows writers to earn money based on the engagement their articles receive from paying Medium members. To join, you need to meet specific criteria, including having a Stripe account for payments. Once enrolled, you can start earning money based on how many members read and engage with your content. Focus on writing high-quality articles that resonate with Medium's audience. Engaging stories and insightful analysis tend to perform well.

Patreon

Patreon is another way to monetize your creativity. Patreon is a membership platform that allows creators to earn a sustainable income by providing exclusive content to their supporters. It's widely used by artists, writers, podcasters, and various other creators who wish to monetize their work and build a loyal community around their content. By leveraging AI tools, creators can enhance their offerings, streamline content production, and maximize their earning potential on Patreon.

Essential AI Tools to Use for Patreon

ChatGPT can generating ideas, writing content, and even drafting messages for their patrons. It's particularly useful for brainstorming new membership tiers, exclusive content, or community engagement strategies. **Canva** can help create visually appealing promotional materials for Patreon, including banners, social media graphics, and promotional images for tier offerings. **Hootsuite** or **Buffer** are social media management tools that can schedule posts to promote your Patreon page across various platforms, keeping your audience engaged without needing to be online constantly.

Mailchimp is an email marketing platform that can help you maintain communication with your patrons. Use it to send newsletters, updates, and exclusive offers to your subscribers. **Descript** is a video and audio editing tool that utilizes AI to simplify the editing process. It's particularly useful for creators who produce podcasts or video content for their Patreon supporters. **Google Analytics** helps track website traffic and user engagement, allowing creators to assess how their promotional strategies are performing and where to focus their efforts.

How to Use AI Tools for Patreon

Use ChatGPT to brainstorm ideas for exclusive content that can be offered to your patrons. Whether it's writing prompts, tutorial ideas, or topics for a podcast episode, AI can help you generate a wealth of ideas quickly. Leverage Canva to design eye-catching graphics for your Patreon page, social media announcements, and newsletters. Create visually consistent branding that reflects your content and appeals to your audience.

Schedule posts with Hootsuite or Buffer to promote your Patreon page on social media. Share highlights of what patrons can expect, and engage your followers with teasers of upcoming content to encourage them to join. Set up automated emails using Mailchimp to keep patrons informed about new content, exclusive offers, or community events. Regular communication helps maintain interest and engagement. If you produce video or audio content for your patrons, use Descript to streamline the editing process. This tool simplifies transcription and editing, allowing you to produce high-quality content more efficiently.

Use Google Analytics to track traffic to your Patreon page and assess the effectiveness of your promotional efforts. Pay attention to which types of content generate the most interest and engagement to refine your strategy.

How to Monetize Patreon

Patreon provides creators with the ability to turn their passions into sustainable income streams. By offering exclusive content and perks to your most dedicated fans, you can build a loyal community that supports your work financially. Here's how you can set up a successful Patreon account and leverage it to earn money from home, alongside other platforms like YouTube, TikTok, and Medium.

Set Up Your Patreon Profile

The first step to monetizing on Patreon is creating a profile that clearly communicates what type of content and benefits patrons will receive in exchange for their financial support. You should be transparent about the kind of work you do, what your patrons can expect, and the specific perks they'll get by joining your membership tiers.

Consider offering different membership levels that come with escalating benefits.

For example:

- A $5/month tier could grant patrons early access to your content (videos, articles, etc.).

- A $10/month tier might include exclusive behind-the-scenes content, access to personalized feedback, or exclusive digital downloads.

- Higher tiers could offer personalized services, such as one-on-one consultations or signed merchandise.

The key is to offer **value** that makes your supporters feel like they're getting something they can't access elsewhere. This will encourage long-term support, as patrons will feel like they have a closer connection to you and your work.

Offer Valuable Perks for Your Patrons

The perks you offer will depend on your niche and the content you create. Here are some ideas to get started:

1. Exclusive Content: This could be anything from early access to videos, behind-the-scenes footage, or extended versions of content that's unavailable to your regular followers. For example, YouTubers can offer their patrons exclusive video tutorials, or TikTok creators can share longer, uncut versions of their viral videos.

2. Digital Downloads & Artwork: If you're an artist, writer, or photographer, consider offering digital prints, downloadable artwork, or writing templates that patrons can use.

3. Exclusive Merchandise: Physical items like signed prints, merchandise, or limited-edition items can be enticing for fans who want to show their support. You could also offer merchandise at a discounted rate to higher-tier patrons.

4. Behind-the-Scenes Content: Show patrons the creative process, whether it's how you film or produce your content, or how you brainstorm ideas. Giving them a "backstage pass" to your creative world can make them feel like they're part of something special.

5. Personalized Services: If you're a coach, consultant, or educator, consider offering one-on-one coaching sessions or personalized feedback on work submitted by your patrons. This type of direct engagement builds strong relationships with your audience.

Promote Your Patreon Across Platforms
Once your Patreon is set up, you need to promote it on all your other platforms to drive traffic and encourage followers to become patrons. Here's how you can do it:

1. YouTube: Add a link to your Patreon in the descriptions of your videos and make sure to mention it in your content. For example, you can let your viewers know that they can support your work by becoming a patron for early access, exclusive content, or personalized shout-outs.

2. TikTok: Use your TikTok videos to share teasers about what patrons can access. For example, you can show behind-the-scenes moments or preview exclusive content, then encourage followers to check out your Patreon for more. You could also promote limited-time offers, such as a special shout-out or exclusive merch for new patrons who join during a specific period.

3. Medium: If you write articles or stories on Medium, link to your Patreon in your profile and within your articles. You can create special, patron-only writing workshops, offer personalized feedback on writing, or provide exclusive written content that can only be accessed by your paying supporters.

4. Social Media: Use Instagram, Twitter, Facebook, and other platforms to direct followers to your Patreon. Engage your community by offering sneak peeks or making announcements about special offers for patrons.

5. Limited-Time Offers: To boost initial patronage, consider offering a limited-time offer. For example, new patrons who sign up within the first week of a launch might receive a free digital download or exclusive merchandise.

Grow Your Patreon Community

As your patronage grows, your community will become an important part of your overall brand. Keep your patrons engaged and motivated to stay subscribed by regularly updating them on your creative process and the exclusive content they're receiving. Show appreciation by offering personalized thank-you messages, shout-outs, or even offering patron-only polls where they can vote on your next content creation.

Maximizing Revenue on Patreon: What You Can Expect

The revenue potential on Patreon varies depending on your audience size, content quality, and engagement. Here's a rough estimate of what you might earn based on your Patreon tiers:

• A **small but dedicated group of patrons** (around 50-100) can earn you anywhere between $250 to $1,000 per month if they're paying $5 to $10 per month. This number grows as you scale your following and offer more valuable perks.

• **Mid-tier creators** who consistently offer engaging content and perks can earn between $1,000 to $5,000 per month if they have between 200 and 1,000 patrons.

• **For top-tier creators**, those with 5,000+ patrons or high-level memberships could easily earn between $5,000 to $20,000 per month, depending on how much value they're offering and the number of exclusive perks available at higher membership levels.

By using the AI tools and strategies shared in this book, you can build a Patreon that not only reflects your passion but also becomes a reliable income stream from home. Diversifying your Patreon tiers and offering different levels of engagement—like exclusive content, early access, or personalized perks—lets you steadily grow your support base while doing what you love.

The real key to success is staying consistent with your content, genuinely connecting with your community, and delivering real value to your patrons. Whether you're an artist, writer, educator, or content creator, you now have the power to build your brand from home using AI. Promote your Patreon on other platforms like YouTube, TikTok, and Medium, and watch as your dedicated followers help support your work financially. Whether you're a writer, artist, creator, or educator, Patreon gives you the tools to earn money from your craft while building long-lasting relationships with your community.

With the right mix of creativity, AI-powered efficiency, and audience engagement, turning your passion into profit from home is more achievable than ever.

Turning Art into Income

Making money from art no longer requires gallery exhibitions or expensive printing costs—thanks to AI-powered tools, you can now create, market, and sell your artwork online with ease. Whether you're a traditional painter, a digital artist, or just someone experimenting with AI-generated designs, there are plenty of ways to turn creativity into cash. The best part? AI tools help you automate tasks like designing, promoting, and even selling your work, so you can focus more on creating and less on the business side of things.

Before diving into creating art, defining your niche and understanding your target audience is crucial. This will guide your design choices and marketing strategies. Identify your niche. Consider digital art, branding, illustrations, logos, or merchandise designs. Research popular styles and trends within your niche. Know your audience. Understand the preferences and needs of your target market. Are they looking for custom logos for businesses, wall art for home decor, or unique branding designs for their products?

Essential AI tools to Creating Art

Here are some of the most powerful AI tools that can help you turn your creativity into income. AI art generators like **Midjourney, Deep Dream Generator, DALL·E, and Adobe Firefly** let artists produce unique, high-quality artwork in seconds. These tools are perfect for creating digital art, abstract patterns, and surreal illustrations that can be sold as prints or stock images.

For artists who prefer customizing and refining their work, **Canva, Adobe Firefly,** and **Visme** provide AI-powered design tools that help with social media content, posters, branding materials, and templates. These platforms are especially useful for artists who want to create printable planners, digital stickers, or branding kits to sell on platforms like Etsy.

Marketing is just as important as creating art, and AI tools like **ChatGPT, Jasper AI,** and **Copy.ai** help artists write product descriptions, Instagram captions, and blog content to attract more buyers. Scheduling tools like **Hootsuite** and **Buffer** allow artists to automate their social media posting, ensuring consistent engagement with potential customers.

For those interested in selling physical products without managing inventory, print-on-demand services like **Redbubble, Society6, Printful, and Teespring** handle everything from printing to shipping. Simply upload your AI-generated designs, and whenever someone makes a purchase, the platform prints the design on T-shirts, mugs, phone cases, posters, and more, earning you a commission.

If digital sales are more appealing, stock image platforms like **Shutterstock, Adobe Stock, and Creative Fabrica** allow artists to upload AI-generated backgrounds, textures, and illustrations, earning passive income every time someone downloads their work. For those looking to break into blockchain-based sales, **NFT marketplaces like OpenSea and Rarible** provide an opportunity to sell unique AI-generated digital artwork with the added benefit of earning royalties on future resales.

How to Monetize Art using AI tools

One of the easiest ways to start earning is by selling AI-generated prints and merchandise. Platforms like Society6, Redbubble, and Printful let you upload your designs and print them on T-shirts, phone cases, mugs, notebooks, and more. The best part? You don't have to worry about inventory or shipping—once a customer buys something, the platform handles everything, and you get paid.

For example, let's say you create a neon cyberpunk cityscape using Midjourney or Adobe Firefly. You can upload it to Redbubble, and suddenly, it's available as a poster, a laptop sleeve, or even a shower curtain. If just 10 people buy your design for $5 each, that's $50 in passive income—all from a single upload. Now imagine having 50+ designs in your store.

If you want even higher profit margins, selling digital art downloads is a goldmine. Platforms like Etsy and Creative Fabrica let you sell digital files that customers can print at home or use for creative projects. You could sell things like:

- AI-generated printable wall art (boho designs, abstract paintings, motivational quotes)

- Custom Canva templates (Instagram posts, Pinterest graphics, business cards)

- Aesthetic sticker packs (cute AI-generated illustrations that people can print and cut out)

Since digital products don't require shipping, you only need to create them once and sell them over and over again. Imagine you create a set of AI-generated watercolor prints and sell them for $10 per download. If 100 people buy them, that's $1,000 in earnings—without lifting a finger after the upload!

You can also sell stock images. Businesses, bloggers, and content creators are always looking for unique visuals to use in their projects. AI-generated backgrounds, textures, and illustrations can be uploaded to Shutterstock, Adobe Stock, and Depositphotos for people to buy and download.

For example, if you create a pastel watercolor texture pack using DALL·E, you can upload it to stock image sites and earn royalties every time someone downloads it. If 50 designers each buy your texture for $5, that's an extra $250 in passive income—and you can keep earning from the same upload for years.

To truly make the most of selling AI-generated art, think like a digital entrepreneur. Don't just upload once and hope for the best—create consistently, test different styles and niches, and pay attention to what people are responding to. Some of your early uploads might not sell right away, and that's completely normal. The magic happens when you treat this like a real business: experiment, learn what works, and double down on what's getting traction.

Another smart move is bundling your products. For example, instead of selling one digital download for $5, create a collection of five coordinating pieces and sell the bundle for $15. People love value, and bundles can significantly increase your earnings per customer. You can also take advantage of seasonal trends—create holiday-themed art, back-to-school templates, or New Year planners that catch people at the right moment when they're searching for something specific.

Branding matters too. Even though platforms like Etsy and Redbubble do the heavy lifting in terms of logistics, building your own brand voice and visual identity will help you stand out. Use AI tools like ChatGPT to write catchy product descriptions and unique shop bios. Design a consistent thumbnail style for your uploads using Canva or Adobe Express. When people recognize your style, they're more likely to come back and buy more.

And don't forget about marketing. Posting your designs on social media platforms like Pinterest, Instagram, or TikTok can drive free traffic to your shop. Show your followers how your AI art is made, give sneak peeks of new products, and share behind-the-scenes content. The more people who see your work, the more likely you are to make sales.

The best part? All of this can be done from the comfort of your home. Whether you're working from your couch, your kitchen table, or your favorite local coffee shop, AI art gives you the power to turn creativity into cashflow without needing to be a traditional artist. Even if you're starting from zero, these tools level the playing field. You don't need a fine arts degree or fancy software. All you need is an idea, the willingness to explore, and a bit of consistency.

In a world that's increasingly digital and automated, creative expression is still one of the most powerful currencies—and now, with AI on your side, it's easier than ever to turn your imagination into income. So whether you want to make a little extra cash each month or turn this into a full-blown business, the tools are in your hands. Start small, dream big, and upload your way to something great.

Sell AI Art as NFTs

If you want to take your AI art business to the next level, selling AI-generated digital art as NFTs can be a highly profitable opportunity. NFTs (non-fungible tokens) are unique digital assets stored on the blockchain, meaning they can't be duplicated or replaced. Because of their exclusivity, collectors, investors, and art enthusiasts are willing to pay premium prices for one-of-a-kind digital pieces. Some AI-generated NFT collections have sold for thousands—even millions—of dollars, proving that the demand for digital collectibles is huge.

How to Create and Sell AI-Generated NFTs

1. Generate Your AI Artwork
Start by using AI art generators like Midjourney, DALL·E, Runway ML, or Deep Dream Generator to create unique, high-quality digital artwork. Think about themes that have a strong appeal to collectors. Some popular NFT categories include:

- **Futuristic portraits** – AI-generated cyberpunk, sci-fi, or fantasy-inspired characters.

- **Abstract AI art** – Surreal landscapes or dreamlike visuals with vibrant colors.

- **AI-enhanced photography** – Digitally altered or AI-processed photography.

- **AI-generated animal avatars** – Unique, collectible animals (think Bored Ape Yacht Club).

For example, let's say you want to create a **futuristic AI-generated portrait series.** You could enter a prompt into **Midjourney** like:

"A neon cyberpunk warrior with glowing robotic eyes, intricate details, and a futuristic city skyline in the background, cinematic lighting, ultra-realistic."

Midjourney will then generate variations of your artwork, and you can refine it by adjusting the prompt until you create **stunning, unique pieces** that are ready for NFT minting.

2. Mint Your NFT on an NFT Marketplace
Once your artwork is ready, you'll need to **"mint" it** on an NFT marketplace. This process turns your AI-generated image into a **blockchain-certified asset**, making it publicly verifiable and sellable as a digital collectible.

Popular NFT marketplaces include:

- **OpenSea** (best for Ethereum-based NFTs)

- **Rarible** (great for artists looking for more control over their royalties)

- **Foundation** (popular for high-end, exclusive digital art)

- **Objkt** (for Tezos-based NFTs, with lower fees than Ethereum)

To mint an NFT, you'll need to connect a crypto wallet (like MetaMask or Coinbase Wallet) to the marketplace, upload your AI-generated image, and set details like:

- **Title and description** – Use **ChatGPT** or **Jasper AI** to write compelling descriptions that **tell the story** behind your art.

- **Price and royalties** – Set a **fixed price** or auction starting bid and define royalties (e.g., 10% every time the NFT is resold).

For example, if you list your futuristic AI portrait NFT for 0.1 ETH ($300 at the time of listing) and it sells, you make $300 instantly. If the buyer later resells it for 1 ETH ($3,000), you get 10% ($300) as passive income.

3. Market and Sell Your NFT Collection

Creating your NFT is just the first step—marketing is what gets sales! Successful NFT collections often go viral because of hype, community engagement, and exclusivity. To promote your AI-generated NFTs, focus on building a presence on platforms where NFT collectors hang out:

- **Twitter** – Post AI-generated teasers, behind-the-scenes creation process, and announce drops.

- **Discord** – Create or join NFT communities and engage with collectors.

- **Instagram & TikTok** – Share short clips of the AI generation process to attract attention.

- **Reddit (r/NFTs)** – Join discussions, share your artwork, and network with buyers.

For example, if you create a collection of 10 unique cyberpunk portraits, you can build anticipation by revealing one new portrait each day on Twitter and Discord. Share AI process videos, engage with NFT communities, and offer whitelist spots (early access) to your first collectors. Exclusivity sells, so making buyers feel like they're getting something rare increases your chances of making a sale.

4. Earn Passive Income Through Royalties

One of the best parts of selling NFTs is that you don't just get paid once—you can earn every time your art is resold. Setting up a royalty percentage (5-10%) ensures that if your NFT becomes more valuable over time, you keep profiting from future sales.

For example, if your cyberpunk AI NFT originally sells for $300, but later the buyer resells it for $5,000, you automatically receive $500 (10%) without lifting a finger. If that NFT keeps trading, your earnings can grow exponentially over time.

Examples of Successful AI-Generated NFT Collections

Some AI-generated NFT projects have already seen huge success:

- **"Botto"** – An AI-generated NFT artist whose works have sold for over $1 million.

- **"Dreaming Machines"** – AI-generated abstract NFT art that sold for thousands of dollars per piece.

- **"AI Art House"** – A collection that blends human and AI collaboration, proving that NFT buyers are open to AI-generated artwork.

These collections succeeded because they leveraged unique storytelling, exclusivity, and community hype—all key ingredients to NFT success.

AI-generated NFTs open a whole new world of opportunities for artists looking to monetize digital art. Unlike traditional artwork, NFTs allow artists to earn royalties forever, making them one of the best ways to create long-term income from your work.

Before you dive headfirst into the world of AI-generated NFTs, it's important to keep your mindset grounded. There's a lot of buzz out there—headlines of digital artists making six or seven figures overnight, viral NFT collections flipping for thousands, and early adopters becoming crypto millionaires. But the reality, especially for newcomers, can look a little different. And that's okay.

The biggest pro of entering this space is freedom—freedom to create art without traditional limits, to work on your own schedule, and to build a potentially global audience right from your laptop or even your phone. The blockchain doesn't care if you're a well-known artist or a beginner with a spark of creativity and a clever AI prompt. You can carve out your niche, define your style, and put your work into a marketplace where buyers from all over the world are looking for the next unique piece to collect.

There's also the long-game benefit: royalties. Once your NFTs start selling, you don't just get paid once. You can keep earning every time your work is resold, which makes this income model scalable. That means one piece of art could continue paying you for years—if it holds value and changes hands in the future.

But with all that said, there are also challenges—and it's only fair we talk about them. Not every piece will sell. In fact, many don't. The NFT market is crowded and highly trend-driven, which means it can be difficult to stand out at first. There's also a learning curve when it comes to using crypto wallets, understanding gas fees, choosing the right marketplace, and marketing your work. If you're expecting fast, guaranteed money with no effort, you might end up disappointed. This isn't a lottery ticket—it's a process, just like any business.

Realistically, you may not see sales right away. It could take time to build your name, understand your audience, and figure out what kind of AI art people are drawn to. Some months might bring in a few hundred dollars, while others might be slow. And some projects may take off when you least expect them to. The key is to treat this like a creative venture with long-term potential rather than a get-rich-quick scheme.

If you're someone who enjoys experimenting with visuals, storytelling, and new technology, NFTs could be a really fun and fulfilling income stream to explore. But like any creative business, success will require consistency, a bit of strategy, and a willingness to adapt. Lean into your curiosity, don't be afraid to put your work out there, and give yourself permission to learn as you go.

At the end of the day, whether you earn $50 or $5,000, the real win is that you're building something from your own imagination—powered by AI, minted on the blockchain, and shared with the world. From your home, on your terms. And that's the kind of future we're here for.

CHAPTER 7

Wealth-Building The Smart Way

Today, technology is transforming the way we manage money, invest, and build wealth. Imagine having a 24/7 financial expert at your fingertips—analyzing market trends, identifying opportunities, and helping you make smarter, data-driven decisions in seconds. That's exactly what AI brings to the table. Instead of relying on gut feelings or spending hours researching stocks, AI tools do the heavy lifting, breaking down complex financial strategies into simple, actionable steps.

From automated portfolio management that adjusts to market shifts to AI-powered apps that track spending habits and recommend smarter budgeting techniques, these innovations are making it easier than ever to take control of your finances. Whether you're just starting out or looking to level up your investment game, integrating AI into your financial strategy can make the journey smoother, smarter, and more rewarding.

In this chapter, we'll dive into how AI can enhance financial planning, investing, and wealth management, giving you an edge in the financial world. Whether you're working towards financial independence, looking to grow your savings, or exploring new investment opportunities, AI can help you make smarter choices with less stress.

Trading: Smarter, Faster, and More Profitable with AI

Trading in financial markets has traditionally been seen as complicated, risky, and time-consuming—requiring deep knowledge, quick decision-making, and the ability to analyze data in real-time. But thanks to AI, anyone can now trade smarter, faster, and more efficiently without spending hours glued to charts or financial reports.

AI-powered trading tools can scan millions of data points in seconds, detect patterns and trends, and provide real-time insights to help traders make informed decisions. Instead of manually analyzing charts and guessing market movements, AI trading bots and predictive algorithms can suggest optimal entry and exit points, manage risk, and even execute trades on your behalf.

Even if you're a complete beginner, AI makes trading more accessible than ever. Platforms like **TradingView, Capitalise.ai,** and **Trade Ideas** provide AI-driven insights that help traders of all levels identify profitable opportunities and minimize risks. If you're interested in hands-free trading, automated bots like those on **eToro** or **Pionex** can execute trades for you based on AI-driven strategies, removing the emotional decision-making that often leads to losses.

The beauty of AI in trading is that it eliminates guesswork and emotion, allowing you to trade based on data and strategy instead of fear or excitement. Whether you're day trading, swing trading, or investing for the long term, AI can streamline your approach and maximize your returns.

As we move forward in this chapter, we'll explore the best AI tools for trading, how to use them effectively, and strategies to grow your wealth using AI-powered investing techniques. With the right tools and knowledge, anyone can tap into the power of AI to trade and invest like a pro—without spending years mastering the markets.

Essential AI Tools to Use for Trading

Trading has always been about analyzing trends, making quick decisions, and managing risks—but let's be honest, keeping up with the markets 24/7 is exhausting. That's where AI steps in. AI-powered trading tools can scan millions of data points in seconds, spot patterns that humans might miss, and even execute trades automatically. Whether you're just starting out or already deep in the world of investing, these tools can help you trade smarter, faster, and with less stress.

Alpaca – Commission-Free AI Trading
For those who want to dip their toes into automated trading, Alpaca is a game-changer. It's a commission-free trading platform that lets you connect AI-powered trading bots, meaning you can let automation do the heavy lifting while you focus on strategy. Even better, Alpaca allows users to build and test their own trading algorithms using historical data before going live, so you can refine your approach without risking real money.

Let's say you want to create a simple crypto trading bot that automatically buys Bitcoin when its price drops by 3% and sells when it rises by 5%. With Alpaca's API, you can program that strategy, run back tests to see how it would have performed in past markets, and then let it trade on autopilot. Instead of staring at charts all day, you can let AI track price movements and execute trades for you.

TradingView – AI-Powered Charting & Market Insights
If you love diving into technical analysis and spotting trends, TradingView is your best friend. It's one of the most popular platforms among traders because it offers advanced charting tools, AI-driven insights, and real-time data across stocks, crypto, and forex markets.

What makes TradingView unique is its AI-powered market scanner, which can identify trends, detect price patterns, and predict market movements before they happen. Imagine you're watching Tesla's stock and wondering if it's about to make a big move. Instead of guessing, TradingView's AI can analyze price action, volume, and historical trends to help you decide whether to buy, sell, or hold.

Another cool feature? You can follow other traders and see their strategies in action. It's like having a built-in trading community where you can learn from experienced investors, compare notes, and even copy successful trades.

MetaTrader 5 – AI-Powered Automated Trading
For those who want to take trading to the next level, MetaTrader 5 (MT5) is a powerful platform that supports Expert Advisors (EAs)— essentially AI-driven trading bots that execute trades based on predefined strategies.

Let's say you have a strategy where you only buy a stock when it crosses above its 50-day moving average and sell when it drops below its 200-day moving average. Instead of manually watching charts all day, you can program an EA to do it for you. The AI will monitor price movements in real time, execute trades when conditions are met, and even adjust stop-losses to protect your profits.

MT5 also includes back testing tools, which means you can test your strategy against years of historical data to see how it would have performed in past market conditions. This can help you fine-tune your approach and minimize risk before trading with real money.

QuantConnect – Algorithmic Trading for Data-Driven Investors
For those who love data science and algorithmic trading, QuantConnect is an incredibly powerful tool. It's a platform designed for traders who want to build, test, and deploy AI-driven trading

strategies using machine learning models.

Imagine you want to trade based on market sentiment. You could build an AI model that scans Twitter, financial news, and earnings reports to determine whether a stock is trending positively or negatively. If your AI detects bullish sentiment, it buys the stock; if sentiment turns negative, it sells. With QuantConnect's AI-driven analytics, you can automate this entire process, eliminating emotional decision-making.

This is a more advanced tool, but for those who enjoy coding and quantitative analysis, QuantConnect opens up endless possibilities for algorithmic trading.

Trefis & Kavout – AI-Powered Stock Forecasting
If you want AI to do the research for you, Trefis and Kavout are fantastic tools for stock market predictions and investment insights. These platforms use AI models to analyze financial reports, earnings trends, and macroeconomic indicators, giving you a data-backed perspective on which stocks might perform well in the future.

Trefis is great for breaking down stock prices visually. Instead of looking at endless spreadsheets, Trefis shows you exactly what factors are driving a stock's value—whether it's revenue growth, market share, or new product launches.

Kavout, on the other hand, utilizes an AI-powered stock-ranking system called the K Score, which assigns stocks a buy or sell rating based on their likelihood of outperforming the market. Let's say you're considering investing in Apple (AAPL) but aren't sure if it's a good time. Kavout's AI will analyze thousands of data points—earnings reports, analyst sentiment, market trends—and give you a clear, objective score to guide your decision.

For long-term investors who don't have time to analyze every stock manually, AI-powered forecasting tools like Trefis and Kavout make investing simpler, smarter, and more data-driven.

How to Use AI Tools for Trading
Determine if you're interested in short-term trading or long-term investing, and assess how much risk you're comfortable with. Many AI tools allow you to adjust settings based on your personal risk tolerance, so it's crucial to know this before diving in. Do not invest any money that you are not willing to lose.

If you're new to investing and want to analyze stock trends, you can use TradingView to identify patterns in price movements. Let's say you want to trade Tesla (TSLA) stock but aren't sure when to buy or sell. Instead of manually tracking stock movements all day, you can use TradingView, which provides AI-powered technical analysis, real-time alerts, and market sentiment tracking. You could set up price alerts that notify you when Tesla hits a key support or resistance level, giving you a strategic entry or exit point. TradingView's AI also analyzes historical trends and can suggest potential buy or sell opportunities based on price action patterns.

If you don't have the time or expertise to make trading decisions manually, Alpaca and MetaTrader 5 (MT5) offer automated trading bots that execute trades for you. Imagine you have a strategy where you buy Bitcoin whenever it drops by 5% and sell when it rises by 10%. Instead of manually monitoring the market 24/7, you can set up a trading bot on Alpaca that automatically follows this rule—buying and selling at the right moments without you having to do anything. MT5's Expert Advisors (EAs) work similarly by executing trades based on predefined AI-driven strategies, helping you trade faster and with fewer emotional decisions.

For those who love data-driven investing, Trefis and Kavout provide AI-powered stock analysis and forecasting. Suppose you're considering investing in Apple (AAPL) but want to know if it's a good long-term play. Kavout's AI scans financial reports, earnings trends, and analyst predictions to give Apple a stock ranking (K-Score), helping you decide if it's a buy, hold, or sell. Meanwhile, Trefis breaks down Apple's stock price visually, showing you exactly what factors—like iPhone sales, subscription services, or international growth—are driving its valuation.

If you're more interested in algorithmic trading, QuantConnect is perfect for building and testing AI-powered trading strategies. Let's say you want to create a machine learning model that trades based on social media sentiment. You can code an AI model in QuantConnect that scans Twitter, Reddit, and financial news headlines, then executes trades when sentiment turns bullish or bearish. This allows traders to tap into market-moving trends in real-time, something that would be impossible to track manually.

By combining these tools, traders can eliminate guesswork, reduce risks, and improve profitability. Whether you're using TradingView for insights, Alpaca for automation, Trefis for research, or QuantConnect for advanced strategies, AI allows you to trade smarter, not harder.

Instead of spending hours analyzing charts and making emotional decisions, AI does the heavy lifting—helping you make better trades with confidence.

How to Monetize with AI-Powered Trading

1. Start with Practice Accounts
Many trading platforms offer practice accounts, allowing you to test AI-driven strategies without financial risk. Take advantage of this by experimenting with various strategies and understanding how each works. You'll be better prepared to start trading with real money by honing your skills in a risk-free environment.

2. Earn Passive Income Through Automated Strategies
One of the most appealing aspects of AI in trading is the ability to earn passive income. By setting up automated trading strategies on platforms like Alpaca, you can continue to earn even when you're not actively managing your trades. Select bots that align with conservative strategies initially, like those based on low-volatility assets or stable market trends.

3. Offer AI Trading Strategy Consulting
If you develop a solid understanding of AI-powered trading, you could start consulting for others interested in the field. Many novice traders seek guidance on setting up trading bots and analyzing market trends. Offering consulting services through LinkedIn or financial forums could be an additional income stream.

4. License or Sell Your Trading Algorithms
For those who have a knack for building effective trading algorithms, some platforms (like QuantConnect) allow you to license or sell your strategies to other traders. This is an excellent way to monetize your expertise, especially if you've developed a consistently well-performing strategy. Alternatively, consider partnering with investors who might fund your strategy.

5. Trade in High-Potential Markets Like Cryptocurrency
Cryptocurrencies are known for their high volatility, which can mean high rewards (and risks) for traders. AI-driven tools are useful here, as they can process crypto market data around the clock and make trades in real time. Trading in crypto can be more profitable than traditional stocks, but it requires a solid understanding of the market's behavior.

6. Utilize AI-Powered Sentiment Analysis

Tools like Trefis and TradingView can provide sentiment data on stocks or cryptocurrencies, helping you decide when to enter or exit a position based on market sentiment. This approach can be especially valuable in high-volatility sectors, where sentiment shifts significantly impact prices.

7. Monetize Your Knowledge Through Educational Content

As you build expertise in AI trading, consider creating courses, eBooks, or YouTube tutorials to share your insights. AI trading is a trending topic, and educational content can be a profitable way to monetize your knowledge. Platforms like Udemy, Skillshare, or even TikTok can be excellent channels for reaching an audience interested in learning about AI trading.

8. Offer Monthly Subscription-Based Trade Signals

Once you've tested and refined your AI-driven trading strategies, you can consider creating a subscription service where users pay for trade signals or market insights. This can be a passive income stream, as AI tools can automatically generate and send trade alerts based on your set parameters.

9. Create and Manage a Trading Community

Another way to monetize your knowledge is by building an online community for AI-driven traders. Using platforms like Discord or Patreon, you can offer exclusive insights, market breakdowns, and live analysis to paying members. Communities are valuable because they provide real-time discussions, mentorship, and collective insights, making them attractive resources for beginner traders.

Dividend Investing: Using AI to Build Passive Income

Dividend investing is one of the most reliable ways to generate passive income, as it involves buying stocks that pay regular dividends—essentially, getting paid just for holding shares in a company. Traditionally, dividend investors spend hours researching companies, analyzing financial reports, and monitoring dividend yields to build a strong portfolio. But thanks to AI, this entire process can be automated, making it easier to identify high-yield dividend stocks, track performance, and reinvest dividends efficiently.

By leveraging AI-powered research tools, predictive analytics, and automation, investors can maximize returns, minimize risk, and optimize their dividend strategy without spending countless hours analyzing data manually. Whether you're a beginner or a seasoned investor, AI can help you build a dividend portfolio that generates steady, long-term income.

What AI Tools to Use for Dividend Investing

AI-powered tools simplify dividend investing by helping you research stocks, analyze financial health, and track dividend income. Here are some of the best AI-driven platforms to enhance your dividend investing strategy.

Simply Safe Dividends (SSD) is one of the most powerful AI-driven platforms for dividend investors. It assigns a dividend safety score (ranging from 0 to 100) to stocks based on factors like payout history, earnings stability, and cash flow. If you're considering investing in Procter & Gamble (PG), SSD's AI will analyze its financial statements, debt levels, and dividend history to determine if the company can sustain and grow its payouts over time. This tool helps investors avoid risky dividend stocks that may cut or eliminate their payouts.

FinChat.io is another AI-powered tool that allows investors to ask natural language queries and receive real-time financial insights. Instead of manually reading financial reports and stock analysis, you can type, "Which dividend stocks have a yield above 4% and a payout ratio below 60%?" and FinChat will instantly pull a curated list of top-performing dividend stocks with detailed financial breakdowns. This makes stock research faster and more accessible, especially for beginners.

Dividend.com is a fantastic platform for tracking and analyzing dividend stocks. It offers AI-driven stock screeners that help investors filter dividend stocks based on yield, growth history, and payout ratios. For instance, if you're looking for stocks with at least 10 years of consecutive dividend increases, Dividend.com will generate a list of reliable companies like Johnson & Johnson (JNJ) or Realty Income (O). The platform also provides real-time alerts about dividend increases, decreases, or cuts, ensuring that your portfolio remains optimized.

AlphaSense is an advanced AI research tool that scans millions of earnings reports, analyst forecasts, and market trends to help investors predict which companies are most likely to increase dividends in the future. For example, if you're considering investing in Microsoft

195

(MSFT), AlphaSense can analyze earnings call transcripts and financial data to determine whether Microsoft has the financial strength to increase its dividend payout over the next year. This kind of predictive insight helps investors make smarter long-term decisions.

For investors looking for automated portfolio management, M1 Finance is an excellent AI-powered platform that allows you to automate dividend reinvestments, rebalance your portfolio, and invest in fractional shares. Let's say you receive $100 in dividend payments from your portfolio—M1 Finance can automatically reinvest that money into your highest-performing stocks, ensuring that your income compounds over time without requiring manual effort. This is a game-changer for investors looking to build wealth passively.

Zacks Investment Research uses AI and machine learning to rank dividend stocks based on earnings growth, valuation, and financial stability. If you're debating whether to invest in Pfizer (PFE) or Merck (MRK), Zacks' AI models will compare dividend yield, payout history, and growth potential, giving you a clear recommendation on which stock is the better long-term investment.

How to Use AI Tools for Dividend Investing

Using AI for dividend investing involves a few simple steps: researching strong dividend stocks, analyzing their financial stability, automating reinvestments, and continuously monitoring portfolio performance.

Start by screening for high-yield dividend stocks using tools like Simply Safe Dividends and Dividend.com. Look for stocks with a dividend yield of 3–5%, a payout ratio below 60%, and a long history of increasing dividends. This ensures that you're investing in stable companies that can maintain their dividend payments.

Once you've identified potential investments, analyze financial strength and future growth using AlphaSense and FinChat.io. These AI tools will break down earnings trends, revenue growth, and analyst sentiment, helping you determine whether the company is likely to sustain and grow its dividend payments.

To make the most of your dividend income, set up automatic reinvestments using M1 Finance or your brokerage's dividend reinvestment program (DRIP). This ensures that every dividend payment you receive is immediately reinvested, allowing your portfolio to grow through compounding.

Finally, monitor and adjust your portfolio using AI insights from Dividend.com and TradingView. These tools will alert you about dividend increases, decreases, or stock downgrades, ensuring that you stay ahead of market changes and keep your portfolio optimized.

How to Monetize Dividend Investing with AI

Select and Invest in High-Yield Dividend Stocks
The first step in making money from dividend investing is finding reliable, high-yield stocks. Using AI-driven platforms like Kavout, identify stocks with above-average yields (generally 4% and higher), a sustainable payout ratio (ideally below 70%), and a solid earnings record. Invest in these companies to start generating regular dividend payments.

Use Dividend Growth Stocks for Increasing Passive Income
Some companies may offer lower dividend yields but consistently increase their payouts over time. AI tools help analyze a company's dividend growth rate, which is important for long-term passive income. Stocks with a steady history of growing dividends provide income and potential for capital appreciation.

Maximize Compounding Through DRIPs
Automating dividend reinvestment is one of the most effective ways to build wealth over time. Many AI-driven robo-advisors offer DRIPs, which reinvest each dividend payment back into the stock that generated it. This compounding effect gradually increases your shares without requiring new capital and can significantly boost your passive income in the long run.

Adjust Portfolio Based on Dividend Safety
Economic cycles can impact dividends, so use AI tools to monitor dividend stability and adjust as needed. For example, if a company's earnings decline, AI-driven analysis will alert you to possible dividend cuts, allowing you to reallocate funds to more reliable stocks.

Establish a Monthly Income Schedule
Some companies pay dividends quarterly, while others pay monthly. Using AI tools like Ziggma, you can strategically build a portfolio that includes a mix of payment schedules, creating a steady monthly income stream. This allows you to rely on dividend payments as a regular source of income.

Set a Passive Income Target and Adjust Accordingly

Establish a monthly or yearly dividend income goal (e.g., $1,000 monthly). Calculate the required portfolio size based on average yields, then use AI tools to periodically assess performance. Tools like Simply Wall St can project dividends based on current holdings and alert you to additional investment opportunities if adjustments are needed.

Minimize Fees to Maximize Returns

AI-powered robo-advisors often have lower fees than traditional brokerage accounts, which means more of your returns stay in your portfolio. AI helps monitor and minimize costs, ensuring your dividends aren't eaten up by management or transaction fees.

Leverage AI Insights for Market Adjustments

AI can analyze market trends and predict potential economic shifts, helping you proactively adjust your dividend portfolio. If a market downturn is projected, focus on defensive stocks (like utilities or consumer staples) that tend to pay steady dividends regardless of economic conditions.

Optimize Tax-Efficiency

Taxes can impact your dividend income, so use AI tools to identify tax-efficient dividend investments. For example, the U.S.'s Qualified Dividend Income (QDI) is taxed lower than regular income. Some robo-advisors offer tax-optimized accounts, which maximize your after-tax returns and increase net passive income.

Mitigate Investment Risks While Maximizing Returns with AI

When I first started investing, I quickly realized how overwhelming it could be. The constant market fluctuations, endless financial reports, and unpredictable global events made it feel like I was always a step behind. No matter how much research I did, I found myself second-guessing my decisions. Then, I discovered AI-driven investing tools, and everything changed.

Instead of manually tracking market trends and trying to decipher stock charts, AI did the heavy lifting for me. It analyzed thousands of data points in real time, highlighting opportunities and warning me about potential risks before they became real problems. It was like having a financial expert watching over my portfolio 24/7, ensuring

AI Income Streams Monetizing Innovation from Home

that I wasn't making decisions based on emotion or guesswork.

What AI Tools to Use for Investment Risk Management

Portfolio Risk Analysis Tools (e.g., Riskalyze, Portfolio Visualizer): These platforms evaluate portfolio risk by analyzing asset correlations, volatility, and sensitivity to market changes, allowing investors to align portfolios with their risk tolerance.

AI-Powered Market Analysis Tools (e.g., AlphaSense, Bloomberg Terminal) monitor global financial data, industry trends, and breaking news, alerting investors to any factors that could impact their investments. Machine Learning Models for Predictive Analytics (e.g., IBM Watson, Alpaca) identify patterns and forecast market movements, allowing investors to anticipate risks and market corrections. Sentiment Analysis Tools (e.g., BuzzSumo, Dataminr) gauge public sentiment on social media, news outlets, and forums, providing insights into market sentiment that can influence stock performance.

Automated Rebalancing Tools (e.g., Betterment, M1 Finance) use AI to automatically rebalance portfolios based on market conditions and individual risk preferences, ensuring alignment with investment goals.

How to Use AI Tools for Managing Investment Risks

Begin by evaluating your current portfolio's risk profile with tools like Riskalyze or Portfolio Visualizer. Input your asset details, and let the AI calculate risk based on diversification, market correlation, and historical volatility. These tools provide insights into potential weaknesses, allowing you to rebalance your portfolio accordingly. Use machine learning-powered tools like IBM Watson or Bloomberg Terminal to stay informed of market trends and anomalies. These tools analyze historical data and economic indicators to offer predictions, helping you anticipate and adjust for risks before they materialize.

Sentiment analysis tools like Dataminr and BuzzSumo can be instrumental in understanding public perception of industries or companies. If sentiment turns negative, for example, regarding a particular stock or sector, this early insight can alert you to potential downturns or volatility, allowing for proactive adjustments. For hands-off management, leverage robo-advisors like Betterment or M1 Finance that offer automated rebalancing based on market shifts and your risk tolerance. These AI tools adjust your portfolio regularly to maintain your preferred asset allocation, reducing risks associated with market volatility.

Many AI platforms, like Portfolio Visualizer, allow you to backtest your portfolio or specific strategies against historical data. By simulating how your investments would have performed in past market conditions, you gain valuable insights to refine your approach and strengthen your portfolio against potential risks.

How to Mitigate Risks and Maximize Returns Using AI in Investment

Diversify and Rebalance Regularly
Diversification is key to reducing risk, and AI tools make it easier to ensure your portfolio is balanced across multiple asset classes, sectors, and regions. Use automated rebalancing features to adjust allocations in response to changing market conditions. A diversified portfolio with AI-managed adjustments reduces exposure to any single asset's risk, creating a smoother investment experience with steady returns.

Leverage Predictive Models for Strategic Entry and Exit Points
Predictive models analyze trends to indicate optimal times to buy or sell assets. By following these AI-generated signals, you can avoid buying high or selling low instead of timing your investments to capitalize on favorable market conditions while avoiding downturns.

Implement Stop-Loss Orders and Hedging Strategies
Many trading platforms allow you to set stop-loss orders or create hedging positions with the help of AI risk analysis. Stop-loss orders limit potential losses by automatically selling assets that dip below a specified price, while AI-driven hedging strategies protect against market downturns by balancing riskier positions with stable assets or alternative investments.

Stay Ahead of Volatility with Real-Time Alerts
Use AI-powered alert systems to notify you of shifts in economic indicators, market sentiment, or geopolitical events that may affect your investments. This gives you an advantage in preparing for possible volatility, allowing you to exit vulnerable positions or invest in sectors expected to thrive under upcoming conditions.

Focus on Defensive and Growth Sectors Based on AI Insights
AI-powered market analysis can help identify sectors positioned for stable growth (like utilities or healthcare) versus those facing potential downturns. By rebalancing to include defensive sectors, you can insulate your portfolio from economic uncertainty while maintaining growth opportunities in areas where AI indicates long-term strength.

Use AI for Tax-Efficient Investment Strategies
AI tools like Wealthfront offer tax-efficient strategies, such as tax-loss harvesting, which allows you to offset gains with strategically selected losses to reduce your tax liability. This strategy, implemented automatically by AI, maximizes your after-tax returns and enhances your overall profitability.

Monitor and Adapt to Interest Rate and Inflation Changes
Inflation and interest rates directly impact returns. AI can analyze macroeconomic trends and predict inflation changes, guiding you to adjust your asset mix accordingly. For example, the AI might suggest allocating more to commodities or real assets during rising inflation, helping you preserve purchasing power and maintain returns.

Utilize AI to Identify and Mitigate Sector-Specific Risks
Different sectors react uniquely to economic cycles and trends. AI can identify sectors under potential risk from industry-specific regulations, consumer demand shifts, or supply chain disruptions. By recognizing these risks, you can allocate fewer resources to vulnerable areas, focusing instead on sectors likely to perform well.

Continuously Backtest and Refine Strategies with AI Models
Use AI tools to backtest your portfolio periodically, ensuring your risk management strategy aligns with your financial goals and changing market conditions. By comparing how different strategies perform historically, you can make data-backed adjustments, staying adaptable in the face of evolving market dynamics.

Engage in Scenario Analysis to Prepare for Different Market Conditions
Scenario analysis allows you to model your portfolio's performance under various hypothetical situations (like a recession, stock market boom, or rate hike). AI tools can run these simulations to determine how well your investments hold up, allowing you to prepare for different outcomes and adapt your risk mitigation strategies accordingly.

Final Thought: Is AI Trading the Right Path for You?

Stepping into AI-powered trading might feel like diving into unfamiliar territory, especially if you're new to finance. But the beauty of this digital age is that you no longer need to be a Wall Street insider or a numbers genius to get started. Thanks to AI, many of the most complex and time-consuming aspects of trading—like analyzing market trends, backtesting strategies, or watching price charts all day—can now be handled automatically.

That said, it's important to go into this with your eyes wide open. AI trading tools are powerful, but they're not magic. Markets are unpredictable, and no algorithm can guarantee profits 100% of the time. There will be wins, and there will be losses—that's the nature of any investment strategy. The key difference is that AI helps you make smarter, faster, and more informed decisions with far less manual effort.

For beginners, AI trading offers a fantastic way to learn the ropes while letting technology do some of the heavy lifting. You can start small—maybe by using copy trading platforms or setting up a bot with conservative strategies—and grow as you become more confident. Most platforms today are user-friendly, with demo accounts, tutorials, and communities to support you as you build your skills.

Monetizing AI trading isn't about getting rich overnight. It's about developing an income stream that can scale with time and experience. For some, it might become a side hustle that earns a few hundred dollars a month. For others, it could evolve into a fully automated system that generates consistent returns as part of a diversified portfolio. The level of success depends on how much you're willing to learn, test, and refine.

So, if you're curious and willing to take it slow, this could be a game-changing opportunity. With AI as your assistant and a solid plan as your foundation, trading from home can shift from a confusing gamble to a calculated income strategy. The technology is ready—now it's just about deciding whether this is a door you want to open.

Real Estate

With the rise of digital technology, making money from real estate no longer requires physically managing properties or even leaving home. AI and digital tools now empower individuals to invest, manage, and profit from real estate virtually. In the final section of this chapter, you will learn how you can leverage technology to enter the real estate market, make passive income, and optimize investments, all from the comfort of your home.

Essential AI tools for Real Estate Investing

Gone are the days of manually scouting neighborhoods or crunching endless numbers. Now, you can analyze, buy, and manage properties with just a few clicks, thanks to smart tech that does the heavy lifting.

Take **Roofstock**, for example—it's a game-changer for remote real estate investing. This platform lets you buy rental properties without ever stepping foot inside them. It provides detailed reports, AI-driven return estimates, and risk assessments, so you know exactly what you're getting into before making a purchase.

Then there's **Zillow** and **Redfin**, which have become essential tools for researching property values and market trends. These platforms use AI to analyze tons of real estate data, helping you figure out whether a property is priced right, how much rental income you could make, and where the market might be heading.

For short-term rental investors, **AirDNA** is a must-have. It breaks down Airbnb and VRBO listings, predicting occupancy rates, expected rental income, and which locations are the most profitable. If you're interested in vacation rentals but not ready to buy an entire property, **ReAlpha** offers a unique way to invest by letting you own fractional shares of short-term rentals—kind of like crowdfunding for Airbnb properties.

And if you're into house flipping or wholesale deals, **DealMachine** is a powerful tool for finding hidden real estate gems. It helps you locate undervalued properties and generate leads without having to drive around searching for "For Sale" signs.

With AI and automation, real estate investing isn't just for the wealthy or industry insiders anymore. These tools make it possible for everyday people to find, evaluate, and invest in properties with confidence—even if they're doing it all from home.

How to Use AI Tools for Real Estate Investing

Now that you know about the essential AI-powered real estate tools, let's dive into how to actually use them to find, evaluate, and profit from real estate investments. Whether you're looking to buy rental properties, flip houses, or invest in short-term rentals, AI can simplify the process and help you make smarter financial decisions.

Finding the Right Investment Property

The first step in real estate investing is identifying a property that fits your goals—whether it's a long-term rental, a short-term vacation home, or a fix-and-flip opportunity. AI tools like **Roofstock** do a lot of the work for you by curating rental properties that are already generating income. Instead of sifting through hundreds of listings, you can filter properties based on expected return on investment (ROI), tenant occupancy, and location trends. This means you can invest in profitable rentals even if they're in a different state—or even country.

For those interested in short-term rentals, **AirDNA** is a must. Simply enter a city or neighborhood, and AirDNA will analyze Airbnb and VRBO data to show you how much similar properties are making per night, their occupancy rates, and seasonal demand. This allows you to predict which locations will generate the highest returns before making a purchase.

Analyzing Property Values & Market Trends
Before you invest in a property, it's crucial to know whether it's a good deal. AI-driven platforms like **Zillow** and **Redfin** provide real-time property valuations based on market trends, recent sales, and future growth potential. You can track price changes over time, compare similar homes, and even get insights into the best neighborhoods for investment. These tools take the guesswork out of pricing and help you avoid overpaying.

For house flippers, **DealMachine** makes scouting for off-market properties easier. It uses AI to help you find motivated sellers and undervalued properties. With just a property address or photo, DealMachine can pull up ownership details, market value, and potential profit margins. This means you can find great deals without having to physically visit dozens of homes.

Automating Real Estate Management
Once you've secured a property, AI tools can help manage it efficiently. If you own a rental, **ReAlpha** allows you to invest in fractional shares of Airbnb properties, meaning you can earn passive income without handling property management. For full owners, Airbnb itself uses AI to adjust pricing dynamically based on demand, ensuring you get the highest nightly rate possible.

For long-term rentals, **Roofstock** and property management platforms like **Buildium** use AI to streamline tenant screening, rent collection, and maintenance requests. These tools can automate nearly every aspect of property management, so you can scale your real estate business without getting bogged down by day-to-day operations.

Making Smarter Investment Decisions
Ultimately, AI tools help you make data-driven decisions instead of relying on guesswork. Whether it's choosing the best rental location, analyzing market trends, or automating property management, AI can give you an edge in real estate investing. By leveraging these technologies, you can minimize risks, maximize returns, and even build a real estate portfolio without ever stepping inside a property.

How to Monetize Real Estate with AI-Powered Solutions

Purchase Rental Properties Remotely
With Roofstock, you can invest in single-family homes and rental properties without physical visits. The platform provides detailed insights into property performance, anticipated returns, and tenant histories. After purchasing, Roofstock's management service can handle day-to-day responsibilities. You earn passive rental income while AI-driven algorithms monitor occupancy rates and adjust rent pricing to maximize returns.

Invest in Short-Term Rentals for High Yields
Short-term rentals (like Airbnbs) often generate higher returns than traditional rentals, especially in popular tourist locations. AirDNA provides essential data on occupancy rates and peak rental seasons. With ReAlpha, you can participate in Airbnb rentals via fractional ownership, earning rental income without owning the entire property. This setup is highly profitable if managed well, and ReAlpha's AI helps optimize rental prices for high yields.

Try Real Estate Crowdfunding
Crowdfunding platforms, such as Fundrise and RealtyMogul, pool investments from multiple people to acquire and manage real estate projects. These platforms use AI to identify lucrative commercial and residential properties, allowing you to invest in larger properties for as little as $500. You receive a portion of rental income or capital appreciation based on your investment. Fundrise, for example, has AI tools that track market shifts and rebalance portfolios for optimal growth.

Utilize House Flipping Platforms and Virtual Wholesaling
For those interested in "flipping" properties (buying low, renovating, and selling high), DealMachine provides lead generation for potential properties, tracking undervalued homes in desirable neighborhoods.

Some platforms also offer virtual wholesaling, which involves identifying a property, finding a buyer, and profiting from the difference without needing to purchase or renovate the property.

Monetize Your Primary Residence as a Rental Property

Renting out rooms or using Airbnb during specific months can be profitable if you own your home. AI-based tools like AirDNA help project expected earnings by analyzing nearby rentals. This option allows you to monetize your home without investing in additional properties, generating income on weekends, holidays, or even while you're away.

Automate Real Estate Management for Passive Income

Once you have one or more rental properties, management tools like Roofstock handle everything from tenant screening to maintenance. Additionally, by integrating smart home systems (like digital locks, automated thermostats, and remote surveillance), you can manage properties entirely from home, reducing costs and increasing security. These automated solutions free up time, allowing you to scale your portfolio and increase earnings.

Use AI to Forecast Market Trends and Adjust Strategy

With access to platforms like Redfin and Zillow, AI tools offer market insights that help anticipate fluctuations in housing prices, rental demand, and market trends. This analysis enables you to make strategic adjustments to maximize returns, such as purchasing properties in emerging neighborhoods or selling properties when prices peak.

Tax Advantages for Real Estate Investors

One of the biggest perks of investing in real estate is the tax benefits that come with it. Unlike many other income streams, real estate offers several deductions that can lower your taxable income and boost your overall profits. If you know how to take advantage of these breaks—and with AI-powered tax tools at your disposal—you can maximize your returns while staying compliant with tax laws.

Key Tax Deductions for Real Estate Investors

As a real estate investor, you can deduct a variety of expenses, including:

- **Mortgage Interest:** If you have a loan on your rental property, the interest portion of your payments is tax-deductible.

- **Property Taxes:** Any local and state property taxes you pay can be deducted from your income.

- **Depreciation:** The IRS allows you to deduct a portion of your property's value each year, even if it's appreciating in market value.

- **Repairs & Maintenance:** Costs for fixing plumbing, painting, landscaping, and general upkeep can all be written off.

- **Property Management Fees:** If you use a property management service—or even AI-driven tools like Roofstock—their fees are tax-deductible.

- **Travel Expenses:** If you visit your rental property for maintenance, inspections, or showings, those travel costs may qualify as deductions.

These tax breaks can add up quickly, significantly reducing the amount of taxable income from your real estate investments.

How AI Tools Help Optimize Tax Savings
Managing taxes manually can be overwhelming, especially if you own multiple properties. AI-powered tax tools can help automate and optimize the process:

- **Stessa** – This AI-driven platform helps real estate investors track expenses, categorize deductions, and generate tax-ready reports automatically.

- **TurboTax & H&R Block AI Assistants** – These platforms use AI to analyze your tax situation and find deductions specific to real estate investors.

- **Zillow & Redfin Property Valuations** – By keeping track of property values, you can accurately report depreciation and adjust your tax strategy accordingly.

With AI handling the calculations and reporting, you can ensure that you're maximizing your deductions without spending hours digging through receipts and paperwork.

Using Tax Strategies to Increase Profits
Beyond deductions, savvy investors use tax strategies to grow their wealth faster:

- **1031 Exchange:** This allows you to sell a rental property and reinvest the proceeds into another property without paying capital gains taxes. AI-powered platforms like RealtyMogul help investors identify potential exchange opportunities.

- **Opportunity Zones:** Investing in designated "Opportunity Zones" can defer or even eliminate certain capital gains taxes. AI-driven real estate platforms can help you find these high-potential areas.

- **LLC & Business Structuring:** Many real estate investors set up LLCs for tax benefits and liability protection. AI-powered accounting tools can help determine if this is the right move for your portfolio.

Final Thoughts: Profiting with AI Tools and Real Estate

Real estate investing used to be a game reserved for the wealthy or those with insider knowledge. The barriers to entry were high, and many people felt like they just didn't have the expertise to navigate the complexities of the market. But with the rise of AI and automation, the landscape has completely changed. Now, anyone with an internet connection can get involved—no matter their background, experience, or budget.

These AI-powered tools make it easier than ever to find lucrative investment opportunities. Imagine being able to search through thousands of potential properties in just minutes, filtering them based on factors like location, price, rental demand, and future appreciation potential. These platforms use advanced algorithms to sift through massive amounts of data that would take a human days, if not weeks, to process. What used to feel like a daunting task now feels like a breeze, thanks to automation.

AI also empowers you to make smarter, data-driven decisions. Rather than relying on guesswork or subjective opinions, you can use predictive analytics to identify properties that are more likely to appreciate in value or generate consistent rental income. Some platforms even offer virtual tours of properties, allowing you to view them remotely and get a clear sense of their condition without ever leaving your home. This not only saves time but also minimizes the risks of making a bad investment.

One of the biggest advantages of using AI in real estate is its ability to minimize the guesswork and risk involved in the process. AI tools can analyze market trends, property values, and local economic conditions to provide you with a detailed picture of potential investment opportunities. They can even help you predict future market shifts, so you can stay one step ahead of the competition. This takes the stress out of the decision-making process, allowing you to make informed choices based on solid data rather than hunches.

Beyond just finding properties, AI can also help you manage your investments. There are platforms designed to automate property management tasks, like screening tenants, collecting rent, and handling maintenance requests. These tools can even help you optimize your rental pricing based on factors like market trends and demand, ensuring that you're always charging the right amount for your property. By automating the day-to-day tasks, AI allows you to create truly passive income streams with less effort on your part.

But perhaps one of the most exciting aspects of AI in real estate is its ability to democratize the market. You no longer need to have a massive portfolio or a network of real estate professionals to get started. AI levels the playing field, giving everyday people the tools and insights they need to succeed in an industry that was once out of reach. Whether you're interested in flipping houses, owning rental properties, or even investing in real estate crowdfunding platforms, there are countless ways to leverage AI to build wealth on your own terms.

So, while real estate investing may have once been an intimidating venture, AI has transformed it into a much more accessible and manageable opportunity. By utilizing the right tools and strategies, you can tap into the wealth-building potential of real estate without the steep learning curve or high upfront costs. The future of real estate investing isn't just about owning properties—it's about using smart, efficient tools to maximize profits, reduce risks, and generate income, all from the comfort of your home. The technology is here, and it's making real estate investing more accessible than ever before. All that's left is for you to seize the opportunity and make it work for you.

With AI and automation, real estate investing isn't just for the wealthy or industry insiders anymore. These tools make it possible for everyday people to find, evaluate, and invest in properties with confidence— even if they're doing it all from home.

The key to success is leveraging these technologies to work for you. Instead of getting overwhelmed by the complexities of real estate investing, let AI simplify the process so you can focus on building wealth.

The future of real estate isn't just about owning properties—it's about using smart tools to maximize profits, minimize risks, and create truly passive income streams. With AI by your side, real estate investing is no longer just for the experts—it's for anyone willing to embrace the technology and take advantage of the opportunities it offers.

CHAPTER 8

Automating E-Commerce and Sales with AI

Running an e-commerce business often feels like juggling endless tasks: managing inventory, answering customer queries, setting up marketing campaigns, and ensuring that everything is running smoothly. At times, it can feel overwhelming, leaving you with little time to focus on growth or strategy. But what if you could automate these everyday tasks, letting AI handle the heavy lifting while you concentrate on scaling your business?

In this chapter, we'll explore how artificial intelligence is revolutionizing the e-commerce landscape, making it easier for business owners to run their operations efficiently and effectively. From automatically restocking inventory and sending personalized marketing emails to streamlining customer support and optimizing ad campaigns, AI has the potential to save you countless hours and improve the overall customer experience.

We'll introduce you to a range of AI tools designed to simplify every aspect of your online store—from managing sales funnels and automating customer interactions to refining inventory and pricing strategies. With the right AI-driven systems in place, your business can run on autopilot, freeing up your time to focus on what truly matters: growth and innovation. Ready to see how AI can transform your e-commerce business? Let's dive in!

Automated Sales Funnels

Running an online business means constantly guiding potential customers from interest to purchase. This process, known as a sales funnel, involves attracting visitors, nurturing leads, and closing sales. Traditionally, this required manual effort—writing follow-up emails, tracking leads, and optimizing marketing campaigns. But with AI, you can automate the entire journey, ensuring that no potential sale slips through the cracks.

Essential AI Tools to Use for Sales Funnels

Creating an effective sales funnel is crucial for converting potential customers into loyal buyers. But managing the different stages of the funnel—lead generation, nurturing, and conversion—can be time-consuming and complicated. Fortunately, AI tools can automate and optimize each stage, allowing you to streamline your process, reduce manual work, and improve your conversion rates. In this section, we'll look at some of the best AI-powered tools that can help you design and manage your sales funnels more effectively.

AI tools like **ClickFunnels** and **Leadpages** allow you to build automated sales funnels, integrating features like opt-in forms, email marketing sequences, and payment processing all in one platform. These tools help you easily capture leads, send them personalized emails, and automatically move them through the funnel until they make a purchase.

HubSpot and **ActiveCampaign** use AI to personalize and automate your email marketing campaigns. These platforms can segment your audience based on behavior, sending tailored messages that speak directly to individual needs. They also track how customers interact with your emails and adjust the messaging accordingly, helping you nurture leads until they're ready to buy.

Chatbots like **Drift** and **Tidio** can be integrated into your sales funnel to engage customers instantly. These AI-powered bots can answer questions, offer product recommendations, and even collect information for follow-up, making sure no lead slips through the cracks. Plus, they can operate 24/7, ensuring that potential buyers always get the attention they need.

Zapier automates workflows between your sales funnel tools, connecting your email marketing software, CRM systems, and e-commerce platforms, so your leads move seamlessly through the funnel with minimal input from you. For example, when a lead fills out a form, Zapier can automatically add them to your email list, tag them with a specific interest, and trigger an automated welcome email.

How to Use AI Tools for Building Automated Sales Funnels

When building a successful sales funnel, start by using platforms like **ClickFunnels** or **Leadpages** to easily create your custom landing page tailored to your target audience. You can use pre-designed templates that are optimized for capturing emails or showcasing specific products, ensuring your page aligns with your goals. The magic happens when you add AI-driven copywriting tools like **Jasper** or **Copy.ai** to create catching headlines, persuasive descriptions, and clear calls to action. These tools make sure the content resonates with your audience's needs and interests, increasing the chances of engagement and conversion. The main goal is to get as much visitors and engagement to your page consistently.

Once visitors land on your page and sign up, it's time to manage leads and automate communication. **CRM tools** like **HubSpot** or **ActiveCampaign** offer AI-powered features that let you automate personalized email sequences. By mapping out common customer journeys—such as sending introductory offers, reminders, or educational content—you can nurture your leads with targeted messages that address pain points and build trust. AI helps personalize these interactions, ensuring the right message reaches the right person at the right time, which ultimately boosts your chances of converting leads into customers.

To amplify your lead generation efforts, pair AI-powered ad copywriting tools like **ChatGPT** or **Jasper** with the robust targeting features of **Facebook Ads** or **Google Ads**. These platforms use sophisticated algorithms to reach potential customers based on their interests, behaviors, and demographics. When you combine engaging, tailored ad copy with precise targeting, you bring highly qualified leads directly into your funnel, optimizing your ad spend and boosting conversion rates.

Incorporating AI chatbots like **ManyChat** or **Tidio** into your landing pages adds another layer of interaction for visitors. These bots are available 24/7 to engage leads in real-time, answer frequently asked questions, guide visitors to relevant pages, and even capture contact information. By keeping visitors engaged and reducing bounce rates, especially during the awareness and interest stages of the funnel, chatbots help push leads further down the path to conversion.

Finally, use tools like **Google Analytics** and **Hotjar** to gain valuable insights into how users behave as they navigate through your funnel. These tools can identify where leads are dropping off, what pages are most popular, and how effective your calls to action are. Armed with this data, you can refine and optimize your funnel to ensure a seamless user experience that minimizes friction and maximizes conversions. With AI tools at your disposal, your sales funnel can run more efficiently, automating many of the tasks that used to take up your time while making smarter, data-driven decisions to increase your bottom line.

How to Monetize AI-Powered Sales Funnels

Making money from AI-powered sales funnels is all about automating the process and making it work for you. The great thing about these funnels is that they help you capture leads, nurture them, and convert them into paying customers without you having to manually do everything. By using the right AI tools, you can set up a smooth, automated system that makes money while you focus on growing your business.

1. Sell Your Own Products or Services
One of the most direct ways to monetize your funnel is by selling your own products or services. Whether you're offering digital products like e-books, courses, or physical items, AI tools help you optimize the sales process. For instance, AI-powered email sequences can guide customers through a journey, leading them to purchase. You can set up automated upsells or cross-sells to maximize the value of each sale. These small, incremental increases in revenue add up quickly, especially when they happen while you're sleeping.

2. Affiliate Marketing
If you don't have your own product to sell, affiliate marketing is a great way to make money through your sales funnel. You can promote other people's products and earn a commission for every sale made through your affiliate link. AI can help you identify products that resonate with your audience by analyzing past behaviors and predicting the best offers. With tools like ClickFunnels or Leadpages, you can easily add affiliate links to your funnel and automate the sales process. These tools even allow you to optimize your ads and landing pages for affiliate offers.

3. Subscription Models
If you're offering something like digital content, software, or services that have recurring value, consider setting up a subscription model. AI can help you manage customer retention and automate billing, making it easier to run a subscription-based business. For example, if you have a membership site, AI tools can analyze user behavior and send personalized emails or offers to encourage renewals, ensuring consistent revenue each month.

4. Sponsored Content or Partnerships
Once your funnel is set up and generating traffic, you can monetize it through partnerships. Reach out to other businesses in your niche and offer to feature their products or services in your funnel for a fee. Whether it's through co-branded content, product placements, or exclusive offers, partnering with the right companies can provide a steady stream of revenue. AI can help you target the right brands and optimize the messaging to increase conversions.

5. Sell Leads or Data
If you've built a funnel that gathers valuable data on your customers—such as their preferences, behavior, and purchasing habits—you can sell this data to interested companies or use it to generate more targeted offers. However, always ensure that you're complying with data protection regulations. AI tools can help you analyze the data and target high-quality leads to sell to businesses in need.

6. Offer Consulting or Coaching Services
If you have expertise in a particular area, like digital marketing, business strategy, or personal development, you can use your sales funnel to sell consulting or coaching services. AI tools can help you manage appointments, automate follow-up emails, and track client progress, making it easier to run a consulting business alongside your automated funnel. You can even create a high-ticket offer that sells your time or expertise in a more personalized way.

7. Running Ads on Your Funnel
Lastly, you can also monetize your funnel by running ads. Once your funnel starts attracting a significant amount of traffic, you can sell ad space to other businesses in your niche or use platforms like Google Ads or Facebook Ads to promote other products or services. AI-powered targeting tools help you reach the right audience for these ads, increasing the chances of generating additional revenue.

The key to monetizing AI-powered sales funnels is automation and optimization. With the right mix of strategies and AI tools, you can build multiple income streams that work for you, freeing up your time while your funnels continue to generate revenue. Whether you're selling your own products, promoting affiliate offers, or partnering with other businesses, AI makes it easier than ever to turn your sales funnel into a profitable asset.

E-Commerce Automation

The e-commerce industry is booming, with more people shopping online than ever before. With the help of AI and automation tools, anyone can create, manage, and grow an online store without needing extensive technical knowledge or a large workforce. You can handle everything from product sourcing to marketing, customer service, and order fulfillment through automated solutions, allowing you to scale your business with minimal effort.

Essential AI Tools for E-Commerce Automation

If you're serious about automating your e-commerce business with AI, you need the right set of tools to streamline everything—from sourcing products to handling customer interactions and running marketing campaigns. Luckily, AI has made it easier than ever to run an online store efficiently, even if you're managing everything solo.

Shopify is one of the most popular platforms for building an online store, and it seamlessly integrates with AI-powered automation tools to handle inventory, order management, and customer interactions. If you're into dropshipping, **Oberlo** and **Spocket** are game-changers. They allow you to find trending products, import them directly into your store, and automate the entire fulfillment process—meaning you don't have to worry about storage or shipping. These tools make it possible to run a successful e-commerce business without ever touching a single product.

Once your store is set up, you'll need engaging product descriptions and social media content to attract customers. AI writing tools like **ChatGPT** and **Jasper** can generate high-converting copy in seconds, from compelling product descriptions to catchy social media posts that keep your audience engaged. If you're running ads, **AdEspresso** and **Facebook Ads Manager** use AI to optimize campaigns, segment audiences, and analyze ad performance, making sure your marketing budget is spent efficiently.

For those looking to boost SEO and keep their website fresh with content, **Zyro AI Content Generator** can create blog posts, product pages, and other website copy automatically—saving you hours of writing while keeping your store active in search rankings. And let's not forget email marketing, which remains one of the highest-converting sales channels. **Klaviyo** is an AI-powered tool that automates email campaigns based on customer behavior, ensuring you send the right message at the right time to maximize conversions.

How to Use AI Tools for E-Commerce Automation

Start by setting up your e-commerce store on Shopify. The platform offers various themes and customization options to make your store visually appealing and user-friendly. Shopify's integrations with tools like Oberlo and Spocket make it easy to add products and automate inventory management. Using Oberlo or Spocket, you can import products directly from suppliers without holding inventory. When a customer places an order, these tools automatically alert the supplier to fulfill it, reducing the need for storage space or manual processing.

Write engaging product descriptions using AI to attract more customers. ChatGPT and Jasper allow you to input product details, specifications, and target audience information, generating polished, SEO-friendly descriptions. These descriptions help convert browsers into buyers by clearly explaining product benefits. Implement AI chatbots to handle customer queries in real time. Shopify integrates with several chatbot options, which can be programmed to answer frequently asked questions, provide order status updates, and resolve common issues. Automating responses reduces the need for manual customer support, freeing up your time.

Use tools like AdEspresso or Facebook Ads Manager to create targeted ad campaigns. These tools use machine learning to segment audiences, test different ads, and optimize spending. With AI analytics, they can adjust campaigns automatically based on performance, increasing ad efficiency and ROI. Email remains a powerful tool in e-commerce. Klaviyo allows you to create personalized email campaigns that reach customers with content based on their shopping behavior. It can automate abandoned cart emails, welcome messages, and promotional offers, increasing the likelihood of repeat purchases.

How to Monetize AI-Powered E-Commerce Automation

The beauty of AI-driven e-commerce is that it allows you to automate processes, save time, and maximize revenue—all without the need for a massive team or deep technical expertise. If you're wondering how to turn AI automation into a profitable business, here are some of the best ways to monetize your store and scale your income.

Implement Subscription Boxes for Recurring Revenue
Subscription boxes are a fantastic way to generate steady, predictable income. Instead of relying on one-time purchases, you can offer customers a monthly or quarterly delivery of curated products tailored to their preferences. AI tools analyze customer data and past purchases to suggest personalized boxes, keeping retention high.

For example, if you run a beauty e-commerce store, AI insights can show which customers frequently buy skincare products. You can then introduce a "Skincare Essentials Box" subscription that automatically delivers their favorite products every month. Shopify and other platforms handle recurring billing, shipping reminders, and order management, making this a hands-off revenue model.

Create Niche Product Bundles to Increase Order Value
AI-driven product recommendations can help you create strategic product bundles that encourage customers to spend more per order. Instead of selling items individually, bundle related products at a slight discount to increase the perceived value.

For instance, if someone is shopping for coffee beans in your store, an AI tool can suggest a "Coffee Lover's Bundle" that includes a French press, specialty beans, and a travel mug—all at a bundled discount. Shopify apps can automate these recommendations based on customer behavior, making it easier to boost revenue without extra effort.

Upsell and Cross-Sell with AI-Driven Recommendations
AI tools can track shopping behavior in real time and suggest the right products at the right moment. Upselling encourages customers to buy a higher-end version of what they're considering, while cross-selling suggests complementary products to go with their purchase.

Tools like Bold Upsell and Fera integrate with Shopify and provide real-time recommendations. For example, If someone adds a smartphone to their cart, AI can suggest upgrading to a premium version or adding a wireless charger and protective case—increasing the total purchase value effortlessly.

Sell Digital Products and Automate Delivery
Selling digital products is one of the easiest ways to generate passive income with AI. Unlike physical products, digital goods require no inventory, no shipping, and no handling. Once a customer buys, AI automation tools deliver the product instantly.

If you're in a creative niche, you can sell ebooks, templates, stock photos, or online courses. For example, if you run a fitness gear store, why not offer a downloadable workout guide as an upsell? AI chatbots can even recommend digital products based on a customer's shopping habits, boosting conversion rates.

Optimize Pricing Strategies with AI Analytics

Setting the right price for your products is crucial, but manually adjusting prices based on demand, seasonality, or competitor activity can be overwhelming. That's where AI pricing tools like Prisync come in—they automatically monitor competitor pricing, market trends, and customer demand to suggest the most profitable price points for your store.

Let's say you sell electronics. Prisync can track competitor pricing in real time, ensuring you stay competitive without sacrificing your profit margins. This dynamic pricing strategy helps you attract customers while maximizing earnings.

Boost Revenue with Retargeting Ads and Personalized Campaigns

Most online shoppers don't buy on their first visit—but AI-powered retargeting can bring them back. Tools like AdEspresso and Klaviyo allow you to track visitors who browsed your store and show them targeted ads or personalized emails reminding them to complete their purchase.

For example, if a customer abandons their cart with a pair of running shoes, AI can automatically send them a reminder email with a limited-time discount. Or, if someone clicks on your product but doesn't buy, Facebook retargeting ads can remind them why they loved it. This kind of personalization increases conversions and keeps your store at the top of their mind.

Use Data-Driven Insights to Scale Your Business

AI tools in e-commerce don't just automate tasks—they provide valuable insights that help you scale smarter. Platforms like Google Analytics and Hotjar track customer behavior, best-selling products, and areas where customers drop off in your sales funnel.

By analyzing this data, you can refine your marketing strategy, improve your product offerings, and tweak your store layout to maximize sales. For example, if analytics show that customers spend the most time on a particular product page but rarely buy, you can use AI to A/B test different headlines, descriptions, or pricing to increase conversions.

Start a Dropshipping Business with Low Upfront Costs

If you want to start an online store without dealing with inventory, dropshipping is a great option. Platforms like Shopify integrate seamlessly with Oberlo and Spocket, allowing you to source trending products, add them to your store with a click, and let suppliers handle fulfilment. You set the prices, and when customers place orders, the suppliers ship directly to them while you keep the profit margin. AI tools can help analyze product trends, ensuring you always stock in-demand items that sell well.

Imagine launching a home decor store. AI-powered trend analysis shows that minimalist LED wall lights are trending. You add them to your Shopify store via Oberlo, set a competitive price, and let AI-driven Facebook Ads target the right audience. Orders come in, and suppliers ship them out—meanwhile, you focus on scaling up.

How to Monetize AI-Powered Dropshipping

Identify a Niche Market and Build Brand Authority

Start by selecting a niche with an engaged audience and demand for specific products, such as eco-friendly home goods, pet supplies, or fitness accessories. Use AI to research audience preferences and trends and select a focused product range that aligns with this niche. Establishing a strong brand identity in a niche market can help you attract loyal customers and stand out from competitors.

Run Targeted Ads with AI-Driven Insights

AI tools within ad platforms like Facebook Ads Manager and Google Ads help target ads based on user behavior, demographics, and preferences. Set up ad campaigns targeting your niche audience, showcasing your best-selling products, or offering special promotions. Track ad performance using analytics tools, and adjust your campaigns based on which products generate the highest ROI.

Automate Email Marketing for Repeat Sales

Use AI-powered email marketing tools like Klaviyo or Mailchimp to create automated email sequences that keep your store top-of-mind. Send welcome emails to new subscribers, abandoned cart reminders to potential buyers, and product recommendations based on previous purchases. Personalized emails increase the likelihood of conversions and encourage repeat purchases, boosting your revenue over time.

Offer Flash Sales and Seasonal Promotions
Flash sales and seasonal promotions create urgency and attract more buyers. Use AI to analyze purchase trends and identify popular times for discounts (e.g., Black Friday, holiday season). Schedule email campaigns, update product listings, and advertise these sales on social media to increase visibility. AI tools can even help determine the ideal discount rates to maximize conversions without hurting your profit margins.

Use AI for Dynamic Pricing Strategies
Dynamic pricing uses AI to adjust prices based on demand, competition, and customer behavior. This strategy ensures your prices are competitive and attractive without sacrificing profit. Use tools like Prisync or Minderest to monitor competitor pricing and set your product prices dynamically, allowing you to stay competitive and increase sales.

Implement Retargeting Campaigns
Retargeting ads effectively bring back potential customers who viewed products but didn't complete a purchase. Use AI tools within Google Ads or Facebook Ads Manager to set up retargeting campaigns. These ads remind visitors of the items they viewed, offering discounts or incentives to finalize their purchase. Retargeting ads are highly effective for converting warm leads and increasing revenue.

Launch Subscription Boxes or Bundled Offers
Subscription boxes or bundled product deals offer customers added value and convenience. For example, if you're selling skincare products, create a monthly subscription for a curated selection of skincare items. Use AI tools to analyze customer preferences and trends to assemble bundles that appeal to customer segments, increasing customer satisfaction and average order value.

Focus on Upselling and Cross-Selling
AI tools can analyze customer purchase history and recommend complementary products, helping you upsell or cross-sell related items. For example, if a customer buys a yoga mat, you could suggest yoga blocks or resistance bands. AI-driven upselling strategies help increase each customer's order size, leading to more significant profits per transaction.

Scale with AI-driven Inventory Management
As your store grows, managing inventory across suppliers becomes more challenging. Use AI tools like TradeGecko or Inventory Planner

for demand forecasting and inventory tracking. These tools help ensure you have enough stock of high-demand items, avoiding out-of-stock situations while preventing overstocking. Efficient inventory management can save costs, improve customer satisfaction, and scale your dropshipping business profitably.

Final Thoughts: AI Turns E-Commerce into Passive Income

AI-powered e-commerce isn't just about automation—it's about building a system that works for you 24/7. Whether you're using AI to find trending products, optimizepricing, personalize customer interactions, or automate marketing, these tools allow you to increase efficiency, boost sales, and create multiple streams of income with less effort.

With the right AI-powered strategies, your e-commerce store can become a self-sustaining business, generating consistent income while you focus on scaling, innovating, or even taking time off. AI isn't just making online selling easier—it's making it more profitable and sustainable than ever before.

Dropshipping allows you to launch an e-commerce store without investing in inventory. Using Shopify with Oberlo or Spocket, you can quickly add products to your store and automate ulfilment. Suppliers handle packaging and shipping as customers place orders, and you earn a profit margin. AI tools also help analyze product trends, allowing you to keep popular items in stock and ensure profitability.

Affiliate Marketing

Affiliate marketing is a popular way to earn passive income by promoting other people's or companies' products and earning a commission on each sale made through your unique link. AI can enhance affiliate marketing strategies, helping you reach larger audiences, tailor your marketing efforts, and optimize content for maximum engagement. You can automate your research, content creation, and analytics through AI tools, making affiliate marketing more efficient and profitable.

Essential AI Tools or Affiliate Marketing

Affiliate marketing is all about creating content that attracts and converts—and AI tools can make that process smoother, faster, and more effective. Whether you're writing blog posts, running email campaigns, or creating social media content, AI can help you optimize your strategy and boost your earnings. Here are some of the best AI-powered tools to help you succeed in affiliate marketing.

Create High-Quality Content with AI Writing Assistants
Content is king in affiliate marketing, and tools like **ChatGPT** and **Jasper** make it easy to create engaging, SEO-friendly content that ranks well on search engines. Whether you're writing product reviews, how-to guides, or social media posts, these AI tools generate persuasive and informative content tailored to your audience.

For example, if you're promoting fitness supplements, Jasper can help you craft a detailed blog post comparing different brands, while ChatGPT can generate compelling Instagram captions and tweets to drive traffic to your affiliate links.

To polish your writing, tools like **Grammarly** and **QuillBot** help refine grammar, structure, and clarity—ensuring your content is professional, engaging, and credible.

Optimize for Search Engines with AI SEO Tools
Ranking high on Google means more traffic and more affiliate commissions. AI-driven SEO tools like **Ahrefs** and **SEMrush** help you find high-traffic keywords, analyze competitors, and track search trends.

If you're writing a blog post about "best noise-canceling headphones," **Ahrefs** can show you the most searched keywords related to that topic, helping you craft content that ranks well. Meanwhile, SEMrush can analyze your competitors' content to identify gaps you can fill, giving you a competitive edge.

Automate Email Marketing and Boost Conversions
Email marketing is one of the best ways to nurture leads and drive conversions, and AI tools like **HubSpot** and **ConvertKit** can help automate the process. For example, if someone signs up for your affiliate newsletter about tech gadgets, ConvertKit can automatically send them a series of emails—starting with a welcome message, followed by a list of top product recommendations, and finally, a limited-time discount to encourage a purchase.

Create Engaging Visuals and Videos for Social Media
A well-designed post grabs attention and boosts clicks, which is why tools like **Canva** and **Lumen5** are essential for affiliate marketers.

With Canva, you can quickly design eye-catching graphics for Instagram, Pinterest, and blog posts—perfect for promoting affiliate products visually. Meanwhile, Lumen5 transforms blog posts into engaging videos, allowing you to reach audiences on platforms like YouTube, TikTok, and Facebook.

For example, if you wrote a review about the latest smartwatch, you can use Lumen5 to turn key highlights into a quick, engaging video—helping you reach more people and increase conversions.

How to Use AI Tools for Affiliate Marketing Income Streams

One of the first steps in affiliate marketing is choosing the right products to promote. Instead of guessing what will sell, AI-powered research tools like **Affilitizer** and **CB Snooper** analyze trends and highlight the most profitable affiliate programs. If AI data shows that smart home gadgets or eco-friendly products are trending, you can focus on those niches, ensuring you're promoting products with strong demand and high commissions. This approach eliminates the trial-and-error phase and helps you start earning faster.

Once you've selected your products, AI can help you create high-ranking content that drives traffic to your affiliate links. **ChatGPT** and **Jasper** generate well-structured, engaging blog posts and product reviews in minutes, while **Surfer SEO** and **Clearscope** ensure your content is optimized for search engines. Instead of struggling to write a detailed article on "Best Wireless Earbuds in 2025," AI can draft it for you, allowing you to focus on refining the content and adding personal insights.

Social media is another powerful way to promote affiliate products, and AI tools make it effortless. Platforms like **Canva** allow you to design eye-catching posts, while **Lumen5** converts your blog articles into short, engaging videos for TikTok, Instagram Reels, or YouTube Shorts. With **Publer** or **Buffer,** you can schedule AI-generated content across multiple platforms, ensuring a consistent online presence without constant manual effort. For example, if you create a blog post about the best fitness gear, AI can turn it into an engaging video and multiple social media graphics, reaching a wider audience and increasing your chances of earning commissions.

AI also enhances email marketing, one of the highest-converting strategies in affiliate marketing. With **ConvertKit** and **HubSpot,** you can automate personalized email sequences that nurture your audience and recommend affiliate products based on their interests. AI analyzes subscriber behavior, allowing you to send targeted offers at the right time. For instance, if someone downloads your free guide on digital cameras, an AI-driven email sequence can follow up with product recommendations, increasing the likelihood of a sale.

To further maximize profits, AI-powered advertising tools like **AdEspresso** and **Google Ads Smart Bidding** optimize paid promotions. If someone visits your site but doesn't make a purchase, AI can retarget them with personalized ads on Facebook or Instagram, keeping your affiliate products top-of-mind. This strategic follow-up increases conversion rates and helps you earn more commissions from visitors who might have otherwise moved on.

Tracking and scaling your affiliate earnings is also easier with AI. Tools like **Google Analytics** and **Hotjar** provide insights into which content is driving the most traffic and conversions, allowing you to double down on successful strategies. **Voluum** takes it a step further by tracking the performance of specific affiliate links, so you know exactly which products and promotions are generating the highest returns. With this data-driven approach, you can continuously refine your strategy and grow your income.

How to Monetize AI-Powered Affiliate Marketing

Build an Affiliate Blog and Drive Organic Traffic
Creating a blog around your niche is one of the most effective ways to earn from affiliate marketing. Use AI tools like ChatGPT and Jasper to write high-quality articles, incorporating keywords from Ahrefs and SEMrush. Content ranking well on search engines can bring steady, passive traffic to your affiliate links. With consistency, your blog can become a trusted source, attracting more clicks on your affiliate links over time.

Grow Your Social Media Presence with Targeted Content
Share product reviews, tutorials, and promotional content on social media platforms like Instagram, Facebook, and Pinterest. Use AI to create captivating captions, eye-catching images with Canva, and engaging videos with Lumen5. Ensure each post provides value and includes a call-to-action (CTA) directing followers to click on your affiliate links. Social media can drive significant traffic to your affiliate products, especially when your posts reach new audiences through shares and comments.

Start an Affiliate-Focused YouTube Channel
Video content is a powerful way to promote affiliate products, as people often seek video reviews before purchasing. You can use AI tools like Lumen5 to turn your blog posts into videos or ChatGPT to draft product reviews and comparison scripts. Monetize your YouTube content by including affiliate links in video descriptions and encouraging viewers to click for more information.

Use Email Marketing for Ongoing Revenue
Email marketing is one of the highest-converting channels for affiliate marketing. Build a list of subscribers by offering something valuable, like an eBook or access to exclusive content, and use AI tools like ConvertKit to automate email sequences. Send product recommendations, reviews, and promotions directly to your audience's inboxes. As you build trust with your readers, they'll likely click on your affiliate links and make purchases.

Capitalize on Seasonal Trends and Promotions
Stay aware of holidays and seasonal trends when certain products are more in demand. Using AI-driven analytics tools, you can predict when your audience might be more likely to buy specific products. Create content, promotions, and email campaigns around these periods, increasing the likelihood of affiliate conversions.

Optimize Your Affiliate Marketing Strategy with Data Analysis
AI-driven tools like Google Analytics and Ahrefs provide insights into which products perform best, where traffic comes from, and which audience segments convert the most. Use these insights to adjust your content and strategy, focusing on high-performing products and channels. You'll improve your earnings potential as you refine your approach based on data.

Utilize Paid Advertising for Targeted Reach
While organic traffic is crucial, you can expand your reach with paid ads. Use Facebook Ads Manager and Google Ads to target specific demographics and direct them to your affiliate content. With AI-powered ad tools, you can create targeted campaigns that bring in high-quality traffic, resulting in more affiliate sales. Paid ads work well when you've identified top-performing products and know your audience's preferences.

Final Thoughts on Monetizing Affiliate Marketing from Home
Affiliate marketing has always been an exciting way to earn money

online, but with AI, it's now more efficient, scalable, and beginner-friendly than ever. Instead of spending hours writing content, manually promoting products, or tracking performance, AI tools do the heavy lifting—allowing you to focus on strategy, creativity, and growth.

Whether you're leveraging AI to create SEO-optimized blog posts, automate email campaigns, or refine your social media strategy, the key to success is consistency. AI doesn't replace the need for effort, but it does remove much of the guesswork and time-consuming tasks, making affiliate marketing a realistic income stream even for those with limited experience.

The beauty of this model is its flexibility. You can start small, test different niches, and let AI guide you toward what works best. Over time, as you refine your approach and build an engaged audience, your earnings can grow into a sustainable, passive income stream—all from the comfort of your home. AI-powered affiliate marketing is not just a side hustle; it's a smart, scalable way to build long-term financial freedom.

Bonus Chapter: Top 50 AI tools used to Monetize from home

The difference between those who thrive and those who merely survive often comes down to how effectively we use the tools. I used to think that achieving my goals meant hustling harder, juggling tasks for countless hours, and constantly being on the grind. But over time, I learned a crucial lesson: working smarter is just as important, if not more so, than working harder.

Thankfully, innovative technologies have transformed how we approach our personal and professional lives, allowing us to streamline processes, enhance productivity, and free up valuable time for what truly matters. From AI-driven project management tools that keep us organized to intelligent budgeting tools that track our expenses effortlessly, there's a smart solution for almost every challenge.

This bonus chapter will introduce you to the top 50 AI tools that can enhance productivity, streamline processes, and boost earnings. Whether you're a freelancer, entrepreneur, content creator, or someone looking to monetize your skills and hobbies, these tools are here to simplify your journey. AI is revolutionizing how we work and earn, from automating mundane tasks to providing insights to help you make smarter decisions.

Content Creation and Writing

1. ChatGPT (OpenAI)
ChatGPT is one of the most versatile AI tools for generating human-like text. Its applications range from answering questions to creating detailed blog posts, writing creative content, and providing customer service solutions. ChatGPT can assist with multiple tasks by helping people understand natural language, saving time, and enhancing productivity.

2. Jasper AI
Specializing in content marketing, Jasper AI helps businesses and freelancers generate high-quality blog posts, social media updates, and even email marketing content. Jasper's template system is highly

customizable, making it easy to produce tailored content based on specific needs or goals.

3. Writesonic
This AI writing assistant is great for anyone looking to generate content quickly. It helps create long-form articles, ads, landing pages, and more. It also provides editing tools to polish the generated text.

4. Grammarly
Beyond being a grammar checker, Grammarly uses AI to improve clarity, tone, and readability. It's a must-have for content creators, writers, and professionals looking to make their writing more effective.

5. Copy.ai
Focused on helping marketers and businesses, Copy.ai allows users to create ad copy, product descriptions, and social media posts. It uses natural language generation to automate much of the writing process, which is particularly helpful in reducing repetitive tasks.

6. INK Editor
INK is an AI-powered writing assistant that helps with content creation and SEO optimization. It analyzes your content and provides recommendations to improve search engine clarity, engagement, and ranking.

7. Peppertype AI
A writing tool focused on content marketing. Peppertype AI helps create blog posts, social media captions, and ads by generating text based on your input and target audience.

Design and Video Creation

8. Canva AI (Magic Write)
Canva AI integrates AI into its design platform, allowing users to generate text-based content for presentations, marketing materials, and social media posts. Canva AI is particularly useful for non-designers who want to create visually appealing and professional content without extensive design skills.

9. Lumen5
Lumen5 helps turn written content into engaging video presentations. It's widely used by businesses and content creators to repurpose blogs and articles for platforms like YouTube and social media. Lumen5 uses AI to handle video creation, including adding visuals, music,

and transitions.

10. Designs.ai
With Designs.ai, users can create logos, videos, and branding materials. It simplifies the creative process with AI tools for fast, professional-level design output. This is great for entrepreneurs or freelancers offering branding services.

11. Pictory AI
Pictory helps transform long-form content into short, digestible videos. The AI automatically identifies key sections of a video or text and repurposes them into short video clips, perfect for social media.

12. Synthesia
Synthesia enables users to create videos using AI-generated avatars and voices. It's often used for corporate training, marketing videos, and customer onboarding, eliminating the need for expensive video production equipment and actors.

13. Runway ML
Runway ML is an AI tool designed for artists, enabling them to create unique videos and images with machine learning models. The tool is particularly popular for creative projects and video editing with the assistance of AI.

14. Descript
Descript is an AI-powered video and audio editing tool. It allows users to edit audio and video files by editing the transcribed text, making removing errors and adding voiceovers easy.

15. AIVA
AIVA (Artificial Intelligence Virtual Artist) composes music using AI. It's useful for content creators, filmmakers, and video producers who need original background music.

16. Animoto
An AI-based video creation platform that enables users to create professional-quality videos from photos, video clips, and music. Perfect for marketing campaigns and social media content.

17. Sonix.ai
AI-powered transcription service that converts audio and video files into text. It benefits content creators, podcasters, and professionals who need fast, accurate transcriptions.

Marketing and Social Media

18. Hootsuite (Amplify)
Hootsuite uses AI to schedule posts, analyze engagement, and optimize social media strategies. It also offers insights on the best times to post, audience interaction patterns, and how to improve reach.

19. Phrasee
Phrasee uses AI to create and optimize marketing language, including email subject lines and social media ad copy. Its algorithm helps to maximize engagement and conversions by providing optimized text based on past performance data.

20. AdCreative.ai
This AI-driven tool helps businesses create high-performing ads. It analyzes previous campaigns and generates creatives tailored for social media platforms, boosting ad engagement and conversions.

21. Surfer SEO
Surfer SEO is a content optimization tool that uses AI to analyze top-ranking content for specific keywords and gives recommendations to improve search engine visibility. It helps marketers ensure that their content is aligned with SEO best practices.

22. HubSpot (AI-Powered CRM)
HubSpot integrates AI to help automate tasks like lead scoring, email marketing, and content creation. The AI component helps businesses nurture leads more effectively and provides actionable insights for improving customer relationships.

23. MarketMuse
MarketMuse uses AI to assist content creators in planning and optimizing content for SEO. It identifies content gaps, suggests topics, and recommends enhancing your content strategy for better organic traffic.

Customer Service and chatbots

24. ManyChat
ManyChat allows businesses to automate customer communication via chatbots on platforms like Facebook Messenger and Instagram. It's ideal for small businesses looking to scale their customer support and marketing through AI-driven interactions.

25. Zendesk Answer Bot
Zendesk's AI-driven Answer Bot helps manage customer support by automatically responding to common questions, reducing the need for live agents. It's often used to handle FAQs and initial customer inquiries.

26. Drift
Drift offers conversational AI to automate lead generation and customer support. It uses AI to engage with website visitors in real time, making it easier to convert leads into customers while offering a seamless user experience.

27. Intercom
Intercom's AI-powered chatbots handle customer queries and help businesses manage customer support more efficiently. It helps improve response times and enhance customer satisfaction with automated assistance.

28. Tidio
Tidio offers a customer service chatbot solution for small businesses. It uses AI to automate customer support tasks and provides seamless communication across platforms like websites, email, and social media.

Automation and workflow

29. Zapier
Zapier is a workflow automation tool that uses AI to connect various apps and services. It helps automate repetitive tasks, such as transferring data between platforms, automating emails, and scheduling posts.

30. IFTTT (If This Then That)
IFTTT enables users to create workflows that automate actions between different apps and devices. AI triggers actions such as sending emails, posting to social media, or managing smart devices.

31. Microsoft Power Automate
This tool allows businesses to automate processes across different applications using AI, helping to streamline workflows and improve productivity across departments.

32. MonkeyLearn

MonkeyLearn is an AI tool for text analysis, including sentiment analysis, classification, and keyword extraction. It automates workflows and analyzes large marketing, sales, and customer service datasets.

33. Notion AI
Notion AI integrates AI features into the popular Notion app to help users generate content, brainstorm ideas, summarize notes, and improve workflows.

34. Airtable (AI-Powered)
Airtable integrates AI to manage complex data and workflows. Its automation features allow teams to optimize project management and collaborate effectively across various departments.

35. Coda (AI-Powered Docs)
Coda uses AI to enhance document creation and collaboration by integrating automation features and data insights, allowing teams to build workflows and automate repetitive tasks.

36. Monday.com (AI Tools)
Monday.com's AI-powered project management platform allows teams to automate workflows, set triggers, and manage projects efficiently using data-driven insights.

E-commerce and Sales

37. Shopify AI
Shopify uses AI for inventory management, product recommendations, and customer insights. The AI tools help store owners predict customer preferences, optimize inventory, and boost sales through personalized marketing.

38. Oberlo
Oberlo, an AI-driven dropshipping tool, automates product sourcing and inventory management. It simplifies e-commerce operations by seamlessly integrating with Shopify and automated order fulfillment.

39. Algolia
Algolia is an AI-powered search and recommendation tool used by e-commerce platforms. It improves product search accuracy and helps customers find the right products quickly, increasing conversions.

40. Yotpo
Yotpo uses AI to collect and display customer reviews, which helps businesses boost their online credibility and conversions. Its AI-

driven review collection and analytics help e-commerce sites improve customer feedback and increase sales.

Design and branding

41. Looka
An AI logo maker that allows users to create professional logos and branding elements without needing a design background. It simplifies the process of building a visual identity for businesses.

42. Logo AI
AI-powered logo design platform that automatically generates logos based on user preferences. It's fast, affordable, and easy to use for small businesses and freelancers.

43. Remove.bg
This AI tool instantly removes the background from images, making it perfect for designers and content creators who need quick edits for their visuals.

44. Let's Enhance
An AI image enhancement tool that improves the quality of photos by upscaling, removing artifacts, and adjusting brightness. It's commonly used for e-commerce, real estate, and professional photography.

45. Artbreeder
Artbreeder is an AI-based platform that allows users to create new artwork by blending images. It's a creative tool for artists, designers, and creators to generate unique visuals.

Data Analysis and Insights

46. Tableau
Tableau leverages AI to analyze large datasets and create visual representations that provide insights. It's used by businesses to make data-driven decisions by identifying patterns, trends, and anomalies.

47. BigML
BigML offers machine-learning algorithms for predictive modeling and data analysis. It's used by businesses to make data-driven decisions, especially in fields like finance, healthcare, and e-commerce.

Customer Experience and Service

48. LivePerson

LivePerson is an AI-based customer service platform that uses bots and AI to automate customer conversations across channels like SMS, web chat, and social media.

49. Kustomer

Kustomer uses AI to provide customer service solutions that help businesses offer personalized interactions across multiple channels. It integrates with chatbots and automation tools to enhance customer support.

50. Tars

Tars is an AI chatbot platform that helps businesses create conversational landing pages, enabling them to automate lead generation and customer interactions.

These tools are transforming industries by automating and optimizing processes, making it easier for businesses, freelancers, and entrepreneurs to thrive in a competitive digital world. AI tools continue to democratize access to advanced technologies, making achieving more with less effort possible.

WRAP UP

As we wrap up this journey through the incredible world of artificial intelligence and its potential to create income from home, it's clear that we're on the brink of something transformative. AI isn't just a buzzword; it's a tool that can change how we work, live, and create value. The opportunities are vast and varied; now is the time to seize them.

You might start small, perhaps with a side gig or a passion project, but as you gain confidence and experience, there's real potential to grow your income. Some individuals are already using AI tools to build thriving businesses that earn five to six figures each month. Success depends on choosing the right niche, crafting effective marketing strategies, and consistently delivering value to your audience.

The key takeaway from this exploration is the importance of staying adaptable and committed to learning. Like any tool, AI is only as good as the person using it. Embracing new technologies and being willing to adapt to changes can set you apart. The strategies and resources we've discussed can guide you, but ultimately, it's up to you to take that first step and shape these opportunities into your unique vision.

By incorporating AI into your work, you're not just safeguarding your future. You're opening doors to new possibilities. Whether you want to set up an online store, freelance with AI-powered tools, or dive into consultancy, the avenues for innovation are wide open.

As we move forward, it's essential to approach the use of AI with an ethical mindset. Understanding the implications of these technologies and navigating the regulatory world is crucial for building trust and credibility in your endeavors. Staying informed will help you comply with laws and foster positive relationships with clients and customers.

Diversification is also key. Explore different income streams, whether it's through digital marketing, online courses, or even investing in AI startups. This approach can help you spread out risks and enhance your financial stability. Those who embrace AI and harness its capabilities will find themselves at the forefront of this new economy, ready to take advantage of the opportunities ahead.

Looking ahead, the future of AI holds even more exciting

developments. It's not just about predicting what will happen but being ready to adapt to emerging trends. A proactive approach to innovation will put you in a position to thrive as AI evolves. Remember, change is the only constant in this journey, and with change comes immense potential.

Let this book serve as your launching pad for an AI-powered venture. Consider it a toolkit filled with insights, strategies, and ideas to inspire action. But remember, having the tools is just the beginning; your actions will define your success.

As you move forward, remember that entrepreneurship is about pushing boundaries and discovering new possibilities. With AI as your partner, you can turn dreams into reality, tackle challenges with creativity, and provide value in ways that were once unimaginable.

This journey toward financial independence through AI is not solely about technology; it's about embracing innovation, staying adaptable, and being open to learning. AI provides numerous opportunities to generate income from home, and it's up to you to transform these opportunities into real success. Embrace the power of AI, trust in your ability to innovate, and embark on this exciting path. It may not always be easy, but it's filled with possibilities for those willing to take the leap.

"Success isn't just about what you accomplish—it's about what you inspire others to do." - Unknown.

Your insights could help someone else succeed!

Sharing your success story and experiences can genuinely make a difference. Let's inspire others together! Consider how you might help someone just like you curious about building wealth from home with AI tools but unsure where to start.

My goal is to make it simple, enjoyable, and accessible for everyone to create income streams with AI.

I'd appreciate your help in reaching more people who could benefit from this book. Most readers rely on reviews when choosing their next book. By leaving a review, you provide feedback and guide someone else on their journey to financial freedom.

Your success story could help one more person discover the potential of AI for their business, one more parent to create income from home and spend precious time with their family, one more budding entrepreneur to turn their side hustle into a full-time success, and one more dream takes flight!

It only takes a moment to make a significant difference. Thank you for being part of this journey and helping others step onto their path to success!

★ ★ ★ ★ ★

Resources

ARTHAOS. (2024). AI for branding: Brand design made easier. Retrieved from https://arthaos.co/branding-in-the-age-of-intelligence-unleashing-the-power-of-ai/

Arek Skuza. (2024). Key trends and challenges in customer experience and project planning. Retrieved from https://arekskuza.com/newsletter-issues/key-trends-and-challenges-in-customer-experience-and-project-planning/

Affpaying. (n.d.). Unlocking passive income: How to earn money with affiliate marketing. Retrieved from https://www.affpaying.com/blog/unlocking-passive-income-how-to-earn-money-with-affiliate-marketing

Business Grow. (n.d.). BGSwk26 - Business grow professional web sites made simple. Retrieved from https://businessgrow.co/bgswk26/

Canva. (2023). Canva. Retrieved from https://internettools.ai/design/canva

CIIM. (n.d.). Digital marketing | Home-based jobs | Freelancing. Retrieved from https://www.ciim.in/how-to-earn-money-through-digital-marketing-home-based-jobs-freelancing/

Digital Kev. (2023). How to build a powerful brand identity for your business in niche markets. Retrieved from https://digitalkev.com/how-to-build-a-powerful-brand-identity-for-your-business-in-niche-markets/

Erik Allen Media. (2024). How to monetize your podcast. Retrieved from https://erikallenmedia.com/how-to-monetize-your-podcast/

Fatcow Digital. (2024). Making money from TikTok. Retrieved from https://fatcowdigital.com/blog/making-money-from-tiktok/

Invisible Beauty Store. (2023). Unleashing AI for optimal SEO content results. Retrieved from https://invisiblebeautystore.com/unleashing-ai-for-optimal-seo-content-results/

Lead Marketing Strategies. (n.d.). 2024 social media trends for NY companies. Retrieved from https://www.leadmarketingstrategies.com/2024-social-media-trends-for-new-york-companies/

Marketing Hacks Media. (n.d.). Fiverr gig SEO: Optimizing for search visibility. Retrieved from https://marketinghacksmedia.com/fiverr-gig-seo-optimizing-for-search-visibility/

Mike Vestil. (n.d.). Dropshipping Retrieved from https://www.mikevestil.com/how-to-start-dropshipping/

Mylance Blog. (n.d.). Selling yourself: The benefits of personal branding for consultants. Retrieved from https://mylance.co/post/selling-yourself-the-benefits-of-personal-branding-for-consultants

Natuerlich-Wittmann. (n.d.). Boosting your YouTube views: Strategies for success. Retrieved from https://natuerlich-wittmann.de/boosting-your-youtube-views-strategies-for-success/

Onetask.me. (n.d.). Affiliate marketing guide: Strategies for success. Retrieved from https://onetask.me/blog/affiliate-marketing-guide

Pixelbuilders. (n.d.). Creative ways to repurpose content. Retrieved from https://www.pixelbuilders.com/blog/our-top-five-creative-ways-to-repurpose-content/

PT SEMrush. (2024). AI in content creation: Best practices & top tools for 2024. Retrieved from https://pt.semrush.com/goodcontent/content-marketing-blog/ai-content-marketing/

Real Estate Figure. (n.d.). The essential steps to starting a property management company. Retrieved from https://realestatefigure.com/the-essential-steps-to-starting-a-property-management-company/

RealtyBizNews. (2024). Meta AI image generator launched. Retrieved from https://realtybiznews.com/meta-ai-image-generator-launched/98780532/

Robin Lee Innovations. (n.d.). Maximize ChatGPT efficiency: Proven workflow optimization strategies. Retrieved from https://robinleeinnovations.com/blogs/elevate-innovate/how-can-i-make-money-using-chatgpt-maximizing-your-online-income

SmallBizTrends. (2023). Cmanva: 22 lucrative ways. Retrieved from https://smallbiztrends.com/2023/12/how-to-make-money-on-canva.html

VAFORX. (2025). ChatGPT secrets revealed: Discover the perfect niche for your virtual assistant career. Retrieved from https://vaforx.com/virtual-assistant-perfect-niche-chatgpt/

WhatTheAI. (2024). Building a content calendar with AI: Tools and tips. Retrieved from https://whattheai.tech/building-a-content-calendar-with-ai-tools-and-tips/

Wordkraft. (n.d.). The role of AI in creating marketing content for startup launches. Retrieved from https://wordkraft.ai/web-stories/the-role-of-ai-in-creating-marketing-content-for-startup-launches/